CASES IN ADVERTISING AND PROMOTION MANAGEMENT

CASES IN ADVERTISING AND PROMOTION MANAGEMENT

Charles H. Patti
University of Denver

John H. Murphy
The University of Texas at Austin

John Wiley & Sons
New York   Chichester   Brisbane   Toronto   Singapore

Library of Congress Cataloging in Publication Data

Patti, Charles H.
  Cases in advertising and promotion management.

  Includes index.
  1. Advertising—Case studies. 2. Sales promotion—
Case studies. I. Murphy, John H. II. Title.
HF5823.P353 1983   659.1   83-1137
ISBN 0-471-87507-4

Printed in the United States of America

10 9 8 7 6 5 4 3

PREFACE

In 1978, our book, *Advertising Management: Cases and Concepts,* was published to present a broad selection of advertising case problems. We wrote that book because we felt there was a need to provide students of advertising with an opportunity to explore a wide variety of advertising issues from a managerial perspective. Essentially, we assembled a set of cases viewed from the perspective of the firm's Advertising Manager.

This book, *Cases in Advertising and Promotion Management,* is an extension of our 1978 book, and it is different in several important ways. First, this book contains no text material as such. We recognize that the fields of advertising and promotion are constantly changing and that it is almost impossible to create brief text material that (1) does not duplicate material found in most introductory texts and (2) reflects the most current theory and practice. Instead, we have organized the cases around a managerial framework for decision making and have briefly described that framework.

Second, the perspective presented in this book has been broadened to include many promotional issues as well as advertising. In today's marketplace, it is nearly impossible to think most effectively about advertising and corporate communication without considering the interaction between advertising and the other elements in the promotional mix. Marketers must learn to make advertising decisions within the context of a promotion mix. You will find this orientation

in our book in two ways. Many of the cases specifically address promotion mix issues. There are cases dealing with sales promotion, public relations, and personal selling and advertising. We have also included promotion by creating cases that encourage you to think beyond advertising issues. For example, a case that deals most directly with advertising creative strategy will contain enough information and emphasis for you to consider the promotion mix implications of any particular creative strategy.

Finally, *Cases in Advertising and Promotion Management* is a book that grew out of specific suggestions from students and teachers. Ever since the publication of our 1978 book, we have been in contact with users and nonusers of our book to determine what people liked and disliked. Preferences, of course, vary widely; nevertheless, several key comments kept coming up. Based on these comments, the main features of *Cases in Advertising and Promotion Management* are:

- The managerial orientation and decision-making framework.
- A variety of case settings, including consumer, industrial, national, and retail market settings as well as cases from both for-profit and not-for-profit sectors.
- Cases of varying length and complexity of data.
- Inclusion of promotion management issues.
- "Real" and "realistic" cases.

The large majority of the cases in this book describe a problem or opportunity encountered by an actual business firm or organization. The remaining cases are fictitious but based on actual business-situations. Often, the names of the individual companies, their executives, and geographic settings have been disguised. All of the situations, however, are based on authentic data and marketplace problems.

Over ninety percent of the cases in this book are new or completely revised. The authors of the cases are noted in both the Contents as well as at the bottom of the first page of each case. At this point we again want to thank each author for contributing to our book.

Also, we would like to express our appreciation to a number of individuals and organizations for their help and support in making this book possible. First, thanks to our colleagues who critically reviewed the book prior to publication: Professor Dean Krugman, Michigan State University; Professor Alan Fletcher, The University of Tennessee; and Professor Charles Frazer, University of Colorado. Second, our gratitude to all the individuals and firms who were willing to share their story with us. Third, our thanks to the very able staff at Wiley and to our universities for their encouragement and support. And, finally, thanks to our students past, present, and future to whom we dedicate this book.

Charles H. Patti
John H. Murphy

CONTENTS

*In these cases, the identities of the companies described have been disguised.

*In these cases, the identities of the companies described have been disguised.

INTRODUCTION

The successful management of the advertising function requires a number of skills. In addition to having many interpersonal skills, the advertising manager must be familiar with the specific principles and concepts involved in the advertising business, such as budgeting techniques, media planning, and the creative process, and must also have the ability to apply these principles and concepts to specific situations. Essentially, these are the two skills taught in most advertising management courses. This book has been created to allow advertising and marketing students to apply principles and concepts in advertising, communications, and marketing to a wide variety of realistic situations.

BENEFITS OF THE CASE APPROACH

On the basis of our collective years of working in the communications industry and teaching advertising and marketing students, we feel that the case analysis approach is the most effective method for helping to develop people who will succeed in managing the mass communications efforts of their employers. The most important benefits of the case analysis approach are:

- *Students learn how to approach a problem or situation.* They begin to understand that marketing problems (like most other problems in life) are most effectively solved by a creative, systematic, and logical application of knowledge and judgment.
- *Students gain familiarity with many different types of businesses and industries.* Too often students are exposed only to those industries with which they are already most familiar—

consumer packaged goods. While it is true that consumer packaged goods marketers *do* rely heavily on mass communications to stimulate demand for their product offerings, most students do not find employment with these companies. Therefore, advertising and marketing students must be exposed to as many types of businesses and industries as possible. For this reason we present cases that deal with a wide variety of situations such as retailing, the not-for-profit sector, industrial marketing, leisure and recreation, and financial institutions, as well as consumer packaged goods.

- *Students learn to appreciate the role advertising plays within the broader contexts of marketing and business in general.* Too often advertising and marketing students become convinced that the solution to a company's problems lies in adjusting some aspect of marketing or advertising. While enthusiasm for a particular business discipline is admirable, there is danger in assuming such a narrow perspective. Advertising alone rarely is responsible for the success or failure of a company. Furthermore, we believe that students who quickly come to appreciate the interrelationships among advertising, marketing, and all of the other functional areas of business will be able to make better management decisions.
- *Students are encouraged to appreciate the position of the promotion management function within the firm.* As previously mentioned, advertising is rarely the most important ingredient in the marketing of a product or service. Also, the person who manages the

advertising function on a daily basis often is not in a top position of authority in the company. To be sure, there are exceptions, but look at almost any organization chart and you'll discover that the person responsible for the promotion function reports to at least two or three layers of management below the chief executive officer. This simply means that although the promotion function may be very important in the marketing of some goods and services, there are distinct limits to the sphere of influence of the advertising or promotion manager. While there is an interaction among promotion and many other aspects of any business, the advertising or promotion manager does not have authority or responsibility for pricing, distribution, product development, or most other aspects of business management.

- *Students learn to appreciate the importance of communicating or "selling" the recommended solution to a particular problem.* It is one thing to come up with a potentially effective solution and quite another to convince top management that the particular solution offers the best opportunity to solve the problem at hand. The case approach can help students develop the skills necessary to sell their ideas.

"REALISTIC" VERSUS "REAL" CASES

Some people attach special significance to cases that describe "real," or actual situations. We don't. Written descriptions of actual situations *can* be extremely useful as class exercises, but so can "realistic" written descriptions. We believe that the overall purpose of the case method is to help develop analytical skills that will be useful in business: ability to identify problems, appreciation for information, capacity to develop and analyze alternative solutions, and ability to communicate recommended courses of action. In advertising and promotion situations, rarely is there a single "right" answer. Take a look at the

advertising campaigns for almost any product category and you will quickly see a wide array of creative approaches. The same is true for budget and media strategies. This, of course, doesn't mean that *any* solution is acceptable; some are more acceptable or more reasonable than others. Cases provide an opportunity for students to develop the skills necessary to formulate the most reasonable solutions. The "realistic" cases that comprise this book are all based on actual situations. The companies or organizations described actually exist, or did at one time; the data are either authentic or approximate the actual situation; finally, the problems or opportunities described are either precisely those faced by the company or ones we know will be encountered in the near future.

As you look through the Table of Contents, notice the asterisk (*) next to the name of several of the cases. In these cases the identities of the companies involved have been disguised. Although a disguised case may restrict the student's search for secondary information (company records, competitive data, and so on), our experience in using these cases in the classroom convinces us that this is simply not a problem. Most cases are not "solved" by locating the company's records or interviewing the company's executives. The best solutions always seem to emerge from the creative application of:

- A careful reading of the case
- A thoughtful analysis of the data presented
- A conscientious search of secondary literature on the industry

Variety of Case Settings

What do the following have in common?

A hospital

A professional basketball team

A machine tool builder

A marketer of plastic lawn bags

A cable TV operator

A lot, we think—particularly with respect to the promotion of their "products."

The commonality of promotion problems is one of the main reasons the cases in this book cover such a diversity of industries. The small advertising budget of a not-for-profit organization needs to be managed with the same amount of attention as the multimillion dollar budget of a consumer packaged goods marketer. Media planning is as relevant for an industrial marketer as it is for a professional sports team.

A second reason is that advertising and promotion are becoming increasingly important to a broader range of industries. Changes in how and where we live are creating opportunities and problems for sellers of virtually everything. For example, we now live longer and we are more interested in physical fitness. Knowing this, the health care industry must find ways to tell us about new services, to inform us about new medical discoveries, to persuade us to donate time or money.

We have more leisure time and more discretionary income. The entertainment industry competes for both. Thus, the professional basketball franchise uses advertising to try to convince us that a basketball game will satisfy us better than soccer, or tennis, or even going to a movie or a concert.

The changing composition of the work force and high gasoline prices have altered the way we shop. Direct marketers use advertising to tell us to shop at home while retailers continue to try to lure us to their stores.

It wasn't very long ago that the use of paid advertising by a not-for-profit organization was unheard of. Today, it is not unusual to see advertising as well as other forms of promotion for churches, schools, hospitals, and many other nontraditional marketers.

The cases in this book also vary in length and complexity. Some are very short, contain little or no data, and focus on a very obvious problem. Others are quite long, with considerable data, and the identification of a single problem is clouded by the complexities of the internal and external environments surrounding the firm. As learning devices, both have advantages. Occasionally, business problems *are* obvious and it is unnecessary to compile and examine pages of supplementary information to determine what issue to address. If, after three months of considering all relevant factors, the company president asks the advertising manager for an opinion on the selection of alternative sizes of promotion budgets, then a simple recommendation (with an appropriate rationale) is in order. If the company is trying to develop a complete advertising campaign for a new brand, then the problems are complex and recommendations require an evaluation of company, consumer, competitive, and industry data. Such data must either be provided to the advertising manager or must be gathered from primary or secondary sources.

Every case contains its own unique problem and we've found that working on a new case is something like solving a puzzle. The more you work at it, the better you will come to understand the situation and yourself. We hope that you will enjoy the cases we have prepared for you.

AN APPROACH TO CASE ANALYSIS

Many undergraduate and graduate courses use the case method. Depending on the purpose of the course and the individual preference of the professor, the formats for analyzing cases will vary somewhat. What follows are our comments and suggestions on the case analysis method. The seven sections presented and described below form sequential steps to be followed in the analysis of case situations. It is strongly suggested that you become thoroughly familiar with each step in this sequence before presenting your analysis of a case in either oral or written form.

1. OVERVIEW

Here is your opportunity to convince your audience that you have a solid grasp of the situation—not only the promotion situation but the environments that affect the total organization. You need to start out strong, demonstrating that you understand key factors regarding the industry, the competition, and the company itself. To do this, it is often necessary to put together information from sources other than the written case. Standard & Poor's *Industry Surveys* is a reasonable starting point. Other useful sources are:

Company annual reports

Financial data available from stock guides like Standard & Poor's or Moody's

The trade press (see Standard Rate and Data Service for pertinent publications)

The general business press (*Business Week, Fortune, Forbes, The Wall Street Journal*, etc.)

The marketing and advertising trade press (*Advertising Age, Sales and Marketing Management, Industrial Marketing, Progressive Grocer*, etc.)

Another good way to get a feel for the industry is to shop for the company's products or services. Go to the grocery store, department store, or other appropriate retail outlet and talk to consumers of the product, the sales clerks, and if possible, the store manager.

Once you have put together this information, think about it in terms of the case situation and then present it to your audience in a way that leads into (*but does not state*) the problem. What you want to do is to convince your audience that you are knowledgeable about matters that are relevant to the problem area.

Essentially, the content of the Overview should follow this diagram.

Information about relevant environments

↓

Information about the industry

↓

Information about the company

↓

Information about the marketing aspects of the company

↓

Information directly related to the promotion problem

Don't just repeat facts from the case. Also, don't take the company's time by telling them things they obviously know, such as the company history, names of company personnel, explanations of the company's products. It is true that the company is likely to know almost everything you tell them in this overview; however, this should not deter you from doing your homework. Three benefits result from a thorough overview.

1. You will convince the company that you have a clear understanding of the task before you.
2. You will be able to do a more effective job of analyzing and solving the case problem.
3. The company will be impressed with your interest and enthusiasm.

2. STATEMENT OF THE ADVERTISING OR PROMOTION PROBLEM

All you need here is a simple, clear statement of the specific promotion problem you are going to address. Remember, *you can solve promotion problems only.* Here are a few examples of appropriate and inappropriate problem statements:

Appropriate Statements

"Determine the advertisability of Product X."

"Determine how much money to invest in advertising Product X."

"Select the most promising creative strategy for Product X."

"Develop a media plan for Product X."

"Design a research project that will measure the effectiveness of this year's advertising campaign for Product X."

"Decide if an advertising agency should be retained."

Inappropriate Statements

"Determine the profitability of Product X."

"Decide if Company A should expand distribution of Product X."

"Establish a price structure for Product X."

"Determine if Company A should remain in business."

3. LIST OF CRITICAL FACTORS

This list should contain brief statements which identify every factor in the case that has a *significant influence on the possible solution of the identified problem in the case.* Remember two things: (1) mention only those factors that are influential on the alternative solutions, and (2) always explain *why* the factor is critical or relevant.

The best way to do this is to say something like this:

Critical Factor: "Small amounts of money allocated to advertising during each of the past seven years."

Critical to Solution Because: It's an indication of the company's reluctance to commit large sums of money to advertising.

Critical Factor: "Agency A is located in New York City."

Critical to Solution Because: Our company's location (small suburb of Indianapolis) creates an extremely inconvenient working relationship.

Critical Factor: "The previous advertising results of creative strategy number 2."

Critical to Solution Because: Our experience with this strategy has been less than satisfactory in the past.

4. ALTERNATIVE SOLUTIONS

You need to list all reasonable alternatives and provide a brief analysis of the pros and cons of each. Here are abbreviated examples:

Possible Solution: Increase advertising budget from $500,000 to $1,500,000 during next campaign period.

Pros: Enhances the possibilities of achieving advertising objectives.
Cons: Substantially increases the company's operating expenses with little assurance of success.

Possible Solution: Retain the services of Agency A.
Pros: This agency has clearly demonstrated familiarity with our product line and provides the creative expertise we require.
Cons: Agency A is located more than 500 miles from our offices, thereby causing inconvenience and additional expense.

Possible Solution: Use creative strategy Alternative B.
Pros: Concept test scores are highest for this alternative and none of our competitors is using this strategy.
Cons: This alternative is the most expensive to implement. Also, it is a complete departure from anything used in the industry and might be too innovative.

5. RECOMMENDED SOLUTION

All that is required here is a one-sentence statement of the alternative solution that you recommend. Make sure that the solution you recommend is clearly identified and has been objectively analyzed in the Alternative Solutions step.

6. RATIONALE/JUSTIFICATION

Defend your choice. Be confident, assured, positive. Avoid statements like:

If you have to have an answer, I guess I'd go with Alternative A, but I really don't think there's any way to solve this problem.

I really don't know why I selected Alternative B. I just think it's better than the other two.

The basis of your rationale should be the analysis presented in the Alternative Solutions step. Your statement should say something like this:

I've selected Alternative A because the advantages of taking this course of action far outweigh any disadvantages. Furthermore, Alternative A is most consistent with the company advertising objectives, marketing goals, and company philosophy. In addition, . . .

Or, something like this will work:

Despite the high cost of implementing Creative Strategy Alternative B, it is being recommended here because at this time in our company's development, cost is secondary to the need for an innovative creative approach. This strategy clearly provides . . .

7. OTHER RELEVANT COMMENTS

Now is the time to rid yourself of the many frustrations you will encounter in the case. Go ahead with suggestions and comments about other marketing and business considerations. Be a little cautious, though. Remember your position within the firm and the need to "win over" your superiors.

ORGANIZATION OF THE BOOK: FRAMEWORK FOR ADVERTISING MANAGEMENT DECISION MAKING

The cases in this book are organized into eight major sections and the sequencing of the sections reflects our view of the process of making effective advertising and promotion decisions. The most successful organizations tend to be those that understand the relationship among the various communications decisions that must be made. For example, a poor creative execution is most likely caused by problems in specifying realistic advertising objectives. And, vague objectives are usually the result of a lack of understanding of the specific role advertising is to play in the total promotion mix.

An understanding of the advertising function within the broader environments of marketing and promotion is fundamental to effective decision making. Since advertising is only a part of these environments, the decision maker must come to appreciate the impact of both marketing and promotion on the series of decisions that follow (Section 1).

As shown in Figure 1, the first advertising management decision area is determining the role of advertising within the promotion mix (Section 2). This decision becomes the major

influence on setting advertising objectives (Section 3). The organization's advertising objectives, in turn, should be the major influence on determining the size of the advertising investment (Section 4).

While we tend to see creative decisions (Section 5) being made before media decisions (Section 6), there are many advertising situations in which media decisions must precede creative ones. One thing is clear—neither creative nor media can be executed until the decision maker knows what funds have been allocated.

Advertising Research (Section 7) simply tells management how effective its decisions have been or how successful they are likely to be (Was the advertising budget large enough? Were the creative strategy and execution effective? Was the media plan efficient?). Measuring the results of the advertising program also gives management its most reliable feedback for preparing for the next campaign period.

Managing the Advertising Program (Section 8) is the last section of the book and frankly it could just as easily be the first. At some point in

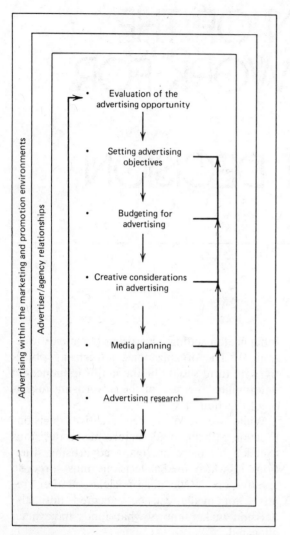

FIGURE 1
Framework For Advertising Management Decision
Making

the development of an advertising campaign the organization must make decisions about personnel. Who will be responsible for creative, media, research, and so forth? Are these tasks ones which we (the advertiser) can, or should perform? Or will they be accomplished more effectively by others? Some organizations begin the advertising process by making this decision. Others prefer to develop at least general advertising plans and strategies before making personnel decisions. The main point is that the personnel decision is an important one for advertising management.

As you experience the advertising industry, you'll find that some organizations make their decisions in precisely the same sequence we are suggesting here. Others have their own decision sequence. We have organized our book around a sequential framework that we believe produces the most effective decisions for advertising and promotion management.

SECTION 1
ADVERTISING WITHIN THE MARKETING AND PROMOTION ENVIRONMENT

Bringing products and services to the marketplace involves a number of complex, interrelated decisions. It is now widely acknowledged that marketplace success depends on the interaction of the internal and external factors surrounding the firm. For all products, it is vital that the qualities that will satisfy the buyers' wants are communicated to the target markets effectively—the right message delivered to the right audience, through the right channels, with the right amount of frequency. However, the communications or promotion variable is not always the most important factor in determining success. Often, one or more other variables—price, product, or distribution, for example—are more significant. Frequently, the external environment determines a company's fate—a new law, a sudden shift in the economy, or a change in social or cultural values.

Further, the advertising effort, just like every company function, competes for company resources. A company can communicate in a number of ways; therefore, in a sense, the advertising department competes with the sales department, the public relations department, and the sales promotion department. In a larger sense, the total promotion program competes for the resources that a company has to allocate to other marketing areas (product development, for example) or to general business areas (such as investment in capital equipment).

To understand how advertising works for any company, it is necessary to appreciate its relationship to broader business decisions. Although the advertising manager is rarely responsible for these broader decisions, he or she must come to understand that advertising both affects and is affected by such decisions. For these reasons, Section 1 contains a series of cases that concern advertising issues within the broader contexts of marketing and promotion. Among the issues to be addressed in this section are:

How an advertising and promotion program can most effectively be initiated

How advertising and promotion can be used to communicate a new shopping concept

The interrelationship among the various forms of promotion

As you read and analyze the cases, you will discover many other issues that are relevant to understanding how the advertising function interacts with other components of the marketing program.

1
VIDEOSHOP—MARK-TELE, INC.

Cable television began to spread rapidly across the United States during the late 1970s. It was promoted to subscribers predominantly as an entertainment media that would provide an expanded choice of high-quality television programming.

Some advertising and marketing experts perceived cable television differently. They saw it as opening a revolutionary new dimension in commercial communications. In the short run, cable television would generate new advertising and direct marketing opportunities. As telecommunication technology improved in the long run, cable television could become a direct threat to conventional shopping systems. Most experts, however, forecasted that significant changes in consumer shopping patterns were at least a decade or two away. Mr. Richard Johnson disagreed. He was the managing director of Mark-Tele, Inc., one of the more innovative and aggressive cable television companies.

During the fall of 1981, Mr. Johnson began to prepare a proposal for presentation to his board of directors at their forthcoming winter meeting. The proposal would suggest that Mark-Tele develop several new television channels. These channels would be unconventional. Most cable channels involved either an entertainment, educational, or public information format. The proposed new channels would involve innovative commercial formats using telecommunications technology that would allow organizations to market and sell directly to consumers in their own homes. A new marketplace would be created. Mr. Johnson named this concept, "VideoShop."

This case was prepared by Professor Michael P. Mokwa and Karl Gustafson (M.B.A., 1981), both of Arizona State University.

THE NEW VENTURE

Several months earlier, Mr. Johnson had created a new ventures task force. The mission of this task force was to generate and study novel programming formats that could be developed into new cable channels in the near term, and possibly into new networks in the long run. These new channels would be used by Mark-Tele to generate additional revenues, to increase its subscription base, and to allocate operating costs more effectively.

The current capacity of the Mark-Tele cable system was 52 different channels, but only 31 were in use. When Mark-Tele began operations, they had only twelve channels but had grown steadily. Costs had been relatively constant regardless of the number of channels that Mark-Tele operated. Thus, Mr. Johnson perceived Mark-Tele's cost structure as highly fixed, and he foresaw the development of new channels as a means of distributing these costs. Mr. Johnson expected that new channels would draw new subscribers, that subscription rates could be raised as more channels were added, and that subscription revenue could grow faster than corresponding operating costs.

The new ventures task force was carefully selected. It included the operations and sales managers from Mark-Tele, two product development specialists from Mark-Tele's parent company, and a consultant from the communications industry. An excerpt of their report to Mr. Johnson is presented in the Appendix.

The task force recommended that Mark-Tele develop several new cable channels using television as the medium for shopping. Each Mark-Tele subscriber could "tune into" these shopping channels. The subscriber could control and execute an entire shopping experience in the home. Products and services could be purchased directly, or the subscriber could gather specific information about a particular product or service and competitive offerings before making an important buying decision. The task force report indicated that eleven different product or service lines appeared viable for the new shopping concept.

Mr. Johnson was thrilled with the new venture idea and the task force report. He wanted to develop and implement the concept quickly. First, he selected a distinctive name for the venture, identifying it as VideoShop. Next, he met informally with some prospective salespeople, distributors, and retailers from different product and service fields. Most of the meetings were casual lunches or dinners. Mr. Johnson sensed some strong but very cautious interest and support from some prospective suppliers. Then he carefully reviewed and screened the list of product and service lines that had been proposed in the task force report.

Mr. Johnson felt that each of the proposed lines was feasible, but he wanted to focus his efforts on those products and services (a) that appeared to be easiest and most profitable to implement in the near term, and (b) that appeared to have the strongest interest among the prospective suppliers with whom he had met. Five lines were selected for development:

1. Catalog sales by regional and national retailers
2. Ticket reservations for concerts, plays, and sporting events, as well as reservations at local restaurants
3. Airline ticket reservations and vacation planning
4. A multiple listing service for real estate companies to display homes and commercial property that were for sale in the area or possibly from areas across the country.
5. Grocery products

Mr. Johnson expected that he could find outstanding firms from each product or service field to participate in the VideoShop venture under terms that Mark-Tele would set forth. He thought the costs to each firm would be small when compared with the benefits of newly accessible markets.

MARK-TELE'S BACKGROUND

Mark-Tele was founded in 1977 as a wholly owned subsidiary of Intertronics, Inc., a large corporation based in New York City. Intertronics was founded in 1973 as a joint venture among three well-respected, multinational firms. One firm was primarily in the information-processing industry, another was a publishing and broadcasting conglomerate, and the third was a high-technology producer in electronics. The mission of Intertronics was to design, develop, and implement innovative, applied telecommunications systems for domestic consumer markets. Intertronics received financial support and full technological cooperation from its parent companies but was operated as an autonomous venture. It managed each of its subsidiaries using the same orientation.

During 1978, Mark-Tele bid to install cable television systems in several large metropolitan areas in the United States. Late that year it was granted the right to install a cable television system in a large growing southwestern metropolitan area. Mark-Tele's management was excited to begin operations and to enter this particular area.

The area had more than a sufficient number of households to support a cable television company profitably according to industry standards. More important, the population was growing rapidly. National and international companies were locating headquarters or building large manufacturing facilities in the area. The growth of industry meant a tremendous increase in the number of families relocating into the area. This growth was projected to continue for at least the next fifteen years, thus representing a very attractive cable market for Mark-Tele. Intertronics would use Mark-Tele's location as the test site for a new type of cable television technology. The traditional type of cable used in cable television systems was a one-way cable because a signal could be directed only from the cable television company *to* the individual households attached to the service.

Recently, Intertronics had developed a two-way cable that was capable of transmitting and receiving signals both from the cable television company and from individual households connected to the system. Thus, a home could send signals *back* to the cable television company. Two-way cable communication processes were used in a few other areas of the country, but these cable systems required the use of a telephone line along with the one-way cable. The cost of the new two-way cable was nearly four times the cost of the one-way cable. Because Mark-Tele was a test site, they and their subscribers received the cable system at a substantially reduced cost.

To implement the two-way cable, Mark-Tele installed an interactive device to the television set of each of its subscribers. These devices facilitated communication between the Mark-Tele building and individual homes. The interactive devices resembled a small desk-top electronic calculator. These devices were expensive to install, but Intertronics absorbed most of the installation cost. The remaining cost was reflected in slightly higher-than-average monthly subscription charges paid by subscribers. The subscription charge for basic cable services from Mark-Tele was $11 per month. The comparable rate that Mark-Tele would charge for one-way cable would be $8.50 per month.

Mark-Tele's first year of operations concluded with 5,000 subscribers and a small negative net operating profit. In the following year, Mark-Tele subscriptions increased to 38,000, generating a net profit of almost 1.4 million dollars. In 1980 Mark-Tele continued aggressively to attract more subscribers, reaching 50,000 total. Net profit increased to exceed $2 million.

Financial statements for 1979 and 1980 are presented in Exhibit 1.

Research by Mark-Tele suggested that the potential number of homes for the cable network in their market area exceeded 400,000 over the next five years. In ten years the market potential was forecasted to be nearly 750,000 homes. A demographic profile of current subscribers is presented in Exhibit 2.

Mark-Tele offered many different channel formats. These channels provided a wide variety of programming for virtually any type of viewer. Several of the channels were "pay television." For these, a household would pay an additional charge beyond the basic monthly rate. Pay

EXHIBIT 1

Income Statement Mark-Tele, Inc.

Fiscal Years Ending December 31, 1979 and 1980

	1979[a]	1980[b]
Revenues		
Subscription revenue	$4,560,000	$6,600,000
Pay service revenue	4,104,000	5,400,000
Total revenue	$8,664,000	$12,000,000
Expenses		
Operation expense (includes salaries)	$3,852,000	$5,248,000
Sales expense	1,913,400	2,610,300
Interest expense	136,200	136,200
Depreciation expense	74,800	74,800
Rent exepense	46,000	46,000
Equipment maintenance expense	32,500	34,700
Total expense	$6,054,900	$8,150,000
Gross profit	$2,609,100	$3,850,000
Taxes @ 47%	$1,226,277	$1,809,500
Net profit	$1,382,823	$2,040,500

[a]Based on subscriptions of 38,000 homes with a subscription rate of $10 per month per home, and average home "pay service" of $9 per month per home.

[b]Based on total subscriptions of 50,000 homes with a subscription rate of $11 per month per home, and average home "pay service" of $9 per month per home.

EXHIBIT 2
1980 Demographic Analysis of
Mark-Tele Subscribers[a]

Family Size		Age of Paying Subscriber	
1	17.6%	18–25	22.4%
2	22.8	26–35	19.2
3	10.8	36–45	19.6
4	19.3	46–55	17.7
5	15.1	56–65	7.1
6	5.8	66–75	8.3
7+	8.6	76+	5.7

Family Income ($000)		Residency	
$0–$8	1.3%	Home owners	71.6%
$9–$18	15.7	Renters	28.4
$19–$28	18.3		
$29–$35	17.5		
$36–$45	19.6		
$46–$59	12.7		
$60,000+	14.9		

Number of Hours Home Television Active per Week		Number of Years of Education of Paying Subscribers	
0–7	2.5%	0–8	1.4%
8–14	15.1	9–11	22.5
15–21	17.2	12	21.8
22–28	40.7	13–15	26.3
29–35	20.8	16+	28.0
36+	3.7		

[a]Based on 50,000 subscribers.

television services were very successful. The revenue nearly matched basic subscription revenue for Mark-Tele in 1980. A schedule for the allocation of Mark-Tele's 52-channel capacity is presented in Exhibit 3. Both current and prospective channels are listed.

CABLE TELEVISION TECHNOLOGY

Cable television became increasingly popular during the 1970s. This can be attributed largely to significant advances in computer and communications technologies, as well as regulatory and legal changes, in the telecommunications industry.

The Mark-Tele cable television system was

EXHIBIT 3
Channel Allocation Schedule

Cable Channel Number	Designated Programming/Service
1	Mark-Tele Channel Listing[a]
2	Program Guide[a]
3	Local Transit Schedule[a]
4	Classified Ads and Yard Sales[a]
5	Weather Radar and Time[a]
6	Dow Jones Cable News[a]
7	Reserved for Future Use
8[b]	Home Box Office[a]
9[b]	Showtime[a]
10[b]	The Movie Channel[a]
11[b]	Golden Oldies Channel[a]
12	Reserved for Future Use
13	Reserved for Future Use
14	Cable News Network[a]
15	Reserved for Future Use
16	UPI News Scan[a]
17	Government Access[a]
18	Music Television[a]
19[b]	Stereo Rock Concert[a]
20	Educational Access[a]
21	Educational Access: New York University[a]
22	Proposed Educational Access
23	Proposed Interactive Channel for Lease
24	Proposed Interactive Channel for Lease
25	Proposed Interactive Channel for Lease
26	VideoShop: *Retail Sales Channel*
27	VideoShop: *Entertainment Tickets and Restaurants*
28	VideoShop: *Grocery Products*
29	VideoShop: Reserved
30	VideoShop: Reserved
31	USA Network[a]
32	WTBS, Atlanta, Channel 17[a]
33	WOR, New York, Channel 9[a]
34	K///, Local ABC Affiliate
35	Christian Broadcasting Network[a]
36	ESPN (Sports) Network[a]
37	K///, Local Station, Channel 15[a]
38	K///, Local NBC Affiliate, Channel 8[a]
39	K///, Local CBS Affiliate, Channel 11[a]
40	Proposed Channel for Lease
41	Concert Connection[a]
42	WGN, Chicago, Channel 9[a]
43	Public Access: Cultural Bulletin Board[a]
44[b]	Proposed Games Channel
45	Public Access: Library Information[a]
46	Proposed Public Access
47	Public Broadcasting System
48	Reserved for Future Banking Transactions
49	VideoShop: *Airline Tickets and Travel*
50	VideoShop: *Real Estate Showcase*
51	Reserved for Future Use
52	Reserved for Future Use

[a]Active channel. [b]Optional pay service.

controlled by a sophisticated configuration of minicomputers with high-speed communications between each processor. Three computers, each used for a different task, ensured that viewers would have access to the cable network at all times.

The main computer transmitted cable signals to each individual home using the two-way cable lines. The second computer's function was to back up the main computer in the event that a system failure occurred. The second computer would be a vital element of the VideoShop system because it could be used as an update system for suppliers to amend information regarding their products or services. This computer also could be used to transmit the orders or reservations placed by shopping subscribers directly to prospective suppliers. The third computer functioned as another backup if system failures occurred simultaneously to the main computers. A very sophisticated software application integrating the communication network and operating system had been developed to assure 99 percent uptime for the cable system. A diagram sketching the Mark-Tele cable system is presented in Exhibit 4.

The cable system incorporated two different types of storage devices. The first type of storage disk (a magnetic disk) was used to store data, such as billing information about a particular subscriber. The second type of disk involved an innovative technology that could be used extensively by the VideoShop system. The disk, called a "video disk unit" (VDU), was capable of storing images or pictures like a movie camera. VideoShop suppliers could store images of their products and services on these disks so that subscribers to the cable system could access the images at any time. Only through the use of the new two-way cable developed by Intertronics would it be possible to incorporate the video disk units into a cable network. The two-way cable allowed signals to travel from the main computer to an individual television, and from the television back to the main computer.

Two-way communication was possible through the use of the interactive indexing device attached to each subscriber's television. This indexing device was a small box, about the size of a cigar box. It contained special electronics allowing the device to transmit data back to the main computer. On top of the indexing device there were twelve keys simply called the keypad. An individual subscriber could use the keypad to call up "menus," sort through a menu, and send data back to the main computer. "Menu" is a computer term used to describe listings of general categories from which additional information can be drawn.

Using a prospective VideoShop example, let's say a menu for a channel containing airline information could first indicate to a viewer the different airlines from which to choose. The viewer could than push the key on the keypad that corresponds to the airline that he or she was interested in using. The next menu could show all the different cities to which the chosen airline flies. The viewer then could push the key on the keypad that corresponds to the city to which he or she wishes to travel. The following screen could provide the flight numbers and times during which flights are available. From the information on that screen, the user could make a reservation which would be transmitted to the airline's computer through the Mark-Tele computer. Finally, the reservation would be logged and confirmed, and tickets would be mailed to the viewer. The entire transaction would take only a few minutes to execute. The shopper would control the entire experience in the home environment, simply, and efficiently.

VIDEOSHOP CHANNELS

Mr. Johnson believed that the most significant factors that would affect the successful acceptance of VideoShop by consumers were: (a) the quality of the picture viewed by the subscribers, (b) the accuracy of the information provided by suppliers to shoppers, (c) the convenience and

EXHIBIT 4
Mark-Tele Two-Way Cable System

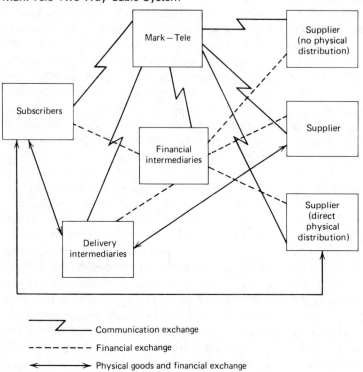

ease of using the system to shop, (d) the technical reliability of the system, and (e) the delivery, billing, and return policies of suppliers. Mr. Johnson felt strongly that control over suppliers would be vital to assure the success of VideoShop. He thought that Mark-Tele should form a small consumer satisfaction department to conduct VideoShop consumer studies, to review the VideoShop policies and operations of all involved suppliers, and to resolve all consumer problems and complaints.

Mr. Johnson felt that the five shopping channels that he had selected from the list generated by the task force would work well given the nature of the success factors that he perceived to be important. He prepared a brief description for each of the prospective shopping channels and a pro forma income statement. He would use these to build his presentation for the forthcoming board meeting and to develop a prospectus to sell the VideoShop concept to suppliers. The pro forma statement is presented in Exhibit 5.

The Catalog Sales Channel(s)

National and regional retailers could use the VideoShop system to sell and promote their entire merchandise lines including their most current items and prices. Shoppers would have the opportunity to view merchandise on the television screen in their own home, avoiding the inconvenience of a shopping trip or the boredom of thumbing through a catalog. Information about products and prices could be presented in a format similar to catalog books,

EXHIBIT 5

Pro Forma Income Statement: VideoShop Operation[a]

Revenue

Catalog Purchase Channel	$ 300,000
Airline Reservation Channel	400,000
Ticket Sales and Restaurant Channel	150,000
Multiple Listing Service Channel	36,000
Total Revenue	$ 886,000

Expenses

Salaries	$ 240,000
Administrative expense	52,000
Communication expense (telephone lines)	19,200
Depreciation expense	15,700
Interest expense	13,820
Equipment maintenance	4,200
Total expenses	$ 344,920
Contribution	$ 541,080

[a]Based on 50,000 subscription base and task force projections.

or innovative action formats could be developed to simulate a store environment or create some novel context.

Retailers would be responsible for developing appropriate video disk units and keeping information current. Mark-Tele could provide a consulting service to help suppliers produce effective video disks. Mark-Tele could also reserve the right to reject any material that was felt to be inappropriate. However, Mark-Tele would attempt to be open-minded. For example, products that consumers find embarrassing to purchase at a store could be considered a prime prospect for Video-Shop, if presentations were tasteful.

A shopper could use the interactive indexing device to direct and control an entire shopping experience. This could involve viewing information about product features and prices from one retailer and then quickly switching to another retailer's presentation for comparative information. In addition, a shopper desiring more

extensive information could access a brief demonstration or informative advertisement about a product. After the shopper selected a product, the interactive device could transmit the order through Mark-Tele's computing system directly to the retailer's processing system. The retailer could present alternative payment programs and specific delivery schedules or instructions. The shopper could charge purchases using national or store credit cards and could pickup the merchandise directly (but conveniently) or could have it delivered.

Mark-Tele could charge each retailer a service fee based upon a fixed percentage of shoppers' invoice values (before taxes). Individual retailers could be billed monthly and various payment programs could be formulated. The new ventures task force estimated that an average home would purchase a minimum of $300 worth of retail merchandise annually through VideoShop. They proposed a service charge rate of 2 percent. Mark-Tele could also generate revenue selling video consulting services to the suppliers.

This shopping and marketing scenario could be the prototype for all the VideoShop channels. Adaptations for different product or service lines and shopping patterns would be relatively easy to implement.

Ticket Sales and Restaurant Reservation Channel

VideoShop could provide to subscribers detailed information concerning local entertainment alternatives. Entertainment organizations could present exciting promotional spots using the video disk technology and sell tickets directly to VideoShop subscribers.

Entertainment shoppers could use video menus to select a particular entertainment form such as movies, theater, or sporting events. On another menu they could view all the relevant alternative events and then access specific promotional spots about events that interested them. These spots could blend information about performance schedules and locations with features about or highlights of the event. The shopper could select an event and a specific performance, then purchase tickets. Tickets could be sold using conventional diagrams of seating arrangements or innovative graphic formats, or the shopper could actually be presented with the view from a specific seat or area of seating using the video disk technology. When tickets were purchased, these could be paid for using credit cards at the time of purchase, or payment could be mailed or made at the time of the event. Likewise, tickets could be mailed or picked up.

Another dimension of this channel could be a restaurant promotion and reservation feature. Restaurant menus and promotional spots could be made accessible for diners. Once diners have chosen a particular restaurant using the menu and spots, they could make a reservation and even select a specific table (if the restaurant developed, as part of its VideoShop system, a seating arrangement routine similar to that of the entertainment organizations).

All VideoShop ticket purchases and reservations could be transmitted directly from the shopper's home through Mark-Tele computers to the restaurant or ticket outlet. Most restaurants and small entertainment organizations would have to purchase or lease a small "intelligence" computing terminal to receive reservations or ticket orders and to keep information updated. Intertronics could supply these.

The task force felt that this channel could generate at least $150,000 revenue per year given the current subscriber base. They recommended a $25 per month minimum charge to restaurants and a $.50 service fee per ticket reservation. They were unsure of a fee schedule for entertainment organizations that would only promote events and would not be selling tickets directly through VideoShop. However, they thought that rates similar to commercial advertising rates would be appropriate.

Airline Ticket Sales and Travel Accommodations Channel

Discussions with the task force concluded that an airline ticket sales channel could be the easiest for Mark-Tele to implement and operate in the short run and also could be most lucrative financially. Projected revenue for the first year of operating this channel was $400,000 based upon a very conservative usage rate and an extremely competitive pricing policy.

This channel could allow subscribers to make airline reservations, purchase their tickets, and select travel accommodations using the same fundamental interactive shopping procedures as other VideoShop channels. Shoppers could avoid the aggravating inconveniences of current airline reservation systems and could quickly do comparative shopping which current systems have inhibited. Research has shown that comparative shopping for airline fares often can save hundreds of dollars. Once a flight has been selected, the subscriber also could make hotel or motel reservations. VideoShop could allow hotels and motels visually to present rooms and surroundings and to promote themselves to *all* travelers.

Perhaps the most important characteristic of this channel could be the potential ease of implementation, once cooperation was secured from the airlines. The format and basic system used within the airlines industry to transmit, display, and process schedules, fares, and ticket information appeared to be compatible with the Mark-Tele system. Mark-Tele computers and cable lines could be used to link shoppers directly with airline ticket reservation systems, bypassing reservation clerks and travel agents. Subscriber's could select itineraries, then secure reservations and pay using major credit cards. Tickets could be mailed or picked up at airport ticket counters or other service locations.

Mark-Tele could record each ticket purchase and charge the appropriate airline a fixed fee of $4 per ticket. This rate was half of the $8 rate charged by most travel agents. The task force believed that a minimum average of two tickets would be purchased by each subscribing household per year. Revenue estimates were not made for the travel accommodations feature of this channel.

Multiple Listing Service Channel

A few large local realtors expressed strong interest in the VideoShop concept. Traditional promotional tools used to stimulate buyers' interest and help them make decisions about what properties to see in person included classified newspaper ads, newspaper supplements, brochures, "for sale" signs, the multiple listing catalog, and photographs of properties posted on an agency's wall. Most realtors and buyers found these boring. More important, these simply did not present most properties effectively. A frequent complaint among realtors and buyers was the high cost in time and dollars wasted traveling to and viewing personally properties that were not represented well in a promotion or informational item. VideoShop could provide an exciting and effective method for presenting realty.

While this VideoShop channel could be accessed by any subscriber, the channel would open a new commercial consumer market for Mark-Tele cable subscriptions—the realty agencies. Many agencies had a television on premise to entertain clients and their children or to provide a means "to catch the news" when business was slow. Some agencies already had purchased cable service from Mark-Tele.

A general issue was raised by the task force whether to charge a commercial subscriber different fees than a residential subscriber. A more specific issue regarding this channel was whether to limit access to realty agencies and others willing to pay an additional fee for it, or to open it for public access. The task force recommended open access and suggested that a minimum of thirty realty agencies would need to participate. Each could be charged a monthly fee of $100 or an annual fee of $1,000. The realtor would be responsible for producing and maintaining high-quality video disks with accurate and updated information. Mark-Tele could provide technical assistance and would monitor this channel carefully.

Grocery Products Channel

One of the most exciting prospects for Video-Shop could be a grocery products channel. It was the most interesting but difficult channel for which to design a format.

Grocery products are purchased very frequently, and everyone must buy. Consumers have tended to develop relatively consistent grocery shopping patterns. Expenditures on grocery items have been swelling. Many consumers find going shoping to be tedious, laborious, and inconvenient. Others such as handicapped people or shut-ins, simply cannot get to stores or cannot shop freely and comfortably in modern superstores. Likewise, groceries producers, wholesalers, and retailers have been threatened by escalating cost structures that reduce their margins substantially.

A VideoShop grocery channel thus could provide consumers with convenience, comfort, low shopping risks, and potential savings. For suppliers, it could generate increased control over operations and costs and higher profits. However, this VideoShop channel would directly attack an expensive, firmly established distribution network and basic, traditional patterns of shopping. Strong resistance from many consumers could be anticipated, and suppliers not involved in the venture could be expected to retaliate competitively. Also, there could be critical barriers to providing shoppers with a total assortment of grocery products including frozen and fresh items and to implementing a cost-effective delivery service or pickup procedure. Undoubtedly, these "bugs" could be worked out. The recommendation for this channel was to maintain its high priority as a channel to develop in the near term, but initially and quickly to invest funds in more design and research before contacting any specific prospective suppliers.

CONCLUSION: A TIME FOR REFLECTION AND/OR ACTION

One more time Mr. Johnson critically reviewed the task force report and his brief descriptions of prospective VideoShop channels. He felt simultaneously excitement, enthusiasm and some frustration. He and the task force had worked hard and creatively to formulate the idea of VideoShop. They thought that most technological barriers could be overcome, and they projected a very favorable cost structure. Definitely, VideoShop was a concept whose time had arrived! Mark-Tele's board, composed largely of Intertronics personnel, would have to be convinced.

Mark-Tele was a small company with only a few people and tight resources. It already was a high-investment and high-risk experimental venture receiving considerable financial support and subsidy from Intertronics. Would Intertronics feel that VideoShop was an extension of the Mark-Tele experiment or a contamination of it? Could the board be convinced to provide more resources and assistance, and what would they expect in return?

If VideoShop received approval and support from the board, Mr. Johnson was not exactly sure in which direction to proceed. He had identified the primary prospective channels, but which specific channel or channels should be developed first? What would be the operational design for a channel, and what type of marketing program would be needed to maximize market awareness and shopper adoption?

Mr. Johnson was also concerned that some of his assumptions and some of those of the task force might be too optimistic, particularly those concerning the costs to suppliers. The task force had recommended that prospective suppliers should incur most of the start-up and maintenance expenses, as well as the risks. Yet, it appeared that Mark-Tele would skim the Video-Shop revenues without much direct cost or risk. Would suppliers accept Mark-Tele's conditions for operations? The entire supply issue would require significant attention. Which specific suppliers would contribute most to VideoShop? Which suppliers would work best with Mark-Tele, and what type of relationships would evolve? How would a marketing program be formulated to reach prospective suppliers?

Suddenly, Mr. Johnson realized that he was vascillating. If Mark-Tele didn't implement VideoShop soon, someone would. VideoShop was a great idea. Mr. Johnson simply lacked the strategic plan that he could use to convince the board and to market VideoShop to suppliers and shoppers.

QUESTIONS FOR DISCUSSION

1. Identify the major advertising and promotion challenges involved in implementing VideoShop.
2. Outline a promotion plan Mr. Johnson could use as part of an overall strategic plan.

APPENDIX
NEW VENTURE TASK FORCE REPORT PROPOSING A TELECOMMUNICATIONS SHOPPING SYSTEM*

We recommend that Mark-Tele design and implement a telecommunication shopping (TCS) system immediately. This proposed new venture appears to be a natural extension of Mark-Tele's experimental mission and an excellent application of Mark-Tele's distinctive technological capabilities in the telecommunications field.

A TCS system would allow a Mark-Tele subscriber to become an active shopper and buyer in the privacy of the home using only the television. Facilitated by Mark-Tele's sophisticated communications and computing technologies, a TCS system subscriber would be able to view and buy a large variety of products and services that conventionally would have required the shopper to leave the home and travel to view and purchase. A TCS system would also serve the suppliers of many different products and services with an opportunity to break away from costly traditional market channels and inexpensively to expand their market coverage and increase sales substantially.

For Mark-Tele, a TCS system would increase revenues, diversify its revenue base, and distribute its high fixed costs efficiently. A TCS system could be used as a promotional tool to build and maintain Mark-Tele's local subscription base. Current subscription rates could be raised with the addition of the TCS system, or an additional fee could be charged to subscribers who desire to participate in the TCS system. Suppliers and shopping subscribers would also be charged for services that Mark-Tele would provide in the development and operation of the TCS system. In the longer run, Mark-Tele could

*This is an abridged version of the committee's report. The authors thank Ms. Sherri Katz for her contribution to this report.

potentially develop TCS networks that could be sold to other cable systems. Clearly, early entry into the TCS field would be lucrative financially for Mark-Tele.

In the remainder of this report we will discuss: (1) significant environmental factors that influence the TCS market; (2) a general strategy for targeting the TCS system; (3) prospective product and service offerings; and (4) developmental issues for promoting the TCS system.

THE ENVIRONMENT OF TCS

Economic, social, technological, and legal and regulatory trends are emerging in support of a TCS system.

Increased consumer spending is predicted to continue, but gains for retailers will be restricted by inflationary pressures. There will be a slower pace of store expansion during the 1980s. Many of the major metropolitan areas are overbuilt with retail space, and developers often are experiencing difficulty obtaining sites and financing. Retailers similarly are experiencing rising rents. Sales growth at many shopping centers has fallen because of slow growth of suburban communities and shrinking distances that consumers are willing to travel to shop as gasoline prices continue to advance.

Retailers are attempting to boost productivity, consolidate store space, and cut costs to improve returns. Inflation has increased operating costs more rapidly than sales during the last ten years. Many retailers have been attracted to discount pricing policies. The catalog showroom has become one of the fastest-growing segments of discount merchandising featuring national-brand products at discount prices while operating on lower overhead than department stores.

Considering sociocultural trends, women are continuing to enter the work force, thus having less time to engage in shopping for staples as well as for discretionary purchases. Greater emphasis on recreational activities continues, and individuals are reluctant to sacrifice leisure time to shop in stores. Convenience is emerging as a high priority.

Consumers are emphasizing their self-identity. They are demanding more individuality in goods and services, often desiring distinctive products that individual stores may not be able to afford to inventory and display. Definitely, there has been more intense consumer preference for specialty items and services difficult to find in the Mark-Tele market area.

An increase in the number of single-parent and single-person households has led to increased in-home shopping. Nonstore innovations such as pay-by-phone, specialty mail-order catalogs, and toll-free phone ordering have become increasingly popular. Catalog shopping currently offers a full line of merchandise together with prices and features that permit a consumer to comparison shop at home without having to spend time inefficiently searching for products in crowded stores, waiting for sales help, or at times being annoyed by overzealous clerks.

In addition, the increasing age of the population, proliferation of retirement communities, and declining mobility of individuals in their later years make catalog shopping very attractive.

There are significant technological advances that will influence the TCS system. In the past, alphanumerics and graphics, but not still or moving "pictures," could be retrieved from a data bank and displayed on a television screen; however, Intertronics' innovative technologies have advanced moving picture capabilities. This new technology has permitted the consumer to control the timing, sequence, and content of information through the use of the keypad. Thus, the convenience of purchasing on impulse without need for either a telephone or advance

credit arrangements is viable. Purchases can be charged automatically to a bank or credit card account.

Development of video disks and video cassettes, which to date have been used by viewers to record television programs, have significant promise for advertising and catalog media. Potential exists for suppliers to mail lower-cost video catalogs on a complimentary basis or in lieu of printed direct-mail offerings.

Consumers are being exposed to and are accepting complex technical items such as videotape recorders, home computers, and debit cards for use with automatic teller machines. Home computers and the development of "videotex," the generic term for home information-retrieval systems, will provide functions compatible with those of the TCS system. Many consumers will easily develop the technical skills and sophistication needed to participate actively in the TCS system.

The political-legal context is confusing. The Federal Communications Commission has decided that cable franchising is mainly the province of local jurisdictions. All cable companies must interact with local governments to obtain and maintain authority to operate. While Mark-Tele has secured exclusive rights in their metropolitan area, changes in federal and local policy must be monitored, and good rapport with local leaders should be cultivated continuously.

The TCS venture raises questions concerning supplier and financial contractual arrangements. The antitrust implications of arrangements with some large institutions should be studied in more detail on a case-by-case basis. Moreover, movement into the retail sector by Mark-Tele through the TCS system will mean closer scrutiny by federal and local consumer protection agencies such as the Federal Trade Commission and Consumer Product Safety Commission. Finally, Mark-Tele will need to carefully consider protection of the privacy of personal, financial, and transactional data about subscribers to the TCS system. Controls must be established to prevent unauthorized access to information in the system data banks and to guard against unauthorized purchasing.

THE GENERAL COMPETITIVE CONTEXT

Industry observers clearly are divided when projecting the evolution of electronic shopping and its acceptance by both consumers and the industry. Consumers appear interested in the potential convenience, extended selections, fuel economies, discount prices, and time savings offered by the concept of shopping at home. Furthermore, at least ten thousand firms have expressed interest in the concept of electronic shopping. Currently, all forms of nonstore retailing are growing rapidly, and continued growth is forecasted. Major developments in nonstore retailing are reviewed below.

Mail-order Catalogs

General department store merchandisers, catalog showrooms, and specialty houses periodically mail catalogs to targeted groups of consumers. An average mail-order house distributes from six to twenty catalog issues yearly at a cost often approaching two dollars each. Circulations range from about one hundred thousand to over a million for each mailing. The results have been outstanding. Over $26 billion was spent by consumers on mail-order items in 1978—an increase of $12 billion in three years. By comparison, in-store retailing sales grew at a rate less than half of the mail-order rate. Mail-order firms' after-tax profits averaged 7 percent during this period.

Specialty firms such as L.L. Bean, Dallas's Horchow Collection, Talbot's of Massachusetts, and Hammacher Schlemmer of New York have become more prominent in the field. Specialty-oriented catalogs are accounting for 75 percent of total mail-order sales, and mail-order catalogs currently contribute 15 percent of the total volume of Christmas season sales.

Telephone and mail-generated orders, received by traditional store retailers such as Bloomingdales, J.C. Penney, and Sears are increasing three to five times faster than in-store sales. Sears found that 9.1 percent of its sales came from outside catalogs in 1977 and an additional 11.4 percent from catalog counters in the stores. Montgomery Ward derived 13 percent of its sales from catalogs.

In-flight shopping catalogs used by major airlines are additional evidence of the increasing popularity of nonstore shopping. Master Card, American Express, and Visa have increased their direct mail offerings to their credit card holders and are expanding their assortments of merchandise.

The Catalog Showrooms

The catalog showroom is one of the fastest growing fields of retailing. Catalogs are used to promote and feature jewelry, housewares, appliances, sporting goods, and toys at discount prices. Customers visit the showroom to inspect merchandise and to make purchases. Analysts suggest that 85 percent of sales are generated by the catalogs and the remainder by test selling products promoted on the showroom floor. Sales for 1980 are estimated to be $7.8 billion, an increase of 11 percent from 1979. Forecasts for 1981 suggest a 20 percent gain in sales revenue. The number of showrooms across the country is nearly 2,000.

Noninteractive Shopping Using the Cable

Comp-U-Card of Stamford, Connecticut, is a seven-year-old telephone merchandising firm. For an annual fee of $18, it offers members a discount on a broad line of durable goods. Members shop around, familiarizing themselves with products and prices. Then they call Comp-U-Card toll-free for specific information about an item's availability and price. If a purchase decision is made, the consumer provides membership and credit card numbers to an operator, and the merchandise is prepared for delivery. An experimental project has been proposed in which Comp-U-Card would use cable systems and satellite transmission to present product and price information to its subscribers. A transmitted schedule would alert subscribers to the time when particular product information would be presented. Subscribers would continue to use the telephone when ordering. In October 1980, Federated Department Stores acquired a substantial interest in Comp-U-Card.

Telephone purchasing systems using cable presentations are currently operating in Europe. In March 1979 the British Post Office, which runs Britain's telephone system, opened a "viewdata" service called "Prestel." Viewers are presented listings of games, restaurants, and consumer product evaluations. Products and services can be purchased on credit by phone. France launched a similar service called "Antiope" in 1979.

A few U.S. companies are testing similar systems. Viewdata Corp., a subsidiary of the Knight-Ridder newspaper chain, proposes to install a permanent system in southern Florida by 1983. First Bank System of Minneapolis will be testing a "videotex" system in North Dakota similar to the Antiope System of France.

Interactive Cable Systems and Videotex

Since December 1977, Warner Communications and American Express have been involved with a $70 million joint venture testing the QUBE two-way system of Warner Amex Cable in Columbus, Ohio. Currently, the system serves 30,000 of the 105,000 homes in its service area. American Express and Warner Communications propose to build other QUBE systems in such metropolitan areas as Houston, Pittsburgh, and Cincinnati. Both Sears and J.C. Penney currently are testing the QUBE system.

In May 1981, American Telephone & Telegraph (AT&T) endorsed a videotex concept in which a home computer terminal must be

purchased. AT&T has set out to develop its own system. AT&T would be a formidable opponent to anyone in the market, considering the firm's capabilities and financial strength. Thus, there are a number of legal actions being undertaken to prevent AT&T's direct entry into the videotex market, in the fear that it could become a monopoly power. However, strong deregulation sentiments may overcome the opposition and facilitate AT&T's entry into the market.

In summary, the TCS market is embryonic. Growth in nonstore retailing is providing a solid foundation upon which TCS systems can build. Over $100 million already has been invested by U.S. firms to design and test various TCS systems, and at least 83 experimental projects are being conducted around the world. As a result, Mark-Tele must be prepared to match formidable competition, and we feel confident that Mark-Tele can.

TARGET MARKET CONSIDERATIONS

The TCS system must be carefully tailored and targeted to meet market demands and expectations. There are two different markets that must be considered when developing this venture: (1) the suppliers, and (2) the shoppers.

We propose that the TCS system be targeted to the ultimate *user*—the subscribing shopper. A TCS system that is designed well will sell itself to suppliers. Suppliers, therefore, should be considered as a dimension of the "total product" that will be offered to target shoppers. This approach will allow Mark-Tele to retain maximum control and autonomy in the design and implementation of this venture.

The Target Market: Shoppers

A careful review of the size and characteristics of the current and potential Mark-Tele subscription base indicates substantial market potential and buying power. However, critical analysis of shopping and buying behavior is necessary to isolate the most lucrative prospective customer segments and to understand their prospective TCS behavior. Three buying factors appear to be very important: (1) risk perceptions, (2) convenience orientations, and (3) buyer satisfaction.

Risk. Buying is a complex experience filled with uncertainty and related risks of unfavorable consequences. Fundamentally, consumers confront the uncertainty of achieving their buying goals and face risks such as embarrassment or wasting time, money, or effort in a disappointing buying or shopping experience. Consumers usually are not highly conscious of these until they face new, different, or very important buying decisions or situations. In general, shopping is used to reduce uncertainty, risk, and potential disappointment. More specifically, consumers shop to help refine their buying goals, to search for and evaluate specific products and terms, to execute transactions, and to favorably reinforce past purchase behaviors.

When consumers consider TCS experiences, they must feel comfortable and in control. All shopping and buying uncertainties, risks, and potential negative consequences must be minimized throughout the total TCS experience. Initially, the consumer must learn how to operate/interface with the TCS system. One positive experience should build into others.

During the TCS experience, some traditional risk-reduction tactics such as personal inspection of merchandise on interaction with salespeople will not be available to the shopper. However, there are significant risk-reduction tactics that will be accessible. These include:

Visual and audio comparison of a wide assortment and range of products and services

Information access and collection controlled by the shopper

Information availability regarding many product features and all terms of sale and delivery

Promotional messages that present products and services in attractive, exciting, and believable formats

Past experiences with the product, service, brand or supplier

Personal experiences shared by significant friends, relatives, or peers

Testimonials from respected celebrities, peers, or experts

Continuous building of positive shopping experiences with the TCS system

These risk-reduction tactics should be incorporated into the TCS system design and promoted during operations.

In short, we suggest (a) that uncertainty and risk can be significantly reduced by presenting TCS, and its products and services, as personal and uncomplicated, and (b) that shopping confidence can be built by involving shoppers in positive TCS experiences. For example, some exploratory studies have indicated that shoppers feel confident ordering merchandise by television when: (1) the product or service is easily recognizable and clearly identified by brand, retailer, size, color, and/or other relevant properties; (2) consumers could access the information when they felt ready to actually make the purchase; and (3) consumers had purchased the product or service previously.

Convenience. Shopping is a problem-solving activity. The TCS system offers solutions to many nagging problems encountered when shopping conventionally. Consider the following common aggravations: having to carry merchandise; adapting to limited store hours; poor and confusing displays of merchandise; difficulty finding desired items; dealing directly with salespeople; spending time and money traveling to the store; crowds of shoppers; boredom and fatigue of going from department to department and store to store. These are some of the inconveniences of conventional shopping systems that TCS can overcome.

A strong need or orientation for convenience is an appropriate base for identifying and understanding the primary target market for the TCS system. The following customer characteristics should be used to identify target market boundaries and to isolate specific segments within the primary target market. In the future, these could be cross-tabulated with other demographic, behavioral, and media characteristics to further refine target segment definitions and to tailor market programs.

Primary target customers for the TCS system are those Mark-Tele subscribers:

With greater than average need or desire for convenience

With restricted mobility because children are at home

With appropriate buying power and media (credit cards)

Who compile shopping lists regularly

Who are frequent catalog shoppers

Who rely extensively on newspaper, magazine, or television advertising

Who are loyal to specific brands or suppliers

Who do not like to travel or find it very difficult to do so

Who do not like to deal with crowds

Who are handicapped physically

Who are actively engaged in time-consuming leisure activities

Who are senior citizens

Satisfaction. A consumer must have a satisfying experience each time that the TCS system is used. Otherwise, it is very likely that the consumer will not use TCS again and may discuss the bad experience with other shoppers and discourage their future use of the system. Thus, Mark-Tele must maintain tight control over suppliers. A consumer satisfaction department should be formed within Mark-Tele. This group should monitor all TCS activities, conduct market research, investigate all consumer complaints, and make certain that all consumers are fully informed and satisfied with TCS.

Supplier Market Implications

After selecting general product and service categories and designing a general format for each TCS channel, Mark-Tele should direct attention to the supplier market. At that time, Mark-Tele should evaluate prospective suppliers regarding the relevance of their product or service assortment, their delivery and financial capabilities, the quality of their promotional strategies, and their desire to enter into this unconventional market. We feel that Mark-Tele's technical competence and captive subscription base will provide substantial leverage in all negotiations with suppliers. The actual marketing effort should involve personal selling programs custom designed for each prospective target supplier.

PROSPECTIVE PRODUCTS AND SERVICES

Preliminary research on TCS systems have uncovered a number of product and service lines that are appropriate for our target market and appear to be financially and technically feasible. As this innovative approach to shopping evolves and consumer acceptance and involvement grow, many other products and services could be incorporated. However, the most feasible products and services currently are:

Standard catalog items

Staple grocery items

Gifts and specialty items

Appliances and home entertainment equipment

Toys, electronic games and equipment, basic sporting goods

Banking and financial services

Classified ads

Multiple listing service of local properties

Ticket, restaurant, and accommodations reservations

Educational classes

Automobiles

We cannot stress too strongly that TCS will involve a high degree of risk perceived by consumers. This must be reduced by offering products and services with which consumers are familiar and comfortable and that involve a minimum number of simple shopping decisions for consumers.

The consumer must *learn* to use the TCS system. Mark-Tele must guide this learning experience and make sure that consumers have consistent, positive shopping experiences that became reinforcing. The following services/features should be incorporated into the TCS system to reduce shopping risks and facilitate consumer satisfaction.

Easy-to-use indexing devices

Top-quality visual and audio representation

Professional promotions

Up-to-date information on specials

Competitive pricing policies and convenient payment methods

TCS availability 24 hours per day, seven days per week

Maintenance service availability 24 hours per day, seven days per week

Accurate order-taking and -fulfilling

Prompt delivery or pickup services

Quick and equitable handling and resolution of customer complaints

Exceptional reliability

Eventually, the TCS product and service assortment could be broadened and channel features changed. However, the products and service lines outlined in this report appear to involve minimal consumer risks, high potential for competitive advantage and target consumer satisfaction, and substantial returns for Mark-Tele.

THE COMPETITIVE ADVANTAGE AND TCS PROMOTION

A competitive advantage over conventional suppliers can be achieved by Mark-Tele if the TCS system is designed to serve the needs and expectations of the identified target market by actively considering their prepurchase deliberations, by guiding their purchase activities, and by reinforcing their postpurchase satisfaction. This must be complemented with accurate and reliable order processing and with prompt, efficient logistical support. Above all, Mark-Tele must communicate and promote its distinctive capabilities. We believe that the following distinctive features of the TCS system should be emphasized.

The extensive variety and depth of product and service assortments

The vast amount of relevant information that is easily accessible and allows consumers to make better choices

The excitement, involvement, convenience, and satisfaction of shopping in the privacy of one's home using space-age technology and the simplicity of television

The insignificant, negligible, and indirect costs to consumers, particularly when compared with the opportunities and benefits

We feel that the best medium for promotion of the TCS system will be the television itself. Promotional information should be presented on all television channels other than pay channels. The TCS system initially should be portrayed as a new, exciting service available to all Mark-Tele subscribers. After this campaign, the theme should be changed to focus on *how* the TCS system works *for* and *with* the subscriber/consumer. A final campaign should be developed to reinforce and to encourage extended usage of the TCS system.

Enclosures and brochures in billing statements should be used extensively in support of the television campaigns to alert subscribers to the availability of the TCS system, to detail operational dimensions, and to discuss changes and additions to the system before these occur. Demonstration projects probably can be executed using the television rather than personal contact.

Mailing, print media, and personal selling appear to be appropriate means for reaching prospective subscribers as the cable system expands, as well as a means to retrack and increase penetration of cable services in areas in which these already are available. However, the TCS system should be promoted as only one dimension of the total Mark-Tele cable package to prospective subscribers.

Finally, word of mouth will be a vital factor underlying acceptance and use of TCS. Active stimulation and encouragement of this free, highly effective form of promotion should be implemented and maintained with use of both creative advertising strategies and other promotional tactics such as special cable rates to subscribers who get friends or relatives to sign up for and use the system.

CONCLUSION

The recommendation of our committee is that Mark-Tele design and implement the proposed new venture concept—a telecommunication shopping system. We have identified the target customer and viable products and services to satisfy their needs and Mark-Tele's objectives. Development of the supplier market and control over suppliers also have been discussed.

Overall, the distinct advantages of the TCS concept would include: (a) the wide variety of products and services that would be available to consumers; (b) the unique and novel process of shopping; (c) the ease, convenience, and privacy of shopping and buying; and (d) the special buying incentives such as comparative sales prices and controlled access to extensive amounts of information regarding products and services.

We recommend immediate action on this proposal to ensure and enact a competitive advantage in this revolutionary marketplace.

2
CENTRAL HOSPITAL

Central Hospital in Bloomington, Illinois, is a 400-bed multi-specialty community hospital providing ambulatory care, acute care, and psychiatric care services to residents living within a 30-mile radius of Bloomington–Normal, twin cities. The nonprofit hospital is located within close proximity to a large state university. Central Hospital is also located close to what is recognized as the poorest neighborhood in the twin cities, an area of rundown homes with a population that is 90 percent black, 5 percent white, and 5 percent "other."

Three years ago the Board of Directors of Central Hospital approved a plan to seek approval to build a new ambulatory care facility to replace its inadequate facilities located within the existing hospital structure. Last year the hospital was awarded a Certificate of Need by the Illinois Health Facilities Planning Board to construct a new 40,000-square-foot ambulatory care building.

The hospital's chief executive officer, health planner, and vice-president of operations worked exclusively with the architect to plan the new facility, taking the plan to the hospital's Board of Directors for ultimate approval.

The plan they took to the board proposed a two-story ambulatory care facility with an attached parking garage, extending from the west end of the existing hospital structure, which housed the current outpatient area. The only drawback of the plan was that the new facility would extend across a section of Moon Street. It was determined by the architect that the facility could not be built over the street and that a portion of Moon Street would therefore have to be purchased from the City of Bloomington to accommodate the new facility.

Twelve of the thirteen board members

This case was prepared by Debra Low, Arizona State University, and Charles H. Patti.

heartily endorsed the plan, provided that the street could be purchased for less than $50,000 from the city. The thirteenth board member, Bill Smith, the board's only black, noted that the proposed street was the only major artery to the poor neighborhood located just south of the hospital. He noted that the local residents would have to drive three blocks around the proposed facility to get to and from the closest boulevard under the proposed plan. Moon Street was currently the most convenient access street.

Paul Jones, the hospital's chief executive officer, noted that the proposed plan was the most efficient and cost-effective plan possible. He further noted that he was certain the neighborhood would support any project that Central Hospital sponsored. "What's more important," he argued, "a health care facility or a three-block detour?"

The Board of Directors voted. Ten approved the project, two voted against the project, and one abstained. The project was passed.

The day before the public hearing, Florence Cummings, an outspoken black who was highly respected in the area, charged that Central Hospital had "ignored the needs of the area residents by proposing to close down our street." She further stated, "Central Hospital is insensitive to our needs. We were never informed of their plans until after the fact. Nobody ever asked us how we felt—or what services we'd like to get from Central Hospital."

Paul Jones' response to the press was:

Central Hospital is providing area residents with the highest quality health care. Our health care professionals have developed this excellent facility for the people we serve. We care.

Florence Cummings and a cadre of 60 local residents picketed the hospital on the day of the public hearing. They also testified against the plan at the public hearing. Despite the protest, the health systems agency voted in favor of the project, and the state ultimately awarded the certificate of need.

On the day of the groundbreaking, Hospital Administrator Paul Jones was quoted by the press as saying, "It is obvious that Central Hospital is sensitive to the needs of our health care consumers." Florence Cummings and a number of persons picketed the groundbreaking ceremonies.

QUESTIONS FOR DISCUSSION

1. What immediate action should Central Hospital take to deal with Florence Cummings and the irritated local residents?
2. What actions would be appropriate for the hospital to take within the next two months?
3. If you had been the Director of Communications for Central Hospital three years ago, what actions would you have recommended to Paul Jones?

3
ALPHA CORPORATION

Alpha Corporation is a marketer of a broad line of consumer household products that are sold nationally. Among the products marketed by Alpha are occasional tables made of high-impact plastic, small decorator lamps, moderately priced Oriental rugs, imported dinnerware, and kitchen utensils. Some of these products hold a very large market share. They are branded products and have been supported by substantial advertising and promotion at both the consumer and trade levels. Other Alpha products haven't done as well. The Oriental rugs, for example, have never really made much of an impact even though Oriental rugs are popular and Alpha's represent a real value to the consumer.

Alpha's advertising programs for all of its various products have been rather loosely run. Money has been assigned to the advertising budget for each of the specific products strictly on the basis of that particular product's percentage contribution to the sales of Alpha. For example, last year, 28 percent of Alpha's sales were accounted for by the sales of dinnerware; therefore, 28 percent of the advertising budget was allocated to dinnerware.

Other advertising management decisions have been made with the same kind of thinking. Whatever is the easiest way to do things is the way Alpha has gone. They hired Jane Browne as Advertising Manager and just let her do whatever she wanted because Alpha's top management was just too busy to get involved in something they didn't know much about. Although Ms. Browne was a conscientious employee, she herself admitted that there were many areas of advertising that she simply was not trained for and didn't know much about. For example, the Advertising Department operated without specific objectives. When asked about

This case was prepared by Charles H. Patti.

the lack of objectives, Jane said that she hesitated in setting objectives for two reasons: (1) she could never get top management to meet with her long enough to discuss objectives, and (2) she herself was uncertain if the department's objectives should be set in terms of sales, market share, or some less direct form of persuasion (improvements in company image or increased awareness of the company's advertising themes).

The major influences on the creative portions of the advertising program were "what we did last year" and "this is how we've always done it."

Media selection was largely determined by three factors:

1. The persuasiveness of media representatives
2. Suggestions and pressure from members of the distribution channels
3. What had been used in the past

Alpha Corporation had never had any type of formal program to measure the effectiveness of its advertising programs. The company seemed satisfied that somehow the advertising expenditure was working. Occasionally, a wholesaler or retailer would write a complimentary letter to Alpha's management about the advertising.

Suddenly, everything changed. Alpha Corporation went public and the new Board of Directors took upon itself the examination of every department within the corporation. The new board was committed to maintaining Alpha's profitability. Last year's sales topped the $250 million mark for the first time and pretax profits reached $42 million.

When the new Board of Directors ultimately got around to examining the Advertising Department, it concluded that the department was just not doing its job effectively and efficiently. Recognizing that neither they nor Jane Browne possessed the expertise to give new direction, they searched for a consultant to provide them with: (1) a complete audit of the current Advertising Department and (2) a procedure or model that could be used to reorganize the department and to illustrate the interrelationships of the major functional decisions required within the advertising program (i.e., objectives, budgeting, media, creativity, etc.).

QUESTION FOR DISCUSSION

1. Using the framework that was suggested in the section, "Organization of the Book," evaluate Alpha Corporation's approach to advertising and promotion.

4
DATAPRO PUBLISHING COMPANY

The DataPro Publishing Company markets a number of publications to the data-processing and computer industry. Among these publications is a bibliography on computers, data processing, and their application to a broad variety of industries (finance, accounting, management, marketing, and so on). This bibliography, called *BiblioDat,* is published every two months and is sold on a subscription basis for $85 per year.

The company has relied exclusively on direct marketing to sell the product, and the primary advertising tool has been direct mail. The number of subscriptions sold during the past year is approximately 2,000. The largest segment of these subscribers is the in-house libraries of companies with large computer installations. However, DataPro is now convinced that there are other potential markets—academic departments of quantitative systems as well as the applications disciplines (finance, accounting, management, marketing, and so on). Also, there

This case was prepared by Charles H. Patti.

are over 30,000 libraries in the United States and these too would be potential customers.

The main copy theme used in DataPro's direct mail pieces has been, "Here's an inexpensive and easy way to build a library on EDP."

As DataPro launches its expanded promotion, their Advertising Manager must answer a number of questions. First, the company would like to learn more about the size and potential of the new markets. They also question the application of the basic selling theme to new markets. The company also needs to select media that will reach the new target most efficiently. Finally, DataPro must set an advertising budget that is large enough to reach the target markets and at the same time must represent a reasonable advertising/sales ratio.

QUESTION FOR DISCUSSION

1. A number of advertising and promotion problems have been identified in the DataPro case. What advice would you give to their Advertising Manager?

5
ST. PETER'S HOSPITAL

BACKGROUND

St. Peter's Hospital, a 200-bed acute care hospital in central Illinois, is owned and operated by an order of religious sisters. In 1978 the hospital's Board of Directors conducted a search to replace its retiring chief executive officer. Within six months a successor was named: John Rowe, 40, who previously served in a similar institution as an assistant administrator. Mr. Rowe was selected for a variety of reasons, but primarily because of his reputation as an aggressive and innovative marketer of new health services. He was also considered an extremely diplomatic administrator with a proven track record in obtaining every Certificate of Need he pursued. This was attributable to his skills in working with the regulatory agencies.

CURRENT DEVELOPMENTS

A Plan of Action

Within six months following Rowe's appointment to St. Peter's, he developed a priority plan for the hospital. Among the areas he hoped to develop were:

1. A home care dialysis center
2. An ambulatory care program (outpatient clinic)
3. Expanded radiologic and laboratory facilities
4. The addition of 20 medical/surgical beds
5. Recognition as an approved Trauma Center
6. Remodeling of 90 percent of the existing facility
7. Designation as a university teaching hospital

In a presentation that Rowe made to the hospital's Board of Directors he outlined his

This case was prepared by Debra Low, Arizona State University, and Charles H. Patti.

seven-point program. The board was receptive to his assessment of needs; however, one member, an oncologist, stated the need to assign an eighth priority area, a hospice program. Dr. Bell, the oncologist, explained:

> Hospice is essentially an innovative program of palliative and supportive services to provide physical, psychological, social, and spiritual care to the terminally ill and their families. St. Peter's is an ideal sponsor of a hospice program because of its already established acute care program.

Another board member, Sr. Marie Davis, noted that hospice care would be consistent with the healing mission of a Catholic health care apostolate. After minimal discussion, the board overwhelmingly approved establishing hospice as the top priority area.

Determining Hospice Feasibility

The first action of the board was to appoint a team to study the feasibility of implementing a hospice program. The in-house team proceeded to visit a variety of hospices around the United States and discovered several existing models. Included in these models were:

Free-standing facilities

Home care programs

Combination home care/inpatient palliative care beds

Multi-institutional arrangements

The team discovered that the pricing of hospice programs was difficult to assess given the variety of existing hospice models, the newness of the hospice concept, and the lack of accurate cost data. They also discovered that the Midland Illinois Health Systems Agency, which served the twelve-county area encompassing St. Peter's service area, would recommend only one hospice per health systems area to the state's regulatory agency. It was learned that three other hospitals within the health systems area were also studying the feasibility of launching a hospice program.

In speaking to hospice program directors, the team learned that most persons in the United States (including many physicians) had never heard of hospice care. Although hospice care had been featured in a number of television news programs and was the subject of numerous newspaper and magazine articles, the fact remained that the hospice movement was suffering from a lack of sustained media exposure.

Three months after its appointment, the team reported its findings to the board. Several conflicting points of view emerged at the meeting. For example:

- Four of the board members proposed to abandon the hospice program until additional information could be obtained on pricing and reimbursement.
- John Rowe stressed that he would like to postpone commitment to the hospice program until the hospital achieved the other seven priority areas.
- Six nuns stressed that the board already made a commitment and should therefore pursue the hospice program as the top priority.
- Four persons believed the proposed St. Peter's Hospice should be a free-standing facility; four believed it should be a home care program coordinated by the hospital's home health department; and three others believed it should be a combined home care/inpatient program.

Ultimately, all of this confusion led the board to decide to hire a marketing consultant to make recommendations. The consultant's mandate was to develop a complete marketing plan for the proposed St. Peter's Hospice. The plan was to focus on:

1. **Service development**

   Major issues:
   a. Determination of the most feasible hospice model to implement.
   b. What needs exist among consumers?
   c. What services should be offered?

2. **Pricing of hospice care**

   Background facts:
   a. The room rate for an acute care bed in the oncology unit was priced at $140/patient day (semiprivate) and a nursing home room was priced at $80 for a similar arrangement.
   b. Blue Cross/Blue Shield would not yet reimburse the costs of hospice care in the State of Illinois (see Exhibit 4).
   c. The availability of federal funds was limited because of a demonstration grant program awarded to 26 hospice programs over a two-year period by D.H.H.S. (previously D.H.E.W.).

3. **Distribution of hospice services**

   Major questions to address:
   a. Twenty-four hours a day or less?
   b. Pain control medication as needed or on demand?
   c. Who will refer patients to hospice?
   d. Who should staff the hospice? Who should direct it?
   e. Should volunteers be used?

4. **Promotion of hospice services**

   Major questions to answer:
   a. Who are the target market(s)?
   b. How best to create awareness among the target market(s)?
   c. How to stimulate ongoing patient referrals?
   d. What media are most effective in achieving communications goals?

Although the board wanted to encourage maximum objectivity and creativity in the consultant's solutions, it decided to supply him with the information contained in Exhibits 1 through 4. The board also told the consultant that:

1. The proposed hospice would service approximately 200 dying patients per year, based on the projections of anticipated cancer deaths in the hospital's service area.
2. The health care environment was extremely competitive.
3. The board was reliant upon his recommendations because of their differing assessments of the situation.

4. He would have no more than three months to complete his analysis. He would also have up to $5,000 to spend on a suitable research project.

QUESTION FOR DISCUSSION

1. The exhibits in this case provide you with pertinent marketing information. Using this information, develop a promotion plan for St. Peter's Hospice.

EXHIBIT 1
Summary of Promotion Studies[a]

Question 1: "Have you heard of hospice care?"

Results: (percent of population responding "yes")

Doctors: 88%
Nurses: 74%
General public: 18%

Question 2: "Indicate your level of knowledge about hospice care."

Results:

General public Very low 42% 28% 20% 8% 2% Very high
Doctors   Very low   0%   5%   8% 34% 53% Very high
Nurses   Very low   4% 12% 43% 23% 18% Very high

Note: Questions 1 and 2 were asked to a nationwide sample of doctors, nurses, and the general public.

Question 3: "How appealing is hospice care to you?"

Results: Very unappealing 21% 10% 32% 22% 15% Very appealing

Question 4: "How likely is it that you would prefer hospice care to conventional care?"

Results: Very unlikely 15% 20% 46% 11% 8% Very likely

Note: Questions 3 and 4 were asked only of the general public. Also, respondents were told to assume that they were in a position to consider hospice care.

Question 5: "If there was a hospice in your area, how likely is it that you would contribute your time as a member of a volunteer staff?"

Results: Very unlikely   8% 12% 62% 15% 3% Very likely

Note: Question 5 was asked to the general public only and they were told to assume that they had an appropriate amount of time available for volunteer work.

Question 6: "How likely is it that you would refer patients to a hospice?"

Results: Very unlikely 20% 30% 23% 12% 15% Very likely

Question 7: "Rank-order the following sources of information in terms of their importance in keeping you up-to-date on current trends in health care facilities. One (1) means the most important source of information and six (6) means the least important source of information."

Results:

Information Source	Rank
Talking with health care professionals	1
Direct mail	2
TV, special topic TV programs	3
Health care journals	4
Health care columns in daily newspapers	5
Medical journals	5

(continued)

Question 8: "Rank-order the following sources of information in terms of their importance to you as a source of general news."

Results:

Information Source	Rank
Newspapers	1
Television	2
Magazines	3
Radio	3
Direct mail	5

Note: Questions 6, 7, and 8 were asked of doctors only.

^aDuring the past few years several studies have been conducted among the various publics that are influential in the potential success/failure of the hospice movement. The above data have been extracted from some of the studies.

EXHIBIT 2
Summary of Distribution-Related Facts

Population of the area which St. Peter's serves is 150,000.

Population growth has averaged 5 percent during each of the past five years.

There are no unusual demographic or economic characteristics of the geographic area in which St. Peter's is located. The city is one of the ten largest in Illinois and is supported by agriculture, light manufacturing, service, and retailing.

There is a rapid development of housing and shopping in areas away from the downtown district. Furthermore, there are no immediate plans for renewal of the downtown area.

EXHIBIT 3
Summary of Service-Related Information

Note: In early 1978, a government health agency conducted a nationwide survey on attitudes about hospice care. The following table has been taken from the final report.

Hospice Care Preferences: Type of Facility

Type of Care	General Public	Doctors	Hospital Administrators
Home Care	53%	5%	23%
Inpatient	15%	82%	62%
Home Care/Inpatient Combination	5%	10%	14%
No Opinion	27%	3%	1%
	100%	100%	100%

EXHIBIT 4
Summary of Price-Related Information

1. The room rate for an acute care bed in the oncology unit was priced at $140/patient day (semiprivate) and a nursing home room was priced at $80 for a similar arrangement.

2. Blue Cross/Blue Shield would not yet reimburse the costs of "hospice care" in the state of Illinois. However, many hospice-type programs are reimbursed through other designations such as 'acute care," "home health care," and "extended nursing care."

3. The availability of federal funds is limited because of a demonstration grant awarded to 26 hospice programs over a two-year period by D.H.H.S. (previously D.H.E.W.).

4. The general public does not consider pricing a highly relevant variable in the selection of the type of health care they can have because most health care is covered by third-party reimbursement. This is particularly true when the health problem involves terminal illness. The cost of health care for terminally ill patients is relevant in the decision process only at the extremes of a cost continuum—that is, both "free" care and care costing $7,000–$10,000 per month are relevant decision variables.

5. Cost is more relevant to relatives of terminally ill patients than it is to the patient.

6. Hospice care *can* be a profitable unit for a hospital, but the nature of the service creates a comparatively low profit potential for doctors.

Texas PetroChem, Incorporated (TP), based in Houston, Texas, is an old, well-established company in the oil refining and petrochemical industries. Since 1909 it has been a major competitor in the oil field production, refining equipment, and chemical fields. Its rapid growth in this highly competitive market was fueled by the oil industries' voracious appetite for better and more economical technology. TP captured an early lead in this field by developing a technique whereby water was separated from produced crude oil, using a revolutionary new method rather than by the less economical methods using heat.

Because of their concentration on research and development, TP and the oil industries grew quickly. However, because of the uncertain political climate for the oil industries which developed in the early 1970s, TP began seeking other markets for its technology. While certainly not abandoning the oil industries, top management felt that it was necessary to ensure the future of the company through expansion into other fields.

In its search, TP discovered what it felt was an excellent opportunity for its progressive technology in the food processing industry. Many methods similar to those used in crude oil refining are used in the food producing industry to manufacture consumer fats and oils. In particular, TP considered the filtering methods used in the hydrogenation of oils (soybean, cottonseed, and so on) to be archaic. In the food industry hydrogenation refers to the process by which an oil of fairly low viscosity is thickened to the proper consistency for products ranging from cooking oils to stick margarine. The nature of the process requires that a nickel catalyst "fine" and diatomaceous earth be added to the

This case was prepared by Tom Wright and John H. Murphy.

oil to be hydrogenated. After hydrogenation, these two additives, which are inedible and discolor the slurry, must be removed from the product oil.

The old, mechanical filters used to remove slurry are known as "plate and frame" or "leaf" filters. These were nothing more than fine sieves, resembling household screening. The structures necessary to house filters capable of accommodating large volumes were massive in size. In addition, the filters themselves were highly inefficient and difficult to clean. Once a filtration pass had ended, the filters would be physically disassembled, shoveled out by workmen, steam cleaned, and then sterilized before the next run, a time-consuming and costly task.

The start-up of a filtration run had to be slow so that a good filter "cake" could be established on the screen. This was necessary because the medium was the slurry material rather than the filter itself. The filter screen supported the slurry buildup, a process that required the constant attention of workmen.

An additional problem with mechanical filtering stems from the fact that the first oil through the filter maintains a high level of impurity even after filtering. Product oil purity increases as the filter "cake" builds up. Unfortunately, as the filter cake accumulates, the processing time increases significantly and many filter runs are necessary in order to achieve the required purity levels. One hundred percent purity can never be attained because the smallest particles in the product oil cannot be filtered out without totally clogging the filter with the cake buildup—a common problem known as "blinding" the filter.

In its attempts to improve the mechanical filtering process, TP utilized the technology it had developed and applied in the petroleum oil industries. TP designed and constructed a small, desk-size vessel with several electrodes and a mineral filter medium. When the electrodes were charged with a high DC voltage, the vessel body acted as a ground. When the product oil (with the catalyst fine and diatomaceous earth in suspension) passed through the vessel, the slurry was attracted to the filter medium. This new filtering process was so efficient that *one* run through it achieved product oil purity never before available to food processors even after multiple filtration runs (see Exhibit 1).

In order to clean the TP electrostatic filter, the power was turned off, releasing the catalyst fines and other entrapped materials much like an electromagnet releases steel when the power supply is terminated. A simple back-flush system removed the filtered materials and the process could begin again after a down time of only minutes. No disassembly of the air-tight, sanitary vessel was required. The filter had no flow, volume, or pore size restriction and could be built to almost any specifications (see Appendix).

The first small pilot filter system (see Exhibit 2) had almost enough capacity to replace a complete room-sized filter in an existing food processing plant that agreed to top-secret testing. After experimentation, the plant bought and installed a slightly larger version for produc-

tion line use, this one the size of a telephone booth. The food processor was very pleased, if not amazed with the results.

After a tour of the TP facilities and a demonstration of the filter, the TP's account executive from the Burke Advertising Agency was asked to develop a complete promotional plan for the introduction of the filter system to the food processing industry. This plan had to include objectives and strategies for the introduction of the system including creative strategy, any recommended media, direct mail pieces, brochures, and so on, plus any sales support materials for use by TP's sales force, a force that, at the onset, would consist of only two engineers in the domestic office. As acceptance of the equipment grew, the sales force could be augmented, but only the domestic office would have the laboratory equipment necessary for sample runs. Other corporate offices in the United Kingdom, France, Italy, and West Germany (second only to the United States in the manufacture of food processing equipment) would be capable of handling requests but would have no direct role in the marketing effort. Full international marketing efforts would follow domestic acceptance. The first fiscal year's budget totaled $50,000.

EXHIBIT 1

Schematic of the Texas PetroChem Filter System

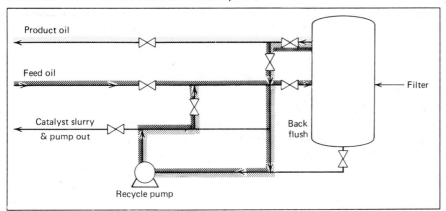

EXHIBIT 2
The TP Electric Filtering System

In analyzing the industry, the agency found that it consisted mostly of old, conservative, large companies, since only the large firms could survive in this highly competitive field where profit margins averaged 1½ percent compared with a national average of 5½ percent. The account executive at Burke felt that it would be difficult to introduce new technology to the processors because of the conservative attitudes and a lack of information exchange between competitors. Since most food processes were impossible to patent, each company functioned under a cloak of secrecy in order to protect the technology they had developed. This cloak of secrecy and conservative stance of companies had kept information and technology relatively stagnant.

With the characteristics of the food processing industry in mind, the account person at Burke working with TP began to develop a recommended plan for the introduction of the filter which was to begin in three months. A crucial first step in developing a set of recommendations would be an appraisal of the coordinated role of advertising and other marketing activities. This seemed especially important given the somewhat unusual product and market environments facing TP.

QUESTIONS FOR DISCUSSION

1. What factors in the external environment are most important in evaluating possible communication mixes for TP? Why?
2. What steps should be followed in developing a communication strategy for TP?
3. How should other marketing activities be coordinated with advertising and promotion?

APPENDIX
DESCRIPTION OF THE TP ELECTRIC FILTER SYSTEM

THE SYSTEM

Clean end product and clean operation—two long-sought-after breakthroughs in petroleum, chemical, and petrochemical filtering processes—are now available with the Texas Petro-Chem electric filtering process.

Essentially complete removal of catalyst fines and other solids from various hydrocarbon streams can be consistently accomplished with the TP system. Filtering of solids from recycling plant solvents, absorption oils, cleaning solvents, and cracked light gas oils; and catalyst/solids removal from hydrocarbons in the production of toulene, diamene, fatty acids, alcohols, formaldehydes, and aniline are well within the capabilities of the TP filter.

Each system is designed and built to handle the flow that you request. Filter limitations no longer place restraints on your capacity, and solids removal is no longer dependent on media pore size, particle size, or flow rate. Since the system is exceptionally compact, transportation and mechanical requirements for placement and installation are of minimal importance.

Regeneration of the filter is as easy as normal operation. When the filter bed has reached capacity (established by customer) a back-flush system incorporated into the process then circulates the solid-laden slurry and returns it to the process stream or to a slurry tank. Regeneration takes only a few minutes of production time and no disassembly of the enclosed pressurized system is required. The security of the airtight environment of the system is maintained at all times.

SYSTEM OPERATION

TP filter system incorporates a unique high-voltage electric field for removing solids from most petroleum and chemical processing streams. The system is designed to process a specified amount of liquid in a selected length of time at temperatures and pressures suitable for solids removal. Operating conditions for the filter system take into consideration existing conditions of customer's operating units. The product delivered from the system is of excellent quality and can be monitored by visual inspection through the use of a sight glass, nephelometer, or other selected monitor installed in the effluent line. Further monitoring as required is accomplished through normal laboratory procedures. Once it is determined that the system requires cleaning, a simple regeneration of the filter is accomplished.

Commencement of the regeneration procedures can be determined by product quality deterioration or projected media bed holding capacity correlated to the amount of solids to be removed. The resuspension of the accumulated solids from the media bed is accomplished by de-energizing of the power supply followed by recirculation of the vessel contents. The slurry volume may be removed from the system by pumping or gas pressuring and delivering to a totally enclosed slurry tank for reuse, back into the process stream, or to a disposal system.

SYSTEM BENEFITS

In addition to safe, clean operation, the system can benefit your filtering operations in many other ways. Consider the following benefits, compare them against any other system on the market. We're sure you'll be convinced that the TP filter system is THE system to handle your filtering needs.

Specifically designed unit for a specific purpose

Continuously removes solid particles ranging in size from submicron to 25 microns and larger

Filtering process is independent of media pore size, particle size, and flow rate

A true filter—not just a strainer

Small, compact unit easily transported and installed

Easy maintenance; no cartridges to change

Safe, simple operation

Easily regenerated

Totally enclosed pressure system operating in an airtight environment

Increased production based on increased filtration rates

7
MEDICAL EMERGICARE CENTER

BACKGROUND

Dr. Jake Christie, an emergency physician, recently opened the Emergicare Center. Located in a newly built shopping center at a dense traffic intersection in a sunbelt community, the Emergicare Center was conceived by Christie as an emergency and ambulatory care (outpatient) center designed to serve the needs of a primarily upper-middle-income residential community in a rapidly growing suburb southeast of a booming sunbelt city. (See Exhibit 1 and Table 1.) This innovative medical concept provides emergency care delivered by a physician and a qualified medical team from 8 A.M. to 12 midnight, seven days a week, every day of the year in a convenient and accessible location. No appointment is necessary and waiting is minimized.

This case was prepared by Debra Law and Daniel Freeman both of Arizona State University.

DESCRIPTION OF SERVICES

The Emergicare Center is primarily an emergency care center providing competent, quality medical services. Although the center is not designed to treat many life-threatening emergencies, it is appointed with a fully equipped cardiac "crash cart"[1] to respond to cardiac emergencies. Primarily, this new concept of medical care is best matched to serving those persons requiring minor emergency care including treatment of cuts, minor burns, sprains, broken bones, asthma, urinary tract infections, stomach pain, and other medical problems.

In addition to emergency care, the Emergicare Center provides general medical care on a walk-in basis. This care, especially designed for episodic treatment, is an effective medical backup when the patient's regular physician is unavailable or when immediate care is required.

EXHIBIT 1
Map of Metropolitan Area Depicting Location of the Emergicare Center

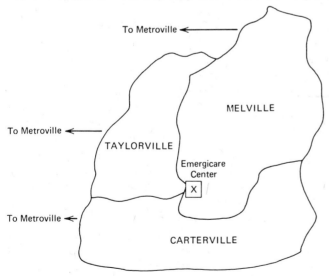

TABLE 1

Population Statistics of Service Area

Melville	(City A)	70,600
Taylorville	(City B)	25,100
Carterville	(City C)	29,673

Race and National Origin (percent)

	White	Black	American Indian	Asian	Other	Spanish Origin
City A	92.2	1.2	0.1	0.1	5.2	9.2
City B	91.5	1.8	0.1	1.5	4.4	8.2
City C	80.7	2.9	1.5	1.0	13.8	20.6
County	86.6	3.2	1.5	0.2	7.8	13.2
State	82.4	2.8	5.6	0.1	8.4	16.2

Age Distribution (percent)

	Service Area	County	State
Under 15	30.3	25.0	25.2
15–44	45.3	45.8	45.5
45–65	17.7	18.3	18.3
Over 65	6.8	10.8	11.0

General Characteristics

	Service Area	County
Median age	23.5	29.9
Median household income	$18,125	$21,933
Percent of households with children under 18	53%	44%
Percent retired heads of households	19%	28%
Median years education of head of household	12.4	19.2

Such procedures as preschool exams, immunizations, and premarital and insurance examinations can also be completed at the Emergicare Center.

The center also offers complete industrial medical services for local businesses. Pre-employment physical examinations, emergency care, and other medical services are available. Written and telephone reports are made to the employer concerning the employee's condition.

A follow-up phone call is part of this innovative concept of care. A call is made the day after the patient's visit to check on the patient's condition. Referrals are also made, when appropriate, to the patient's personal physician or a specialist. A prescription phone-in service is also provided to the patient's personal pharmacy.

THE FACILITIES AND STAFF

The Emergicare Center is located in a 2,000 square-foot site in a strip shopping mall (see Exhibit 2). Emergency and handicapped parking is available at a rear emergency entrance, as well as regular spaces located to provide easy access.

The Emergicare Center has four examination rooms, a fully equipped X-ray unit, a laboratory for performing routine blood, urine, and chemistry work, a minor surgery/treatment room, and a waiting room. (See Exhibit 3.) It is also equipped with an EKG, cardiac monitor, and fully-equipped "crash cart" for coronary patients, as well as all supplies for suturing, splinting, and performing other minor surgical procedures. The staff consists of Dr. Jake

EXHIBIT 2
Plan of Shopping Center

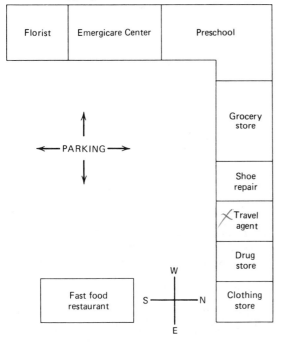

EXHIBIT 3
Floor Plan of Emergicare Center

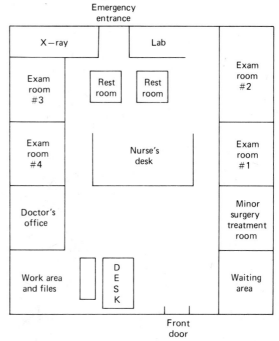

Christie, a physician specializing in emergency medicine, four full-time medical assistants, and four part-time medical assistants.

PRICE

The Emergicare Center concept is designed to provide competent medical care at prices that are substantially lower than hospital emergency rooms. Most medical insurance policies will reimburse patients for acute care, whether the care is delivered at a hospital-based emergency room or an ambulatory/emergency care center such as the Emergicare Center. Patients receiving treatment at the center with charges of $100 or less are expected to pay at the time the services are rendered, and then may file for reimbursement with the medical insurance company. If medical charges exceed $100, or if any injury or minor surgery is involved, or if it is a work-related injury, or if hospitalization is required, the Emergicare Center will accept the patient's insurance card instead of direct payment.

ANALYSIS OF THE COMPETITIVE CARE MARKET

Within the service area of the Emergicare Center are four existing hospitals, one proposed hospital, and two satellite facilities; all offer various levels of emergency care, in addition to the services of the Emergicare Center. (See Exhibit 4.) Traditionally, hospital emergency rooms have provided the majority of emergency care, presumably because they have been perceived to be best equipped to handle emergency cases by most health care consumers. In addition, consumers have had no alternative to traditional hospital-based emergency rooms.

EXHIBIT 4
Proximity of Competing Services

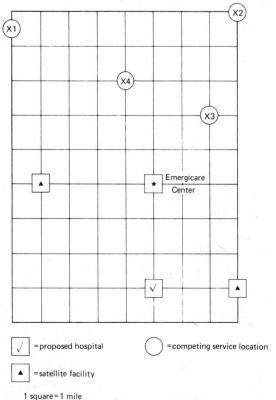

□ = proposed hospital   ○ = competing service location

▲ = satellite facility

1 square = 1 mile

TABLE 2
Emergency Services Offered

Procedure	Health Care Facility				
	1	2	3	4	Emergicare Center
Gastric lavage	√	√	√	√	√
Gastroscopy	√	—	√	√	—
Incision and drainage	√	—	√	—	√
Cauterization	√	—	√	—	√
Eye dilation	√	√	—	√	√
Cryotherapy	√	√	—	—	—
Wash wounds	√	√	—	√	√
Crash cart	√	√	√	—	√
Lumbar puncture	√	√	√	—	—
Sigmoidoscopy	√	√	√	√	√

√ = Services offered
— – Not available

As an alternative to the traditional hospital emergency rooms, the Emergicare Center is in direct competition with those area hospitals that provide emergency and ambulatory care. The Emergicare Center is located within four miles of a well-known community hospital (part of an aggressive multi-institutional system) and within four miles of a small community hospital. Each hospital provides emergency care. (See Exhibit 4 and Tables 2 and 3.) The Emergicare Center is at a relative disadvantaged to the hospital's emergency rooms because, as an innovative concept, it is not yet widely known. Because it is not affiliated with a hospital, the center has the additional problems of low name recognition, potential misunderstanding among health care consumers who are as yet not familiar with this concept of care, a smaller amount of money to allocate to advertising and public relations than the hospital-sponsored emergency rooms (see Tables 4 and 5), and the potential for being poorly accepted by the hospital community who may view the Emergicare Center as a competitive force.

THE ADVERTISING AND PUBLIC RELATIONS PLAN

The center has primarily relied on publicity to generate awareness of its services in the communities it serves. A press release was sent to the newspapers, radio stations, and television stations in the metropolitan area to announce the opening of the Emergicare Center and to generate usage.

Advertising has been used in the print media, primarily in a local weekly shopping guide and in a zoned regional edition of the metropolitan daily newspaper. In addition, an informational brochure was distributed in the weekly shopping guide. It reached approximately 72,000 house-

TABLE 3
Price Comparisons

Procedure	Average Hospital-Based Emergency Room[a]	Emergicare Center
Minimum fee	$37.50	$25.00
Incision and drainage	$55.80	$80.00 —
Cauterization	$13.55	$12.50
Eye dilation	$ 8.20	$ 7.50
Clean wounds (simple)	$ 3.83	$ 3.50
Crash cart	$58.63	$53.50

[a]This table is only for the basic Emergency Room fee. It does not include the physician's fee, supplies, or additional procedures.

TABLE 4
Advertising and Promotional Budgets Allocated to Hospital-Based Emergency Rooms ($000) and Emergicare Center

Budgets	Health Care Facility				Emergicare Center
	1	2	3	4	
Advertising					
TV	$—	$—	$—	$10	No budget
Radio	—	2	1	4	No budget
Newspaper	1.5	1	2	6	No budget
Magazines	.5	.75	1	2.5	No budget
Billboards	—	1	—	1.5	No budget
Other	.5	1.5	—	2.1	No budget
Public Relations	1.5	1	.75	3	No budget
Sales Promotion (collateral)	2	1	1	5	No budget
Research					
Advertising	—	—	—	2	No budget
Marketing	1	2.5	2	10	No budget

holds one time in the local communities. Personal contact was also perceived to be important in diffusing the concept. A representative personally contacted every pharmacy in the service area.

Dr. Christie's brother-in-law, David Barnes, recently offered to shoot a 16-mm commercial at no cost; Barnes takes home movies as a hobby. Dr. Christie gladly accepted Barnes' offer. The two are presently writing the script. Dr. Christie and his staff will be the talent although none has ever appeared in commercials.

No budget has been allocated to cover advertising and promotional costs. An "all-we-can-afford" budget strategy has been implemented. Additionally, no formalized advertising/promotional objectives or plans have been specified. The target market has been identified as "women" because "they make health decisions," according to Dr. Christie.

TABLE 5
Estimated Advertising and Promotional
Expenditures of Emergicare Center
($000) (First Six Months of Operation)

	Emergicare Center
Advertising	
TV	$5[a]
Radio	—
Newspaper	7.5
Magazines	1
Billboards	—
Other	1
Public Relations	1.5
Sales Promotion	5
(collateral)	
Research	
Advertising	—
Marketing	—

[a]Television time not yet purchased; however, this figure was being discussed as "feasible" by Dr. Christie.

ENDNOTE

1. A "crash cart" contains intravenous solution, a cardiac defibrillator, a cardiac monitor, and various drugs used in resuscitation.

QUESTIONS FOR DISCUSSION

1. How effective do you feel the current advertising and public relations plan has been for the Medical Emergicare Center?
2. What promotion recommendations would you make to the Medical Emergicare Center?

SECTION 2
EVALUATION OF THE ADVERTISING OPPORTUNITY

In the marketing of goods and services, every seller attempts to stimulate demand through a combination of promotional methods. Personal selling, public relations, sales promotion, and advertising are all means of persuading customers and prospects to specify a particular brand. The major decision facing the firm should not be which *one* of these tools to use but rather what combination will maximize the effectiveness and efficiency of the total promotional effort.

Ideally, a marketer would like to be able to specify the precise contribution of each of these promotional tools to the stimulation of demand. Such specification begins with an understanding of the limitations and the advantages of each element in the promotional mix. If marketers have a means of appraising the opportunity of each of these tools to contribute to stimulating brand demand, they could establish more realistic, attainable objectives and allocate the firm's marketing resources in line with the task assigned to the particular tool.

The primary questions facing the Advertising or Promotion Manager attempting to evaluate the advertising opportunity are:*

Under what conditions is advertising most likely to help expand demand?

How can the conditions be evaluated?

FACTORS INFLUENCING THE ADVERTISING OPPORTUNITY

The conditions or underlying factors to be considered in evaluating the advertising opportunity fall into three main categories: *product factors, market factors,* and *financial factors.*

---

*For a more complete discussion of the concept and application of evaluating the advertising opportunity, see *The Economic Effects of Advertising* by Neil H. Bordon (Homewood, Ill.: Richard D. Irwin, Inc., 1942), and "Evaluating the Role of Advertising" by Charles H. Patti (*Journal of Advertising,* vol. 6, no. 4, 1977).

Product Factors

While it has always been possible to advertise "parity" products successfully, advertising is most effective and efficient when the product or service being marketed:

Possesses unique, want-satisfying attributes

Contains hidden qualities (characteristics that cannot be detected by physical inspection and/or through use yet are relevant to the prospective buyer)

Can be sold largely on the basis of powerful, emotional motives

Market Factors

Successful use of advertising also depends on existing marketplace conditions. Among the marketplace conditions that influence the opportunity to use advertising successfully are:

A rising generic demand trend in the product category

Adequate market potential expressed in terms of market size and profitability

Economic conditions that are favorable to the sale of the advertised product or service

A favorable competitive environment

Financial Factors

Finally, advertising cannot be expected to make a significant contribution to demand stimulation unless the organization is financially able and willing to spend the amount of money required to launch a significant advertising campaign. At the same time, the organization needs to possess sufficient expertise to market the product or service. This includes access to the appropriate channels of distribution, knowledge about the importance of pricing and packaging, and sensitivity to the behavior of buyers, both the end users and those within the channels of distribution.

EVALUATING THE FACTORS

There are a number of ways to evaluate the opportunity to use advertising successfully, ranging from a simple "yes–no"/"for–against" response to the presence of each of the underlying factors to a quantitative determination of the relative importance and extent of existence of each factor. There are limitations to all these evaluation methods; however, the organization will improve its chances of using advertising successfully by experiencing the process of evaluating the advertising opportunity.

THE VALUE OF EVALUATING THE ADVERTISING OPPORTUNITY

We believe that advertising works best when organizations have specified the precise role it is to play in the promotional mix. The fundamental purpose of evaluating the advertising opportunity is to provide the organization with a guide that can be used to make a number of other important advertising and promotion decisions. The appraisal concept was never intended to provide management with a tool to make a "go/no–go" decision about advertising. Its primary benefits are the following:

1. *It forces management to examine the purposes of advertising.* Rarely is advertising alone the main sales stimulant; for many marketers its important role is to communicate relevant information to customers and prospects. Through the experience of evaluating the advertising opportunity, management can come to a clearer understanding of the specific role advertising should play in the promotional mix.

2. *It assists management in establishing advertising objectives.* Although the stimulation of brand demand is the long-range goal of most advertising, it is now generally accepted that more modest communications goals must first be achieved. Through an analysis of the advertising opportunity, the Advertising Manager can set more realistic, attainable advertising objectives. When the advertising opportunity is high—when most of the underlying factors favor the use of advertising—advertising can be assigned tasks closer to the buying or action end of the communications hierarchy. When evaluating the advertising opportunity is used to help set advertising objectives, objectives can be developed that are sensitive to conditions within the firm, the market, and the economic environment.

3. *It encourages a "task" method of advertising budgeting.* Once the advertising opportunity is appraised and advertising objectives established, setting the advertising budget can then be related directly to the established objectives. This method of budget determination is far superior to other methods and relates advertising directly to an assigned task—an objective that has been determined *after* an evaluation of the role of advertising.

The cases that follow provide an opportunity to consider the specific role advertising can or should play in marketing efforts. As you read and analyze the cases, think about advertising in the context of a promotional mix. Put yourself in the position of the Advertising or Promotion Manager who must make decisions about the extent to which advertising can be expected to fulfill demand stimulation goals.

As opening day of the 1981–1982 National Basketball Association season approached, Phoenix Suns' General Manager Jerry Colangelo found himself in an enviable, but frustrating, position. Colangelo was at the helm of one of the most successful and progressive franchises in the entire NBA. The Phoenix Suns had just completed their most successful campaign ever in terms of club wins (57 wins, .695 percent), fan attendance (92.9 percent of arena capacity), and the final standings (Pacific Division Champions).

The team was exceeded only by the World Champion Boston Celtics (62 wins, .756 percent), the Philadelphia 76'ers (62 wins, .756 percent), and the Milwaukee Bucks (60 wins, .732 percent) in total number of wins and won–lost percentage. In overall percent of arena capacity filled, the Portland Trail Blazers (100 percent), Milwaukee Bucks (98.9 percent), and Boston Celtics (94.8 percent), were the only NBA clubs to attain higher marks (see Table 1). In addition to these successes, Colangelo himself had been named NBA Executive of the Year by *The Sporting News*—the second time that he had been the recipient of this honor.

Yet, with all of this good fortune, Colangelo remained somewhat dissatisfied. The primary source of this dissatisfaction was the fact that his team had once again been disappointed in the NBA playoffs. A gritty Kansas City Kings club had defeated his Suns, four games to three, in the 1980–1981 Western Conference semifinals. For Colangelo and the Suns the defeat represented the fifth time in the last six years that the Suns had made the playoffs but had failed to bring home the championship.

This case was prepared by Professor Vincent J. Blasko, Arizona State University. The original version of the Phoenix Suns case was written by Charles H. Patti and appeared in *Advertising Management: Cases and Concepts*, by Charles H. Patti and John H. Murphy, Grid Publishing, Inc. 1978.

The upcoming season also posed a number of difficult off-the-court decisions that Colangelo did not look forward to making. The team's advertising agency had recently presented their recommendations for the 1981–1982 Suns' advertising/promotional campaign and Colangelo found himself in disagreement with many of the agency's proposals. The agency had called for a substantial increase in the Suns' media budget and for a much expanded promotional effort. In view of the Suns' many accomplishments the previous year, Colangelo had serious doubts concerning the need for such an extensive program.

In evaluating the agency's performance over the last few seasons, Colangelo had also decided that the team's advertising had lacked a basic continuity and focus. This represented an additional area of concern for the Suns' management since the agency recommended the same overall strategies for the upcoming campaign.

MARKETING CONSIDERATIONS

The Product

Jerry Colangelo and the Suns' top management have always strived to improve their product offering from year to year. Since the beginning of the franchise's history in 1968 (when the team struggled through their worst season ever—16 wins), Colangelo has worked tirelessly to improve all areas of the business. Fortunately, he has seen those efforts pay major dividends. That first season, a grand total of 753 season tickets were sold and attendance ran at a rather embarrassing 4,340 fans per home game. The team's second year saw season ticket sales jump to 1,752 and average home game attendance nearly doubled (7,617). From that point to the present, with the exception of the 1974–1975 season, the Suns have steadily increased both

TABLE 1
1980–1981 NBA Attendance Figures and Percent of Arena Capacity Filled

	Total Attendance	Average Attendance	Arena Capacity	Percent Capacity
1. Portland Trail Blazers	519,306	12,666	12,666	100.0
2. Milwaukee Bucks	448,366	10,936	11,052	98.9
3. Boston Celtics	595,454	14,523	15,320	94.8
4. Phoenix Suns	482,693	11,773	12,660	92.9
5. Golden State Warriors	413,480	10,084	13,239	76.2
6. Los Angeles Lakers	537,865	13,119	17,505	74.9
7. San Antonio Spurs	440,553	10,745	15,964	68.4
8. New York Knicks	544,641	13,284	19,591	67.8
9. Philadelphia 76'ers	469,355	11,448	18,276	62.6
10. Utah Jazz	307,825	7,508	12,143	61.8
11. Houston Rockets	385,354	9,399	15,676	59.9
12. Denver Nuggets	423,307	10,325	17,271	59.8
13. Seattle Supersonics	675,097	16,466	27,894	59.0
14. Indiana Pacers	408,839	9,996	16,924	59.0
15. Atlanta Hawks	595,454	8,846	15,700	56.3
16. Chicago Bulls	389,718	9,505	17,374	54.7
17. Kansas City Kings	336,585	8,209	16,638	49.3
18. Washington Bullets	375,360	9,155	19,035	48.1
19. Dallas Mavericks	319,347	7,789	17,134	45.4
20. San Diego Clippers	257,597	6,283	13,841	45.4
21. New Jersey Nets	302,059	7,367	21,100	34.9
22. Cleveland Cavaliers	224,489	5,475	19,548	28.0
23. Detroit Pistons	228,348	5,569	22,366	23.9

their individual game ticket sales and their season ticket figures (see Table 2).

The chief reason for the team's success at the gate is, of course, the overall success that the Suns have realized on the court over the past thirteen seasons. Like most teams, the Suns have experienced their highs and lows—with most of the lows occurring between the dismal first year and the 1974–1975 season. In that period, the Suns' record (including playoff contests) was 255 wins and 326 losses (.434 percent). The Suns had five coaches in those seven years and managed to make it to the playoffs one time—in the 1969–1970 season.

The next six seasons (1975–1976 through 1980–1981) however, provided a totally different scenario. In that period, under Coach John MacLeod, the team notched an outstanding record. The Suns gained a playoff berth five times in those six years and earned a trip to the NBA World Championship Series in the 1975–1976 season. In addition, the Suns' won–lost percentage, including playoff competition, rose to .575—a record exceeded by only Philadelphia, Los Angeles, and Boston for that same time period.

What is perhaps most impressive is the fact that this record was achieved without the presence of a true superstar on the team. While the Suns have had some very solid players, they have never built their attack around a specific individual. As a result, the Suns have gained the reputation for exciting team, rather than individual, performance.

TABLE 2
Phoenix Suns' Home Attendance: 1968–1969 through 1980–1981

Year	Season Ticket Sales	Dates	Attendance	Average
1968–1969	735	37	160,565	4,340
1969–1970	1,752	37	280,868	7,617
1970–1971	3,204	41	332,945	8,120
1971–1972	3,510	41	342,922	8,364
1972–1973	4,396	41	342,117	8,444
1973–1974	4,503	41	284,424	6,934
1974–1975	2,900	41	253,103	6,173
1975–1976	3,500	41	295,293	7,202
1976–1977	5,030	41	411,294	10,032
1977–1978	5,500	41	470,009	11,463
1978–1979	6,800	41	465,010	11,342
1979–1980	8,010	41	480,659	11,723
1980–1981	8,026	41	482,693	11,773

In preparing for the coming 1981–1982 season, the Suns' management made a number of transactions that they believe will add even more strength to the team's already impressive roster. Larry Nance and Craig Dykema, the Suns' number one and three draft picks in the 1981 college draft, were signed and second-year guard Dudley Bradley was acquired in a deal with the Indiana Pacers. Returning to the Suns are a number of standout performers including All-NBA defensive performer Dennis Johnson, all-star forward Walter Davis, and last year's impressive rookie, Kyle Macy. The Suns' aggressive, breakaway style and well-balanced attack, combined with these individual player personalities, make the Suns a very marketable product.

THE MARKET

Fan Loyalty

In the formative years of the team's existence, General Manager Colangelo felt that the Phoenix market contained a number of negative characteristics with regard to the establishment of a successful NBA franchise. The most disturbing of these was the fact that the Phoenix area has been growing so rapidly that it was difficult to build true fan allegiance to the Suns.

Many of the new Phoenix area residents (from the East and Midwest) still felt a strong loyalty to teams such as the Milwaukee Bucks, New York Knickerbockers, or Boston Celtics. In fact, a study conducted for the Suns in 1975 supported Colangelo's beliefs. Over one-third of the study's respondents selected a team other than the Suns as their favorite NBA club.[1]

The problem of building a loyal following, however, seems to have been rectified as witnessed by the recent success of the team, near capacity attendance figures, and a later study which reported only 9 percent of the respondents selecting a team other than the Suns as "their favorite."[2] The study sampled 525 attendees at the first three home games of the 1978–1979 season and was conducted by marketing research students at Arizona State University. The study was designed to answer the following two questions:

1. What demographic characteristics do the Phoenix Suns' fans possess?
2. What effect do various promotional activities have upon the fans' decision to attend the games?

See Tables 3 through 7 for the results of the study.

TABLE 3

Occupation Characteristics of Population Attending Suns' First Three Home Games in 1978

Occupation	Total Number of Responses	Percent of Total
Laborer	28	5.3
Clerical	31	6.0
Professional	168	32.0
Technical	34	6.4
Service worker	26	5.0
Farm worker	4	.8
Sales	64	12.2
Student	54	10.3
Self-employed	48	9.1
Unemployed	21	4.0
Retired	19	3.6
Other	28	5.3
Totals	525	100.00

TABLE 4

Education Characteristics of Population Attending Suns' First Three Home Games in 1978

Education	Total Number of Responses	Percent of Total
Finished grade school	16	3.0
1–3 years high school	37	7.0
Graduated high school	105	20.0
1–3 years college	189	36.0
Graduated college	178	34.0
Totals	525	100.0

Lack of Blue-Collar Market

Another major hurdle that the Suns have managed to negotiate successfully is the fact that a large portion of the Suns' spectators are employed in a professional capacity. This means the makeup of the Suns' target audience is quite a bit different from most NBA franchises. Typically, the blue-collar worker represents the largest portion of the professional sports team market; however, 32 percent of the Suns'

TABLE 5

Income Characteristics of Population Attending Suns' First Three Home Games in 1978

Income	Total Number of Responses	Percent of Total
No response	26	5.0
Under $8,000	52	10.0
$8,000–$14,999	100	19.0
$15,000–$24,999	137	26.0
$25,000–$39,999	121	23.0
$40,000 and more	89	17.0
Totals	525	100.0

audience are employed in a professional category. In addition, 70 percent of the Suns' home game attendees have attended college for one to three years or are college graduates.

Colangelo has been successful in turning this "disadvantage" into a marketing opportunity by employing an approach emphasizing season ticket institutional buys. Under this program, a large company purchases a block of season tickets and then uses the seats for various marketing a promotional activities (public and customer relations, employee incentives, customer contests, etc.). The Suns were the first NBA club to adopt this strategy—an approach now considered standard in the marketing of professional sports teams.

Stadium Expansion

Suns' management expects both season and individual ticket sales to be boosted even further with the expansion of the Phoenix Coliseum that was completed at the start of the 1981–1982 NBA season. A $1.2 million loan, approved by the Arizona State Legislature, allowed for the addition of 2,100 seats to the existing arena. The new capacity brings the total seating to approximately 15,000, a figure that closely parallels that of other NBA arenas.

Colangelo believes that the addition will

TABLE 6
Age Distribution of Population Attending Suns' First Three Home Games in 1978

Age	Total Number of Responses	Percent of All Sampled		
		Males	Females	Total
Under 18	39	4.8	2.6	7.4
18–24	78	9.8	5.2	15.0
25–35	141	17.5	9.3	26.8
35–49	179	22.0	12.0	34.0
50–64	64	8.1	4.1	12.2
65 and over	24	3.1	1.5	4.6
Total	525	65.3	34.7	100.0

TABLE 7
Effectiveness of Promotions on Fans' Decision to Attend Suns' Games (Data Collected at Suns' First Three Home Games in 1978)

	Reduced Price Tickets (percent)	Giveaways, T-shirts, etc. (percent)	Opposing Team (percent)
Always influenced	36.0	16.0	53.0
Occasionally influenced	9.0	12.0	4.0
Never influenced	55.0	72.0	43.0
Total	100.0	100.0	100.0

increase season ticket sales by 1,000 and that overall attendance will be increased by 2,000 per game. It is estimated that an increase of 2,000 fans per game will mean over a half million dollars to the Suns in gate receipts.

Effects of a Championship

Colangelo feels that the best way for the Suns to increase attendance revenues would be to win the NBA World Championship. The experience of the Portland Trail Blazers, NBA Champions of 1977, would seem to confirm Colangelo's beliefs. The Portland club has consistently sold out their home dates since winning the championship and shows no signs of any attendance loss four years later (see Table 1). Colangelo also cites the 1976–1977 season (the year following the Suns' defeat by Boston in the championship series) as proof of what that title could mean. Average attendance per game during the 1976–1977 season jumped 39 percent (from 7,202 in 1975–1976 to 10,032) and season ticket sales increased 25 percent (from 3,500 in 1975–1976 to 5,030).

In addition to improving performance at the gate, Colangelo feels the championship would increase the profitability of the team's television market also. The Suns sell television rights to KPNX, a Phoenix TV station, and have also entered into a contract with the American Cable Company. American Cable will televise a total of 37 Suns' games (20 home, 17 away) beginning with the 1981–1982 season. The NBA championship would undoubtedly increase the price of these rights substantially. The Suns' radio market is controlled by the team, who purchase the air time from KTAR, a Phoenix radio station. The Suns then sell the advertising time to produce profit from the broadcast. An NBA championship title would, of course, raise the price of that advertising time.

The Competition

The Suns find themselves in an excellent marketing position because there is only one other major league team in the Phoenix metropolitan area. The other professional sports franchise competing with the Suns is the Phoenix Inferno, a member of the Major Indoor Soccer League. The Inferno, who also play in the Phoenix Coliseum, begin their second full season in 1981 and compete in 22 contests at home. Two other professional sports franchises, the Phoenix Racquets (World Team Tennis) and the Phoenix Roadrunners (World Hockey League), had been located in the market but both teams experienced only limited success, for various reasons, and were forced to discontinue play.

The Suns must also compete with a major collegiate sports power, Arizona State University, an institution located in nearby Tempe and well known for its top-flight baseball, football, and basketball teams. ASU is a member of the competitive PAC-10 Conference. In addition, ASU's stadium is the home of the Fiesta Bowl football game, which takes place every December.

In the spring four major league baseball teams (Oakland A's, Milwaukee Brewers, San Francisco Giants, and Chicago Cubs) make the Phoenix area their annual training ground. Also, the Phoenix Giants (the AAA minor league baseball team of the San Francisco Giants) play a 70-game home schedule that extends from April through August. See Exhibit 1 for a summary of team sports located in the Phoenix metropolitan area.

In addition to the organized team sports in the Phoenix area, Suns management realizes that the many outdoor recreational activities that the Phoenix area is well-known for must also be considered direct competition for the sports enthusiast's dollar. Because the weather in the area is comfortable throughout most of the year, the many activities (golf, hiking, boating, tennis, etc.) available to Phoenix residents comprise a negative factor with regard to professional sports attendance.

EXHIBIT 1
Team Sports in Phoenix

Team	Season	Home Games	Average Attendance	Ticket[a] Price
Phoenix Suns	October–April	41	11,723	$4.50
Phoenix Giants	April–August	70	5,255	2.50
Phoenix Inferno	November–April	22	7,191	4.00
ASU football	September–December	6	63,683	7.25
ASU baseball	January–May	35	2,160	2.50
ASU basketball	November–March	14	8,703	5.00
Major league baseball (spring training)	February–April	40	2,500	3.00

[a]Denotes general admission ticket price.

PAST MARKETING EFFORTS

Promotional Strategy

Basically, the Suns' management conducts two promotional campaigns. The first is geared toward the building of season ticket sales and the second attempts to increase individual game ticket purchases. Season ticket sales are promoted primarily through personal sales calls made by a Suns' representative on large Phoenix area businesses. The primary purpose of these visits is to discuss with company executives the advantages connected with the purchase of a large block of Suns' season tickets. The Suns' representative outlines a variety of promotional ideas and programs that these organizations can implement through the use of season tickets. Many large Phoenix firms (such as Armour Dial, Carnation, and First National Bank) take advantage of this program and have used the season seats to accomplish a variety of their own marketing and promotional objectives (increased traffic, better customer relations, et al.). The Suns have also used newspapers and direct mail in the promotion of season tickets. These media, however, play a much less important role in the marketing of these seats since the majority (78 percent) of season purchases are made by area businesses.

Although the 1978 survey profiles the Suns' primary target audience quite well, Suns management believes that the market for individual home games is, in actuality, much broader than this. The Suns feel that any sports enthusiast who lives in the area and has the means available ($4.50) for a general admission ticket is an excellent prospect for a single game ticket sale. The Suns have used a number of promotions to help encourage attendance at individual games, including giveaway nights (team posters, T-shirts) and numerous discount ticket nights in cooperation with local businesses (Basha's Night, Circle K Night and the like).

Other secondary markets that the Suns management feel are important in individual game sales are out-of-town businesses that will be holding conventions in the Phoenix area and the many area clubs and organizations that might be interested in a Suns outing. These prospects (convention directors and club officers) receive a mailer that offers selected home games at specific group rates. Since the target market for individual game tickets is a good deal broader than that for season tickets, the Suns rely more

TABLE 8
Phoenix Suns' Media Expenditures: 1977–1981

Medium	1977–1978[a]	1978–1979[b]	1979–1980[c]	1980–1981[d]
Newspaper	$52,100	$49,614	$40,984	$44,382
Radio	21,523	19,786	21,260	20,380
Magazine	855	988	71	185
Television	750	2,380	1,970	2,560
Outdoor	1,756	—	1,037	1,065
Totals	$76,984	$72,768	$65,322	$68,572

[a]Does not include $42,625 of media purchased by trading tickets for space and/or time.
[b]Does not include $40,757 of media purchased by trading tickets for space and/or time.
[c]Does not include $41,145 of media purchased by trading tickets for space and/or time.
[d]Does not include $44,320 of media purchased by trading tickets for space and/or time.

heavily on a wider range of media (television, newspaper, radio, and outdoor) to deliver their advertising message.

Creative Strategy and Execution

In attempting to increase attendance, for both season ticket sales and individual game ticket sales, the Suns have adopted a number of creative concepts which have served as a basis for their advertising executions. These concepts and executions have been built around a number of consumer sales points and consumer benefits. The majority of the Suns' advertising messages are delivered through radio and newspaper, with television, magazine, and outdoor also used but to a mucher lesser degree (see Table 8). A description of the creative themes and executions are outlined below.

1. *Stars on other teams.* Frequently, Suns' ads have featured prominent players on other teams, such as Julius "Dr. J" Erving of the Philadelphia 76'ers (see Exhibit 2) and Ervin "Magic" Johnson of the Los Angeles Lakers (see Exhibit 3). Used to promote individual games, this theme has highlighted the playing ability of NBA superstars as well as the personality of their respective teams.

2. *Suns player/company discount promotions.* The Suns have also used ads featuring their own team members (such as Walter Davis and Alvin Scott) in conjunction with company promotional nights to boost individual game attendance (see Exhibits 4 and 5). The strategy behind these ads is to capitalize on the performance/personality of the Suns players and to promote the company ticket discount. In addition, the Suns have promoted company discount nights quite frequently on radio.

3. *Season ticket promotions.* Ads intended to increase season ticket sales have generally centered around a specific Suns player (see Exhibit 6) or on the Suns' team personality (see Exhibit 7). Because the majority of season ticket sales are made to businesses

EXHIBIT 2

THE DOCTOR MAKES A HOUSECALL!

Julius Erving

SUNS VS. 76ERS

Monday, Oct. 19 / 7:35

See Dr. J, Darryl Dawkins and the rest of the Sixers in one of only two Coliseum appearances this season. Get tickets early for best seat selection.

TICKETS:
Suns office—2303 N. Central
Coliseum Box Office
Diamonds Box Office*

*50¢ service charge per ticket at Diamonds

EXHIBIT 3

SUNS VS. LAKERS
SATURDAY / 7:35

Magic Johnson

TICKETS:
Suns Office—2910 N. Central
Coliseum Box Office
Diamonds Box Office*

50¢ service charge per ticket at Diamonds

EXHIBIT 4

SUNDAY /7:05

SUNS
VS. WARRIORS

Walter Davis

ARMOUR DIAL NIGHT

Bring a wrapper from Dial soap to the Suns office and get a $3 discount on $8 tickets, a $2 discount on $6 or $7 tickets. Offer good only at the Suns ticket office and is subject to ticket availability.

2303 N. Central

(through personal sales and direct mail), these themes have been used rather infrequently in Suns advertising.

4. *Giveaway promotions.* The Suns agency has also included the team's many giveaway nights in advertising designed to build single game attendance. These ads have featured

such promotions as Team Poster Night (see Exhibit 8) and Suns T-Shirt Night (see Exhibit 9). These giveaways are usually advertised as part of an overall promotion being sponsored by a local company (other giveaway promotions include Coors Cup Night and Pepsi-Cola Tote Bag Night).

5. *Family-oriented promotions.* Top management has always felt it important to reinforce the belief that Phoenix Suns basketball is family entertainment, packaged in a highly appealing team and augmented by numerous family-oriented promotion nights. This theme has been advertised through a variety of execu-

EXHIBIT 5

THURSDAY/7:35

SUNS
VS. HAWKS

Only Coliseum appearance by Atlanta this season

Alvin Scott

BASKIN-ROBBINS 31 FLAVORS NIGHT

Ticket discount coupons available at Baskin-Robbins 31 Flavors Ice Cream stores

$8 tickets — $3 discount per ticket with coupon
$6 & $7 tickets — $2 discount per ticket with coupon

Redeem coupons at any Suns ticket outlet,* including the Coliseum right up till gametime. Subject to ticket availability. Children 12 years & under get $8, $7, or $6 adult tickets FOR HALF PRICE.

PHOENIX SUNS

TICKETS:
Suns office — 2303 N. Central
Coliseum
Diamonds Box Office*

*35¢ service charge per ticket at Diamonds

EXHIBIT 6

MACY!

In Indiana, his high school talents earned Kyle Macy the title of "Mr. Basketball." At the University of Kentucky, he was a three-time All American. As a pro with the Suns...the beat goes on.

And the best way to see it, is with your own season tickets. For your family. For your business.

Tomorrow, call or visit the Suns office to get complete information on the many season ticket packages available. It's the best entertainment around.

PHOENIX SUNS

2303 N. Central
258-7111

EXHIBIT 7

Intensity!

You see it in every Phoenix Suns fast break, in every steal, in every John MacLeod time-out. And it's contagious!

Catch it yourself, 41 nights a year, with season tickets. There isn't a better entertainment act in town.

PHOENIX SUNS

2303 N. Central   **258-7111**

EXHIBIT 8

HOME OPENER!

P H O E N I X   S A N   A N T O N I O

SUNS VS. SPURS

TUESDAY, NOV. 3 / 7:35 p.m.

CIRCLE K NIGHT
Save on tickets to the Suns' home opener with special discount coupons available at Circle K stores throughout the Valley. Or use the coupon below.

FREE SUNS CALENDAR POSTERS
to everyone attending the game, compliments of Circle K!

TICKETS:
Coliseum Box Office, Diamonds Box Office*
Suns Ticket Office—2303 N. Central
  (2910 N. Central effective Nov. 2)

SUNS TICKET DISCOUNT COUPON

PHOENIX SUNS

SUNS VS. SPURS / Nov. 3

This coupon good for a $2.00 discount on $7.00 adult tickets or a $2.50 discount on $9.50 adult tickets purchased for the above game. Discount ticket prices for children 12 years & under are one half the regular adult ticket price. To receive discount, coupon must be redeemed at the time of ticket purchase. Redeem the coupon at the Suns office, Diamonds Box Office* or at the Coliseum Box Office right up until game time. Offer is subject to ticket availability.

*50¢ service charge per ticket at Diamonds   Code B 1

---

tions and in a variety of media (see Exhibit 10).

CURRENT SITUATION

As the Suns face the 1981–1982 season, very few obstacles would seem to stand in the way of successful ticket sales and further improvement in attendance figures. However, there are two negative factors that must be considered when one begins to construct an objective-oriented advertising plan. These problem areas, as outlined by the Suns' advertising agency, are as follows:

1. *Lack of "choice" season tickets* Because of excellent team performance in the past few

EXHIBIT 9

WEDNESDAY/7:35

SUNS
VS. WARRIORS

Mike Bratz

CIRCLE K NIGHT
**Ticket discount coupons available
at all Valley Circle K locations**

$8 tickets — $3 discount per ticket with coupon
$6 & $7 tickets — $2 discount per ticket with coupon

Redeem coupons at any Suns ticket outlet,* including the
Coliseum right up till gametime. Subject to ticket availability. Children 12 years & under get $8, $7, or $6 adult
tickets FOR HALF PRICE.

FREE SUNS T-SHIRTS
to the first 3,000 16 years & under at the game, compliments
of Circle K.

PHOENIX SUNS

TICKETS:
Suns office — 2303 N. Central
Coliseum
Diamonds Box Office*

*35¢ service charge per ticket at Diamonds

EXHIBIT 10

SUNDAY/1:45 p.m.

SUNS
New Jersey
VS. NETS

Alvan Adams

SMITTY'S
FAMILY PLAN

Pick up Family Plan ticket discount coupons at any Valley Smitty's location. Redeem at a Suns ticket outlet and save $3
on $8 tickets; $2 on $6 & $7 tickets. Subject to ticket availability.

PHOENIX SUNS

TICKETS:
Suns office — 2303 N. Central
Coliseum
Diamonds Box Office*

*35¢ service charge
per ticket at Diamonds

seasons and a low season ticket attrition rate,
many of the best season seats are no longer
available for purchase.

2. *Economic factors.* Double-digit inflation,
possible fuel shortages, and other demands
on personal income are likely to cut into
discretionary funds and impact leisure-time
activities.

The Suns' agency has also pointed out that the team has a number of items in its favor. These are:

1. *Increase in attendance.* The previous year saw the team enjoy their best season in terms of overall attendance and season ticket sales.
2. *Team performance.* The Suns are also coming off their best year in terms of on-court performance, with the team recording a mark of 57 wins against only 25 defeats.
3. *Team charisma.* The Suns are a team characterized by youth, personality, and a break-away style of play. These attributes combine to make the team a very marketable product.
4. *Realignment of NBA schedules.* The weighting of schedules toward more frequent play within conferences and divisions will serve to create two areas of opportunity:
   a. The more frequent exposure to teams within the division will heighten rivalries and place more significance on intradivision contests.
   b. One-time visits by top teams outside the conference (Boston, Milwaukee, Washington, and Chicago) will give tickets to these games a premium status.
5. *Promotional nights.* The various premium and discount offers conducted with local businesses provide an incentive for the occasional ticket buyer to become exposed to Suns basketball more frequently. This may heighten a fan's interest in the Suns and may also make the individual a prospect for future season tickets. (See Exhibit 11 for the agency's proposed promotion game schedule).
6. *Healthier local economic outlook.* Despite the many negative influences nationwide, the Phoenix economy is likely to suffer less than other parts of the country. Local economic indications are quite strong, with personal income and employment figures at all-time highs.
7. *Additional 2,000 coliseum seats.* The expansion of the Veteran's Memorial Coliseum provides an excellent market opportunity for the Suns in both season and individual game ticket sales.
8. *Influx of new residents.* As the Phoenix metropolitan area continues to grow, new markets for both season tickets and individual game ticket sales will be further expanded.

After evaluating the advertising and promotion plans prepared by the Suns' advertising agency for the 1981–1982 season, General Manager Jerry Colangelo finds himself hesitant in approving the agency's recommendations. For the past three years the Suns have been spending between $65,000 and $73,000 for advertising media (see Table 8). The cost of giveaways, salaries, production, and media time and space purchased in exchange for tickets is not included in these figures. To further increase both season ticket sales and individual game ticket sales, the Suns advertising agency is recommending (based on the aforementioned positive factors) a substantial increase both in the media budget (see Table 9) and in individual game promotions. (see Exhibit 11).

The agency is recommending a $100,000 media budget and is also requesting an expanded promotional effort consisting of 29 promotion games. (This is an increase of 38 percent over the previous year, in which 21 promotion nights were held.) The agency feels that the Suns are a very salable commodity and that the current situation warrants increased expenditures to take full advantage of an excellent market opportunity. Mr. Colangelo, on the other hand, is not convinced that the agency's media and promotion recommendations are particularly sound. It is his feeling that the team is now in a position to rely more on it excellent record and proven personnel to increase attendance.

Mr. Colangelo has always believed that a team's success at the gate is directly related to its performance on the court. He backs up this contention by citing the 1970–1971 and 1971–

EXHIBIT 11
Suns' Promotion Games: 1981–1982 Phoenix Suns

Date		Opposing Team	Promotion
November	3	San Antonio	Circle K Night
			Poster Calendar Night
November	5	Dallas	Armour Dial Night
November	25	Houston	Bashas' Night
November	27	Chicago	Pepsi-Cola Night
December	1	San Diego	Armour Food Night
December	5	Utah	Phoenix Gazette Night
December	10	Portland	Sun Giant Night
			Coors Cup Night
December	12	Washington	Circle K Night
			Carnation YMCA Night
December	19	Kansas City	Pepsi-Cola Team Poster Night
December	23	Golden State	J.C. Penney Poster Night
December	30	Portland	Rossie Ford Night
January	2	Seattle	Greyhound Night
			Gorilla T-Shirt Night
January	14	New York	Carnation Night
January	16	San Diego	Circle K T-Shirt Night
January	19	San Antonio	Bashas' Night
January	22	New Jersey	Pepsi-Cola Tote Bag Night
January	23	Detroit	Carnation Girl Scout Night
February	3	Golden State	Checker Auto Night
February	10	Boston	Coors Cup Night
February	12	Atlanta	Earl's Sporting Goods Night
			Wristband Night
			Carnation Boy Scout Night
February	26	Denver	Circle K T-Shirt Night
March	3	Utah	Armour Food Night
March	5	Kansas City	Pepsi-Cola Night
March	7	Houston	Armour Dial Night
March	21	Seattle	Pioneer Take-Out Night
March	24	Dallas	Circle K Night
March	26	Milwaukee	Nike Poster Night
April	4	Kansas City	Bashas' Night
April	8	Portland	Circle K Night

1972 seasons, when team attendance was growing rapidly without large advertising expenditures (about $30,000) and with about half the number of promotions that are currently being recommended. During these two seasons the team had excellent records and therefore generated expanded interest and support. He also brings out the fact that after the Suns' exciting 1975–1976 season, ticket sales soared and the team was spending only $50,000 on advertising media. It is Mr. Colangelo's contention that, after the Suns' best season ever, the fans will not have to be coaxed into coming to see the team play.

TABLE 9
Proposed Phoenix Suns' Media
Budget: 1981–1982

Medium	Proposed Budget[a]
Newspaper	$55,000
Radio	31,000
Magazine	6,000
Television	6,000
Outdoor	2,000
Total	$100,000

[a]Does not include approximately $45,000 of media space and/or time that will be purchased by trading tickets.

In addition, Mr. Colangelo has his doubts concerning the viability of the giveaway and discount ticket promotions. His feeling is that teams with excellent records should not have to rely so heavily on giveaways and discounts to attract fans. A successful team, in Colangelo's opinion, is the best promotion that management can possibly have. For these reasons, and the fact that the Suns are currently the only proven major league sports franchise in the area, Mr. Colangelo would like to see the media budget set at $50,000 and the number of promotions reduced by half of what the agency suggests.

Finally, the Suns' management feels that a clear statement of advertising objectives is needed to provide the team's overall communications effort with a basic focus and direction. Without these goals, Colangelo feels that a unified program is impossible.

ENDNOTES

1. McGuire Research Co., Dallas, Texas, December 1975.
2. *Phoenix Suns Marketing Research Study,* College of Business Administration, Department of Marketing, Arizona State University, Tempe, Arizona, October 1978.

QUESTIONS FOR DISCUSSION

1. What is your opinion of the advertising and promotion programs used by the Phoenix Suns?
2. What is the opportunity for advertising to contribute to the stimulation of demand for both season ticket and individual game ticket sales?

The All-Sweet Sugar Company is a relatively small refining and distributing company located in Indianapolis. Nearly 75 percent of company sales come from a five-state area: Indiana, Illinois, Ohio, Kentucky, and Michigan.

The company produces a full line of bulk and packaged sugar for industrial and home use. About 30–35 percent of All-Sweet's output is sold to wholesalers, chain organizations, and retail grocers for use in the home. Approximately 65–70 percent of company sales go to food processors, bakers, and manufacturers of such products as candy, ice cream, and soft drinks. See Exhibit 1.

COMPANY AND INDUSTRY PROBLEMS

The All-Sweet Sugar Company and the entire industry are bothered by a number of problems: excess refining capacity, keen competition, inability to develop brand preferences, no control over prices, and a decline in the per capita consumption of sugar throughout the United States. See Tables 1, 2, and 3.

The sugar industry is overexpanded and the current level of demand is able to consume only about half of the total productive capacity of the industry in any one year. Because of the standardized, undifferentiated nature of the product, it has been virtually impossible for one company to gain any degree of control over price. Any reduction in price by one refinery is met almost immediately by other companies, so that the price cut usually results in a narrower operating margin for all competitors.

The relatively low utilization of plant capacity and low prices result in high production costs, low efficiency, and low gross margins. The cost of

This case was prepared by Nugent Wedding, Professor Emeritus, University of Illinois, and Charles H. Patti.

production of companies in the industry usually averages well above 80 percent of net sales.

ALL-SWEET COMPANY PROBLEMS

Profit Margin

The influence of these industry problems on All-Sweet's financial position is apparent by examining a typical company operating statement:

Net sales	$15,000,000	100.0%
Cost of goods sold	13,125,000	87.5%
Gross margin	1,875,000	12.5%
Administrative and marketing expense	1,800,000	
Net profit	$75,000	.5%

A cost of production figure of 87.5 percent, resulting in a 12.5 percent gross margin, leaves very little opportunity for an active, aggressive marketing program. With a narrow net profit of ½ to 1 percent, small declines in sales or prices may very quickly result in losses.

EXHIBIT 1
Consumption Levels of All-Sweet Sugar Output

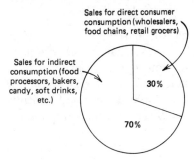

TABLE 1
U.S. Supply of Sugar

Year	Supply (in thousands of short tons, raw value)	Percent Gain/Loss
1960	4,009	—
1965	5,370	34
1970	5,874	9
1973	6,061	3
1974	5,662	−7
1975	6,300	11
1976	6,798	8
1977	6,089	−10
1978	5,602	−8
1979, preliminary	5,799	4

Source: Statistical Abstract of the United States: 1980.

TABLE 2
U.S. Consumption of Sugar (Refined)

Year	Civilian Per Capita Consumption in pounds
1960	97.4
1965	97.0
1970	101.8
1974	96.5
1975	90.2
1976	94.6
1977	95.7
1978	93.1
1979, preliminary	91.3

Source: Statistical Abstract of the United States: 1980.

TABLE 3
U.S. Prices of Sugar, Beet, and Cane

	Cents per Pound		
Year	Raw	Refined	Retail, Granulated
1960	6.3	9.3	11.6
1965	6.8	10.0	11.8
1970	8.1	11.7	13.0
1972	9.1	13.1	13.9
1973	10.3	14.1	15.1
1974	29.5	34.4	32.3
1975	22.5	31.4	37.2
1976	13.3	19.2	24.0
1977	11.0	17.3	21.6
1978	13.9	20.9	24.0
1979, preliminary	15.6	23.2	24.9

Source: Statistical Abstract of the United States: 1980.

low prices and profit margins. Wholesale, retail, and chain grocers are not usually able to secure a markup sufficient to cover all costs of handling sugar. The result is that sugar is handled as a loss leader. Because of the low margins, many retail store managers would not stock sugar at all if they had a choice. Because sugar is a household staple, however, they have no option. As a result of this low interest, retailers rarely stock more than one or two brands of sugar. This situation makes it difficult for All-Sweet to compete for shelf space with the larger, better-known companies such as American, National, and C and H.

Distribution

In another area of marketing, distribution, All-Sweet also faces a troublesome problem. Adequate distribution at the retail level is an essential ingredient in a successful marketing program for sugar. All-Sweet has had difficulty getting and maintaining an adequate distribution system.

At the retail level keen competition results in

Advertising and Sales Promotion Efforts

Advertising, increased personal selling, point-of-purchase materials, and innovations in packaging were among the promotion possibilities most frequently discussed by All-Sweet's management. All of these promotion tools seemed to offer some opportunity for increasing sales and retail distribution. However, they all involve considerable expense.

Each additional salesman hired by the company costs about $50,000 a year, considering both salary and expenses. Estimates for point-of-purchase costs are extremely difficult to gather, but P.O.P. has never been particularly effective for this product category. The low interest of retailers in handling sugar tends to minimize their interest in handling P.O.P. materials.

New packaging ideas were also met with some skepticism. All-Sweet had in the past experimented in the design of special packages or cartons, but these devices seemed to have been most successful in marketing such low-volume specialty items as powdered sugar. The experience of All-Sweet and other companies in the industry offered rather strong evidence that consumers were unwilling to pay an additional amount per pound for granulated sugar sufficient to cover the added costs of packaging.

Several All-Sweet executives expressed interest in the possibilities that advertising offered, both in promotion of the All-Sweet brand and as a means of counteracting the overall decline in sugar consumption. This attitude existed in spite of the fact that advertising had not played a major part in the marketing programs of sugar refiners. American and National, the two largest companies in the industry, had spent relatively modest sums, principally in newspaper advertising for a number of years. Their budgets had averaged between $200,000 and $400,000 per year, which was considerably less than 1 percent of sales. The results had not seemed to be overly impressive. It was the general opinion throughout the industry that this advertising had not succeeded in building a degree of brand preference for either company sufficiently strong to permit a control over price. It did seem, however, that brand recognition and acceptance by consumers had been helpful in gaining interest and support of wholesalers and retailers in the food field.

Years ago the Sugar Institute attempted to expand total consumption of sugar by implementing an industry-wide advertising program. This effort took place during the depression years of 1930 and 1931, when the Institute spent about $400,000 each year in magazine advertising. No noticeable change in generic demand resulted.

CURRENT SITUATION

Realizing that they were facing a number of promotion problems, All-Sweet management decided to seek professional advice. They contacted a highly respected advertising agency and, after several meetings between the agency and All-Sweet management, the agency presented its recommendations. An excerpt from the agency's recommendation follows:

In summary, we recommended that the All-Sweet Sugar Company allocate $500,000 for a regional advertising campaign (see Exhibit 2). The objective of this campaign is to significantly increase market share of the All-Sweet

EXHIBIT 2
Advertising Agency Proposal

Proposed Budget	
Consumer advertising	$250,000
Trade advertising	150,000
(to food retailers and wholesalers)	
Business advertising	100,000
(to food processors and	
manufacturers)	
Total Budget	$500,000
Media	
Magazines	300,000
Business	
Consumer	
Trade	
Newspapers	75,000
Radio	50,000
Outdoor	75,000
	$500,000

TABLE 4
All-Sweet Advertising Investment

Year	Advertising Budget	Annual Sales ($000)	A/S Ratio
1973	$ 64,900	$12,980	.5%
1974	48,900	12,222	.4
1975	27,900	13,971	.2
1976	87,900	14,644	.6
1977	85,300	12,189	.7
1978	41,000	13,675	.3
1979	71,600	14,321	.5
1980	60,700	15,182	.4
1981	88,600	14,770	.6
1982	76,200	15,240	.5
1983[a]	500,000	16,400 (projected)	3+

[a]Proposed by advertising agency.

brand—at both the direct and indirect consumption levels. We believe a major reason for the industry-wide lack of price control is the void of brand advertising. We see no reason why we cannot move the All-Sweet brand beyond the brand recognition level. With the creative approaches we are suggesting, we are fully confident that our two-front campaign (one aimed directly at consumers and the other to the trade) can move the All-Sweet brand to at least the brand preference level.

Naturally, All-Sweet management was enticed by such optimism, but at the same time they wondered if the sizable investment in advertising was prudent—particularly when they had no historical evidence to suggest advertising could affect the demand curve. See Table 4, which presents the All-Sweet advertising budget and sales over the 10 year period 1973–1982.

QUESTIONS FOR DISCUSSION

1. Should All-Sweet's management accept the advertising agency's recommendation? Why or why not?
2. What is the opportunity for advertising to stimulate brand demand for All-Sweet?

10

PLAS-TECH CORPORATION (B)[1]

In late 1957 George Atkin left an important position with a major oil firm to start his own business. Although Atkin was fully aware of the high failure rate of new business ventures, he possessed a combination of talents and experience which he believed would contribute heavily to the success of his new business.

After graduating from MIT as a chemical engineer, Atkin went to work for one of the country's largest oil companies. Within three years he was put in charge of an industrial products development project that was to explore new ways of adapting polyethylene for industrial use. As part of this project, Atkin supervised and then directed the commercial development of polyethylene film.

Polyethylene film became so popular with industrial customers that within six months after its development Atkin was made general manager of a new operating division. The objective of this new division was to manufacture and market polyethylene (plastic) film to a variety of industrial markets.

Under Atkin's direction, this new division developed into a highly profitable operation. Sales grew rapidly and demand soon began to exceed supply of the raw material.

Although the production and manufacturing of plastic film is not technically complicated, Atkin was among the few in the industry with firsthand experience in both production and marketing the product. He had the unique combination of engineering-manufacturing know-how and proven administrative abilities. At age 30, George Atkin felt the time was right for him to try his own business. In October of 1957 he moved to Des Moines, Iowa, and started the Plas-Tech Corporation to manufacture and market a line of disposable polyethylene film for industrial and consumer use.

POLYETHYLENE MARKET

Polyethylene represents both the fastest growing and the largest segment of the plastics packaging industry. In 1960 the dollar volume of polyethylene sold was $660 million. In 1971 the same figure was $3.3 billion. Of the 2.5 billion pounds of plastic packaging materials produced in 1970, polyethylene accounted for nearly 1 billion pounds, or 35 percent of the total. In 1980 the figures were 6.9, 2.5, and 36 percent respectively (see Table 1).

Among the factors influencing the rapid growth of polyethylene are its relatively low price (polyethylene is the lowest-priced transparent material in the world), its strength and versatility, and the development of high-speed and dependable equipment that prints, bags, and wraps.

Industrial Market

Nearly 65 percent of the polyethylene film is consumed by the industrial market (shipping bags, liner film, and construction film). The balance of film production is accounted for by the consumer market (household wrap and bags). Although now growing very rapidly, consumer applications of plastic film were developed several years after the introduction of the product to the industrial market.

The industrial market is made up of government, industrial, commercial, and institutional users. Major users of the product are building material suppliers, mobile home manufacturers, hospitals, food processors, contractors, and apparel manufacturers.

This case was prepared by Charles H. Patti. The original Plas-Tech case was prepared by Charles H. Patti and appeared in *Advertising Management: Cases & Concepts*, by Charles H. Patti and John H. Murphy, Grid Publishing, Inc., 1978.

TABLE 1
Production of Plastic Packaging Materials
(in millions of pounds)

Type	1967	1968	1969	1970	1975	1980	1985[a]
Plastic containers							
Bottles	357	380	443	491	791	1,273	2,051
Tubes	20	24	25	23	32	42	57
Molded polystyrene containers	350	360	375	400	607	864	1,229
Transparent films							
Cellophane	385	360	350	340	350	375	392
Polyethylene	735	795	895	975	1,670	2,514	4,199
Other plastic film	198	240	277	300	918	1,832	2,493
Totals	2,045	2,159	2,365	2,529	4,368	6,900	10,421

[a]Projected

Consumer Market

Disposable plastic bags are sold in a variety of sizes and used for several household purposes—lawn and garden care, garbage and waste containers, food storage, and the packaging of miscellaneous household items. The total market for disposable plastic bags at the consumer level was approximately $520 million in 1975, $810 million in 1980, and projected to over $1 billion by 1985 (see Table 2).

Although brands are not very important in marketing plastic film to the industrial market, almost all of the film produced for consumer use is sold under a brand name—the brand name of

TABLE 2
Industry Sales of All Disposable Plastic Bags

Year	Retail Dollar Volume ($000)	Percent Increase
1967	$ 10,000	0
1968	25,000	150
1969	100,000	300
1970	275,000	175
1975	520,000	125
1980	810,000	31
1985[a]	1,231,000	52

[a]Projected.

either the manufacturer or the distributor. The rapid growth and high profit potential of consumer plastic bags and wrap have attracted many competitors. While today there are literally dozens of brands on the market, three brands dominated the field during the early stages of the product's life cycle (see Table 3).

GROWTH OF PLAS-TECH CORPORATION

Because Atkin had extensive experience in manufacturing and marketing film to the industrial market, he directed Plas-Tech's initial efforts along these same lines.

During the late 1950s and early 1960s, Plas-Tech manufactured a variety of sizes and gauges of plastic bags and film for industrial users. The product was manufactured in the company's 150,000-square-foot manufacturing and warehouse facility in Des Moines and marketed by a staff of six full-time, "inside" salespeople and fifteen sales agents located throughout the United States.

Although competition was keen, a favorable economic climate, a rapidly increasing demand for the product, and a continuing supply of raw materials needed to manufacture the film combined to make Plas-Tech a successful operation.

TABLE 3
Retail Sales of Plastic Bags: 1971

Type of Bag	Estimated Sales (in $ millions)	Brand	Sales (in $ millions)	Share of Market (percent)
Household/lawn	200.0	Brand "A"	74.0	37.0
		Brand "B"	46.0	23.0
		Brand "C"	34.0	17.0
		All others	46.0	23.0
Food storage	45.0	Brand "C"	22.5	50.0
		Brand "A"	9.9	22.0
		Brand "B"	4.5	10.0
		All others	8.1	18.0
Waste disposal	155.0	Brand "A"	55.8	36.0
		Brand "B"	51.2	33.0
		Brand "D"	23.3	15.0
		All others	24.8	16.0
Total market	400.0	Brand "A"	139.7	34.9
		Brand "B"	101.7	25.4
		Brand "C"	56.5	14.1
		Brand "D"	23.3	5.8
		All others	78.9	19.7

In addition to factors beyond his control, Atkin felt his company was enjoying success because of manufacturing efficiencies and low marketing costs. Selling to industrial markets required almost no advertising. Also, sales personnel were being paid on a commission system; therefore, there were few fixed costs in the promotion program.

DEVELOPMENT AND MARKETING OF "BIG BOYS"

1970–1975

During the late 1960s Atkin began planning for entry into the consumer goods market. Several firms were already marketing plastic film for consumer household use, and the products of these firms were eagerly accepted by consumers. Consumer sales were increasing rapidly and the profit margins on plastic film were considerably higher at the consumer level than at the industrial level. In 1970, after eighteen months of product development and testing, Plas-Tech entered the consumer market with Big Boys, a line of plastic bags for household use.

Creative Strategy

Plas-Tech's advertising agency suggested that Big Boys be positioned as the bag offering the consumer the best value. Although most plastic bags are identical in construction, Big Boys' reinforced bottom seam provided more strength than any other bag on the market. Furthermore, all of the leading brands were priced approximately 10 to 15 percent higher than Big Boys. Therefore, a creative strategy built around "Big Boys—the extra-strength bag with the lowest price" appeared to offer a strong selling idea with high saliency for the consumer.

Distribution and Promotion

The normal chain of distribution for this product is from manufacturer to wholesaler to retail outlet to the ultimate consumer. The leading

TABLE 4
Advertising Expenditures and Market Shares of Leading Brands of Plastic Bags and Wrap for Consumer Household Use: 1971, 1976, 1981

	1971			1976			1981		
Brand	Advertising Expenditure ($000)	Share of Advertising (percent)	Market Share (percent)	Advertising Expenditure ($000)	Share of Advertising (percent)	Market Share (percent)	Advertising Expenditure ($000)	Share of Advertising (percent)	Market Share (percent)
A	$ 3,500	34.3	34.9	$ 7,307	33.0	32.4	$12,740	35.0	34.3
B	2,750	26.9	25.4	6,665	30.1	28.9	9,246	25.4	24.4
C	2,500	24.5	14.1	4,473	20.2	16.7	6,188	17.0	12.1
D	812	8.0	5.8	2,318	10.7	7.1	4,041	11.1	5.1
E	600	5.8	3.0	1,271	5.6	4.1	3,895	10.7	3.9
Big Boys	50	0.5	0.4	105	0.4	2.3	291	0.8	3.0
All others	N/A	N/A	16.4	N/A	N/A	8.5	N/A	N/A	17.2
Totals	$10,212	100.0	100.0	$22,139	100.0	100.0	$36,401	100.0	100.0

national brands were all heavily advertised via television, magazines, newspapers, and radio. There was also a need for promotion and advertising to the trade; therefore, co-op advertising, trade deals, cents-off coupons, and point-of-purchase materials were used extensively. However, it was generally felt that mass consumer advertising was the most important promotional tool in stimulating and controlling brand demand (see Table 4).

In 1971 Plas-Tech decided to introduce Big Boys on a market-by-market basis. Big Boys were first introduced in Des Moines and sup-ported by little consumer advertising. Distribution was secured primarily through personal selling and price discounting. During the brand's first year in the market, Plas-Tech spent $50,000 for Big Boys advertising and most of this was spent on material to support the selling effort of wholesalers. While advertising costs were kept at a minimum, distribution was slow. Fourteen months after the product had been introduced, Big Boys had limited distribution in Des Moines, Iowa; Lincoln, Nebraska; Rockford, Illinois; and several other medium-sized Midwest markets.

EXHIBIT 1
Polyethylene bags have become a household staple. It is estimated that nearly 75 percent of all U.S. households use plastic garbage bags and trash can liners.

1975–1981

During the late seventies the plastic bag market continued to expand at a rapid pace. The product category became a household staple as consumers learned to appreciate the convenience, flexibility, and low cost of polyethylene.

By 1980 nearly 75 percent of all households

TABLE 5
Big Boys Advertising Media Analysis:
1971, 1976, 1981

Year	Advertising Budget	Advertising Media Used
1971	$ 50,000	Direct mail to wholesalers and retailers
		Newspapers (co-op)
		Outdoor
1976	$105,000	Newspapers
		Outdoor
		Radio
1981	$291,000	Newspapers
		Sunday supplements
		Outdoor
		Radio
		Television

TABLE 6
Plas-Tech Corporation Sales: 1957–1985

Year	Total Sales	Sales of Big Boys	Percent of Total Sales
1957[a]	$ 5,000	$ 0	0
1960	240,000	0	0
1965	2,870,000	0	0
1970[b]	8,565,000	428,250	5.3
1971[c]	14,000,000	1,680,000	13.6
1975	38,044,000	14,260,000	59.9
1980	61,868,000	24,300,000	64.7
1985[d]	103,341,000	45,547,000	78.8

[a]Company was formed in October 1957.
[b]Big Boys brand introduced.
[c]First full year of Big Boys sales.
[d]Projected.

TABLE 7
Geographic Distribution of Big Boys: 1971, 1976, 1981

Big Boys Markets	Time Period Distribution Achieved		
	1970–1971	1972–1976	1977–1981
Illinois			
Alton		✓	
Aurora		✓	
Belleville		✓	
Bloomington			✓
Champaign-Urbana			✓
Decatur			✓
DeKalb	✓		
East St. Louis		✓	
Elgin		✓	
Freeport	✓		
Galesburg		✓	
Moline	✓		
Normal			✓
Pekin		✓	
Peoria		✓	
Rockford	✓		
Rock Island	✓		
Springfield			✓
Iowa			
Ames	✓		
Burlington		✓	
Cedar Rapids		✓	
Council Bluffs		✓	
Des Moines	✓		
Ft. Dodge	✓		
Ft. Madison			
Iowa City		✓	
Marshalltown	✓		
Mason City		✓	
Ottumwa		✓	
Waterloo		✓	
Kansas			
Lawrence		✓	
Topeka		✓	
Wichita			✓
Missouri			
Columbia		✓	
Independence			✓
Jefferson City		✓	
Joplin			✓
Kansas City			✓
Springfield			✓
St. Joseph		✓	
St. Louis			✓
Nebraska			
Grand Island		✓	
Hastings		✓	
Lincoln	✓		
North Platte			✓
Omaha	✓		

used plastic garbage bags and trash can liners and 70 percent of all households used plastic sandwich bags or food bags (see Exhibit 1).

Attracted by the continued growth of this market and its profitability, private brands began appearing in the early 1970s. The private or store brands were eventually joined by generics, and by 1980 the consumer had a wide choice of brands. As the national brands continued to fight to hold their market share, national advertising intensified (see Table 4).

Although the Big Boy brand was able to survive the seventies, George Atkin was less than completely satisfied. Although he had developed a good product and was able to survive a ten-year market struggle against companies much larger than his, he knew he really had not seriously penetrated the market positions of the industry leaders. He frequently wondered if his original marketing plan of minimal consumer promotion and market-by-market introduction had been the best strategy. With ten years of data to examine, he was often bothered by the correlation between industry share of advertising and market share. Tables 5, 6, and 7 present a summary of past Big Boy advertising, Plas-Tech sales, and Big Boys distribution.

CURRENT SITUATION

Next week George Atkin would present a new long-range plan for Big Boys to his Board of Directors. Industry projections were quite encouraging and he didn't want to let another opportunity escape him.

ENDNOTE

1. The data presented in this case were taken from a number of sources including *Industry Surveys,* Simmons Market Research Bureau, Inc., the National Flexible Packaging Association, and *Advertising Age.* Also, much of the information has been disguised and does not describe the actual situation in the plastic bag and wrap industry.

QUESTION FOR DISCUSSION

1. Evaluate the opportunity for advertising to stimulate brand demand for Big Boys at two different time periods—1971 and 1982.

SECTION 3
SETTING ADVERTISING OBJECTIVES

One of the ironic aspects of advertising management is that while great amounts of time, energy, and money are typically devoted to the creative, media, and research portions of a campaign; minimal attention is directed to advertising objectives. A media plan, for example, often consists of a multipage report which includes details on dollars invested, media vehicles used, target markets reached, and the like. On the other hand, advertising objectives are all too often expressed in one or two short, vague statements about improvements in the organization's market share or image.

Traditionally, advertising management has had difficulty in formulating advertising objectives that are: (1) meaningful expressions of the expectations of advertising and (2) acceptable to top management. Part of the difficulty stems from the fact that the fundamental purpose of advertising is to cause some type of action (sales, inquiries, attendance, votes) and top management evaluates success in terms of achieving the specific action goal. At the same time, advertising management has come to recognize that achievement of an action goal generally must be preceded by one or more preliminary tasks (increase in awareness, attitude change, alterations in beliefs or perceptions, etc.). This situation often results in two different kinds of advertising objectives. The type of objective that is most appealing to top management is the sales-oriented objective which is reflected in such objectives statements as, "increase sales by 10 percent," "improve market position," or "increase distribution." The advertising objectives that frequently are recommended by advertising management or the advertising agency, however, include such statements as, "enhance the company image," "create a favorable impression about our brand," or "increase awareness of our product."

The purpose of advertising objectives are to provide:

1. An expression of the common understanding of what is expected of the advertising effort.
2. Direction to all of the other components of the advertising campaign.
3. A standard against which success can be measured.

We have already recommended that the foundation for setting advertising objectives should be the evaluation of the role of advertising. Once an organization has evaluated the factors that compose the environment within which advertising must work, it should have a clearer understanding of what advertising can reasonably be expected to accomplish. In almost all cases, advertising can and should be expected to accomplish one or more communications tasks (increase awareness, expand knowledge, change opinions or beliefs, etc.). In the rare situation in which advertising is the sole communications link between the marketer and the buyer (mail-order situations, for example), advertising objectives and sales objectives become almost identical.

Advertising objectives that best fulfill their purposes are those that are *realistic* and *specific* in terms of intended effects, target market, message content, measurement criteria, and time frame. Further, in most situations advertising objectives should *address one or more of the steps that are preliminary to the organization's action objectives.*

Because the Advertising or Promotion Manager does not always have full control of the process through which advertising objectives are formulated, there are two basic challenges facing the manager. The first is to be able to formulate sound advertising objectives through a consensus of those involved in the process. The second is to be able to evaluate the appropriateness of advertising objectives developed by others. Sometimes the advertising objectives are developed by top management or the advertising agency, and the Advertising or Promotion Manager, who is ultimately responsible for the entire advertising campaign, must be able to critically analyze the objectives upon which all subsequent work is based. If the Advertising Manager feels the objectives are inappropriate, this should be communicated to the others involved and some mutually agreeable solution sought.

11
MAYES LAMP COMPANY

BACKGROUND

In 1948 John and Tom Mayes started their own business of manufacturing and marketing a line of domestic lamps and fixtures for household use. The Mayes brothers marketed several different lamp styles but eventually specialized in small, portable electric lamps. They purchased a small warehouse and production facility in the Chicago area and concentrated their sales efforts on the large retail chains—Sears, Wards, Penneys, et al. Their efforts were considered successful but their total sales were modest in terms of the total industry. (See Table 1.)

During the fifties the company grew and continued to add new products to the line, additional direct salesman, and more warehouse and production facilities. At this time, they also began to search for production help because they had started to rely more on the subcontracting of lamp production.

As population and disposable income increased, Mayes Lamp prospered. The sixties were generally a period of great growth for the total industry and for Mayes. In 1961 Mayes had sales of $13 million, by 1970 their sales had reached $24 million, and their estimated sales in 1982 were $55 million.

MARKETING CONSIDERATIONS

Distribution

The distribution chain for lamps, lighting fixtures, and lamp shades is as follows:

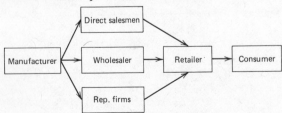

This case was prepared by Charles H. Patti.

TABLE 1
Sales of Lamps, Lamp Fixtures, and Shades
(in millions of dollars)

Year	Total Industry	Mayes	Mayes Percentage of Total
1940	$ 500	—	—
1945	$ 620	—	—
1950	$ 700	$ 3	0.4
1955	$ 780	$ 6	0.8
1960	$ 850	$12	1.4
1965	$1,400	$18	1.8
1970	$2,500	$24	0.96
1975	$3,300	$32	0.97
1980	$4,100	$42	1.0
1982	$5,100	$55	1.1

Mayes Lamp followed this distribution pattern and in 1982 had a direct sales staff of 12 covering "house" accounts and 27 representative firms covering the entire United States.

Promotion

Advertising has not been considered a major factor influencing generic or selective demand in this industry. Studies have shown that consumers have a very low interest in lamps, light fixtures, and lamp shades. Over 80 percent of new lamps are bought for "redecoration" purposes. In general, the industry has been largely unsuccessful in creating much consumer interest in the product classification.

With little success in developing direct consumer interest, manufacturers have concentrated most of their marketing efforts on co-op advertising, trade advertising, and point-of-purchase materials.

Product and Price

Since 1975 Mayes has moved toward specializing in small, portable electric lamps. Such lamps are

TABLE 2
Advertising of High-Intensity Lamps

	1960	1965	1970	1975	1980	1981	1982	1983
Competitor A	$200,000	$200,000	$125,000	$155,000	$157,000	$161,000	$164,000	Not available
Competitor B	$150,000	$175,000	$105,000	$125,000	$155,000	$136,000	$162,000	Not available
Competitor C	$ 30,000	$ 50,000	$ 50,000	$ 75,000	$125,000	$150,000	$155,000	Not available
Competitor D	$ 40,000	$ 35,000	$ 20,000	$ 50,000	$ 90,000	$ 90,000	$ 80,000	Not available
All foreign	$ 25,000	$ 70,000	$100,000	$125,000	$200,000	$250,000	$275,000	Not available
Mayes	$ 5,000	$ 10,000	$ 25,000	$ 45,000	$110,000	$125,000	$131,000	$350,000[a]

[a]Proposed.

known by consumers as "high-intensity" lamps and are ideal for use in detail work, such as reading in bed, sewing, or reading at a desk.

Mayes' high-intensity lamps are comparable in quality to those of the industry leaders. Furthermore, Mayes retails its lamps for 10–15 percent less than competing, comparable models. Since high-intensity lamps retail from $7 to $20, the Mayes lower price means a savings to the consumer of roughly $.70 to $3 per lamp.

CURRENT DEVELOPMENTS

The Mayes brothers are very pleased with the developments and growth of their company but are now anxious to assume greater command of the industry. They are convinced that they can become the leader in high-intensity lamp sales by stimulating consumer demand for their brand. The two leading brands spend little on advertising high intensity lamps (see Table 2) but combined account for 33 percent of this market (see Table 3).

The Mayes brothers believe that consumer advertising can do three things to increase their sales:

1. Attract new users to the market—get more people to buy a high-intensity lamp.
2. Attract a sizable market share away from the

industry leaders by showing the value of a Mayes lamp.
3. Stimulate and encourage distribution.

At the present time John and Tom Mayes are planning next year's (1983) advertising program. They are considering the launching of a $350,000 national consumer advertising campaign for high-intensity lamps.

The Mayes brothers have very little experience in consumer goods advertising; therefore, they have been looking for an advertising agency to handle their account. During the past several weeks John and Tom have interviewed several agencies but so far they have not found one they feel comfortable with. They realize that their $350,000 budget is not large—particularly for a national, consumer-oriented campaign. Therefore, they are looking for an agency that is willing and able to put together an effective yet efficient media program.

To assist the various agencies in pitching the Mayes Lamp account, John and Tom have put together the information in Exhibit 1.

QUESTIONS FOR DISCUSSION

1. To what extent are the Mayes brothers' expectations about advertising realistic?
2. Create a statement of advertising objectives for the Mayes Lamp Company.

TABLE 3
Sales of High-Intensity Lamps

Firms	1960 Sales in $MM	Percent of Market	1965 Sales in $MM	Percent of Market	1970 Sales in $MM	Percent of Market	1975 Sales in $MM	Percent of Market	1980 Sales in $MM	Percent of Market	1982 Sales in $MM	Percent of Market
Competitor A	$ 6.0	30	$ 60	58	$ 25	24	$ 28	20	$ 36	20	$ 39	19
Competitor B	$ 5.0	25	$ 16	15	$ 20	19	$ 22	16	$ 28	15	$ 29	14
Competitor C	$ 2.0	10	$ 5	5	$ 8	8	$ 10	7	$ 9	5	$ 15	7
Competitor D	$ 2.0	10	$ 4	4	$ 6	6	$ 10	7	$ 11	6	$ 10	5
All foreign	$ 3.0	15	$ 8	8	$ 16	15	$ 22	16	$ 33	18	$ 39	19
All private brands	$ 1.8	9	$ 8	7	$ 20	19	$ 31	21	$ 38	21	$ 42	20
Mayes	$ 0.2	1	$ 3	3	$ 10	9	$ 18	13	$ 28	15	$ 33	16
Totals	$20.0	100	$104	100	$105	100	$141	100	$183	100	$207	100

EXHIBIT 1

Information for Advertising Planning

Target Markets

  Primary: married, unemployed women, 21–49, households of 3+ people

  Secondary: professional men and women, 21–49, incomes of $15,000–$25,000

Seasonality of Sales

  Insignificant monthly variations

Marketing Objectives

1. Increase total sales by 33⅓ percent during the 1983–1985 period.
2. Increase market share of high-intensity lamps to 25 percent by January 1985.
3. Expand distribution penetration from 40 percent to 65 percent of available retail outlets by January 1985.

Advertising Objectives

1. Create brand awareness.
2. Build conviction/belief that the Mayes product is a superior value to consumers.
3. Stimulate consumer action to buy the Mayes product.
4. Attract attention of potential distributors (retailers).

12

CLIFF PECK CHEVROLET

Whenever a new Chevrolet automobile dealership was opened, a thorough amount of front-end planning was required. The Cliff Peck dealership established in Austin, Texas, several years ago was no exception. The relatively new dealership was located in the growing northwest section of Austin with over 10 acres of cars and 900 feet of frontage on a major traffic artery.

The two principals who established the dealership, Mr. Harold Pannel and Mr. Jack Izard, were extremely pleased about the prospects for their new dealership. They were confident that widespread consumer acceptance of the Chevrolet product line coupled with the healthy Austin market would produce a winning combination. In fact, the success the dealership had enjoyed during its first few years had supported their confidence, and prospects for even greater success in the future appeared bright.

THE AUTO INDUSTRY

No motor vehicle manufacturer has control of any part of the market. There are striking variations in customer acceptance of each manufacturer's products—variations by product groups, car lines, and geographic area. Although repeat sales are highly prized, the evidence has been overwhelming that customer preference must be earned anew with each sale.

Motor vehicle producers also face competition from the large stock of used vehicles in the United States. The great reservoir of unused mileage and the repairability of motor vehicles give customers the option of continuing to use existing vehicles rather than purchasing new ones. This interaction between new and used vehicles is an integral part of competition in the industry. Since motor vehicles are durable and

This case was prepared by John H. Murphy.

represent a major family decision, cyclical swings in employment and in consumer confidence create amplified swings in new car demand.

THE AUSTIN MARKET

According to published estimates, the Austin Standard Metropolitan Statistical Area (SMSA) ranked in the top 100 markets while the city of Austin was ranked in the top 50 of the United States Commerce Department's list ranking cities by population. Automobile dealer sales per capita for the Austin SMSA were estimated to be at or slightly above the national average.

Austin had been breaking growth records over the past few years for population increases, although the tide of immigration had eased from its peak period. The city's economic picture had continued to be bright, and a recent survey by The University of Texas' Bureau of Business Research indicated that Austin led all major Texas cities in economic growth. With an almost recession-proof economy firmly rooted in government, education, tourism, and a growing industrial complex, Austin officials were optimistic about the city's continued growth.

A study conducted by a respected national news magazine listed Austin as among the top 15 "most pleasant places to live." The magazine pointed to its recreational opportunities, combined with one of the lowest cost-of-living indexes in the country, which had proven to be an irresistible lure to both retirement people and industries looking for attractive leisure facilities for their employees.

AUSTIN AUTO DEALERS

The two Austin Chevrolet dealers in competition with Cliff Peck were Capitol and Henna Chevrolet. Henna led in sales, with Capitol at an estimated 85% of Henna sales and Peck at 80% of Henna sales. Capitol has been in Austin for over 50 years, and they tended to use more TV advertising than Peck or Henna. Capitol called themselves "Your Chevrolet Capitol."

Henna Chevrolet was located in the nearby town of Round Rock for 30 years before they moved to Austin more than a decade ago. Henna tended to advertise heavily in newspapers, and their slogan was "Austin's Favorite Dealer."

Austin dealerships selling other makes of cars included Austin Toyota, Covert Buick, Cen-Tex Datsun, Charles Maund Cadillac-Olds, George Coffey Lincoln-Mercury, McMorris Ford, Leif Johnson Ford, Town Lake Chrysler-Plymouth, Rio Dodge, Bob Miller and Lamar Volkswagen, Continental Cars—Mercedes/Honda, and Bill Munday Pontiac/AMC. In addition to these Austin dealers, dealers in surrounding communities such as Round Rock, San Marcos, and Georgetown provided a fair amount of competitive pressure on the Austin auto market.

CLIFF PECK'S PAST ADVERTISING EFFORTS

Since the dealership opened, Peck had changed advertising agencies twice. For approximately the first three months of the dealership's operation the firm had used an out-of-state agency but it quickly became apparent that this arrangement was unsatisfactory. Next, an agency based in Austin was hired to facilitate communication and to add a new creative punch to the firm's advertising.

Exhibit 1 presents a representative Austin *American-Statesman* newspaper ad for the dealership. Exhibit 2 presents representative radio spots.

Two major reasons were cited for the decision to drop the second agency in favor of another local agency. These reasons were: (1) Peck owners' feeling that the agency had failed to produce creative flair on behalf of the dealership, and (2) their feeling that the agency's casual attitude toward research resulted in a failure to properly initiate and utilize research in planning Peck's advertising efforts.

RESEARCH PROJECT

In order to provide continuous research input for use in advertising planning and evaluation, the dealership and the new agency commissioned a series of ongoing research studies. A local advertising and marketing research firm was retained to conduct an initial benchmark study and additional follow-up surveys. After a series of meetings with the client and the agency, the research firm developed a research plan to collect the necessary data. This program is described in the following paragraphs.

The ongoing research project was identified as, "Awareness, Knowledge, and Attitudes Toward Automobile Dealers Among Adults, Residing in Selected Areas of Austin." Phase I had just been completed. This initial study provided a benchmark measure of the awareness, knowledge, and attitudes of target prospects toward Cliff Peck Chevrolet and the competition. Such measures, repeated at regular intervals, were to be used in establishing objectives and as a control device for evaluating the effectiveness of the promotional communications activities of the dealership.

In each phase a random sample of target prospects in selected geographic areas of Austin located reasonably close to the dealership were to be interviewed. In addition to being relatively accessible to the dealership, these areas contained the best prospects for the dealership based on socioeconomic considerations.

Telephone interviews were used to collect the data. Three hundred male and female adult household-heads were contacted by using a random sampling procedure. A structured questionnaire was used to measure respondents'

EXHIBIT 1
Representative Newspaper Advertisement

CLOSE OUT 82...

1982 CITATIONS—CHEVETTES—CAVALIERS

Our Entire Citation, Chevette and
Cavalier Inventory on Sale.
Take your Pick
At $1.00 Over Invoice
More Than 100 Available For
Immediate Delivery.

$1.00
ONE DOLLAR

OVER INVOICE*

*Original factory invoice. Does not include holdbacks
or possible future rebates. Plus tax, title and license
and financing charges, where applicable.

NOW
OVER 400
NEW CHEVY CARS & TRUCKS PRICED FOR LESS!

1982 CORVETTES

FANTASTIC SAVINGS

CLOSE OUT PRICES CAPRICES

CLOSE OUT PRICES CELEBRITYS

CLOSE OUT PRICES PICK-UPS

CLOSE OUT PRICES MONTE CARLOS

CLOSE OUT PRICES CAMAROS

GOOD CLEAN USED CARS

81 MALIBU WAGON 4800 Miles, Immaculate... $6999	80 THUNDERBIRD Weekend Special............ $5777	81 GMC ½ TON 6 Cyl. — Special............ $5444
81 CORVETTE 3900 Miles — A Puff... $15,750	80 PHOENIX HATCHBACK Low Mileage — Clean... $4666	80 FORD COURIER Camper — Sharp............ $4999
80 CORVETTE Black — Glass Tops... $13,500	79 FORD LTD WAGON Clean — 43,000 Miles...... $4555	77 CHEV. SCOTTSDALE Air — Power — Clean... $3888

CLIFF PECK CHEVY COUNTRY

Northwest on Hwy 183 at 11400 Research Blvd.   345-7890   *Across From Balcones Woods
Open Evenings till 8:00 p.m.*

EXHIBIT 2
Representative Radio Spots

"Jingle"

Chorus: Pick a Peck Chevrolet—you can do it today—with a Cliff Peck Chevrolet. Take it from the folks who save. Pick a Cliff Peck Chevrolet. The dealer who will help keep your car new. It's waiting here for you to help you keep your car new. Cliff Peck's waiting here for you. Cliff Peck Chevrolet.

"Crazy Day Sale"

Anncr: Time is running out at Cliff Peck Chevrolet. Chevy's national sales campaign ends April 5, and we are desperate to meet our goal. So we've gone a little crazy. We want to move cars more than make profits. So this is your chance to save big on a beautiful new Peck Chevrolet car or truck. We're forgetting the sticker price—it's what you can buy it for. Now that's what really counts. Come on out—we've got hundreds in stock. Cliff Peck Chevrolet, on 183 north at eleven four hundred Research.

"Door Slammer Sale"

Anncr: Cliff Peck Chevrolet is slammin' the door . . .
Sfx: (DOOR SLAMS)
Anncr: . . . on inflation with a door slammer sale. Because all new Chevys coming in are factory priced one hundred dollars higher than those now in stock, the cars and trucks we have at the old price will go fast, so hurry in now. New Monte Carlos are priced from _____
Sfx: (DOOR SLAMS)
Anncr: Citations from _____
Sfx: (DOOR SLAMS)
Anncr: Come to Peck's door slammer sale for your best deal in Austin.
Chorus: (SINGS JINGLE)

"Image Trucks"

Anncr: The trucking life in Texas starts at Cliff Peck Chevrolet. Cliff Peck knows what a Texan wants in a pickup, and handles the trucks at the prices to fit that lifestyle. Chevy pickups are built to stay tough, and tough in the right places. Cliff Peck has the Chevy truck to fit your needs, whether it's rugged ranch work, or comfortable in-town cruising. For your best truck deal in Austin, come to Cliff Peck Chevrolet.
Chorus: (SINGS JINGLE)

unaided recall and aided recall of automobile dealerships and of Cliff Peck Chevrolet.

Identification of slogans, attitudes toward automobile dealerships, automobile purchase decisions, and several demographic variables were also included in the questionnaire. Selected portions of the research instrument are presented in the Appendix. Tables 1 to 8 present the findings of Phase I of the continuing research project.

Phase II of the research program was to be conducted twelve months after a new advertising campaign was launched. During the time between Phase I and Phase II the advertising slogan and the theme used by Cliff Peck in its campaign was to be modified. Also, other changes were to be introduced, such as the models being advertised at different times, the total budget being allocated to the campaign, and the emphasis on specific variables such as location, service, and price which were to be promoted in Peck's advertising.

Phase II would use the same data collection methodology as Phase I (although a new random sample would be interviewed). The purpose of the Phase II study would be to evaluate whether or not differences had occurred in the way potential buyers perceive local dealers and

specifically Cliff Peck. Also, other attitudinal and demographic measures that were made in Phase I and repeated in Phase II and later phases would provide a longitudinal study of the effectiveness of Cliff Peck's campaign and would be useful in monitoring other changes in the market.

Phase II would provide a comparison which it was hoped would indicate both the past success and future directions for changes in advertising

TABLE 1
Top of Mind Awareness, All Car Dealers (Q.1)

	First Mention	Any Mention[a]
Capitol	13%	28%
Covert	4	10
Henna	18	29
Johnson	13	22
Coffey	7	15
Maund	10	22
McMorris	5	17
Peck	5	11
Other	25	47
Don't know	0	
	100%	

[a]Multiple responses (first three mentions recorded).

TABLE 2
Why Dealership Was Selected (Q.2)

1.	Offered "best deal," price, cheapest, best price	32%
2.	Only dealer in town.	15
3.	Had car wanted, model, etc.	15
4.	Convenient location	8
5.	Friends with owner or employee	8
6.	Dealt with dealer before	5
7.	Reputable, honest	4
8.	Service	4
9.	Friend or relative recommended	3
10.	Sales personnel	2
11.	Good trade-in	2
12.	Easy credit	1
13.	Advertising	1
14.	Others	—
15.	Work there	—
16.	No reason	—
		100%

TABLE 3
Most Important Qualities of Car Dealers—Any Mention (Q.3)

Service	77%
Location	5
Reputation	13
Price	33
Sales staff	13
Personal attention	13
Other	32

TABLE 4
Top of Mind Awareness, Chevy Dealers—(Q.4)

	First Mention	Any Mention[a]
Capitol	44%	65%
Henna	37	66
Peck	15	33
Other	4	21
	100%	

[a]Multiple responses (first three mentions recorded).

TABLE 5
Slogan Identification (Q.5)

	Correct	Incorrect	Don't Know
Capitol	50	9	41
Henna	27	13	60
Peck	0	2	98

TABLE 6
Awareness of Cliff Peck Chevrolet (Q.6)

(A) Ever heard of Cliff Peck	
Yes	66%
No	34
	100%
(B) Make of cars Cliff Peck handles (among those who had heard of Cliff Peck)	
Chevrolet	90%
Other	3
Don't know	7
	100%
(C) Cliff Peck location (among those who had heard of Cliff Peck)	
Correct ID	82%
Incorrect ID	3
Don't know	15
	100%

by Cliff Peck. In addition, information from the study would help management to determine whether current advertising expenditures were sufficient, given the firm's objectives.

FUTURE DIRECTIONS FOR CLIFF PECK'S ADVERTISING

Set against the background of this research project, the new agency's task was to develop a complete advertising campaign for the upcoming fiscal year. For initial planning purposes the agency was told that they could make any reasonable assumptions about the level of the advertising appropriation for the coming year. It was noted that in past years the firm had invested between $150,000 and $200,000 in their total advertising budget.

In developing campaign recommendations, the agency's first step was to develop a set of specific, appropriate, and realistic advertising objectives. More specifically, the agency was asked to prepare a written statement of advertising objectives for Peck which met Steuart Britt's four criteria of sound advertising objectives (1) what basic message is to be delivered, (2) to what audience, (3) with what intended effects, and (4) what specific criteria are to be used to measure the success of the campaign. (See "Are So-Called Successful Advertising Campaigns Really Successful?" *Journal of Advertising Research,* June 1969, pp. 3–9.)

Mr. Izard and Mr. Pannel both firmly believed that by their developing advertising objectives consistent with Britt's philosophy and using a comparison of the Phase I and II research findings, some valid conclusions could be reached regarding the effectiveness of the new advertising campaign. Both of the principals in the dealership had indicated that they were eager to confer with the agency to go over the agency's proposed statement of objectives. Individuals at the agency realized how important this task of formulating objectives was, not only in

TABLE 7
Cliff Peck Compared with Other Chevrolet Dealers[a]

(A) "Best" service dept. (Q.7)		(B) "Best" prices (Q.8)	
Capital	9%	Capitol	9%
Henna	12	Henna	7
Peck	8	Peck	9
All same	1	All same	3
Don't know	70	Don't know	72
	100%		100%

(C) "Best" selection (Q.9)	
Capitol	8%
Henna	10
Peck	15
All same	4
Don't know	63
	100%

[a]Three dealers compared were Capitol, Henna, and Peck.

TABLE 8
Sample Demographics

(A) Household size (Q.12)		(B) Age (Q.13)	
1	9%	Under 18	0%
2	37	18–24	8
3	18	25–34	27
4	23	35–49	32
5+	13	50–64	18
	100%	65+	12
		Refused	3
			100%

(C) Annual household income (Q.14)		(D) Race (Q.15)	
Under $10,000	9%	White	95%
10,000–14,999	13	Other	5
15,000–24,999	26		100%
25,000	28		
Don't know/refused	24	(E) Sex	
	100%	Male	55%
		Female	45%
			100%

terms of directing all of the other decisions in the campaign planning process but also in terms of proving to the owners of Cliff Peck that they could handle the account properly.

QUESTIONS FOR DISCUSSION

1. What are the limitations and strengths of the Phase I research study? What modifications or additions would be appropriate? Why?

2. What additional data from the Phase I study beyond what is presented in the case would be useful?

3. How can the data presented in Tables 1 to 8 be used to develop a statement of advertising objectives?

4. Which of the four component parts of advertising objectives identified by Britt is most important? Why? Which involves the most uncertainty? Why?

List statement of obj.

APPENDIX
DATA COLLECTION INSTRUMENT

CAPITOL CITY RESEARCH SERVICES   **AUTO DEALERS ATTITUDES STUDY**

Telephone #_____   Questionnaire_____
                                          Census Tract_____
                                          Interviewer _____

Note day and time of contact_____ 2nd contact_____

May I speak with the male or female head of the household? (If neither head is available, arrange a call back)

Hello, my name is _____. I work for Capitol City Research Services, a public opinion survey firm. We are interested in finding out what selected Austin residents think about automobile dealers.

1. When you think of new car dealers, what are the first three that come to mind?

	Capitol	Covert	Henna	Johnson	Coffey	Maund	McMorris	Peck	Other	D.K.
1st mention	1	2	3	4	5	6	7	8	9	0
2nd mention	1	2	3	4	5	6	7	8	9	0
3rd mention	1	2	3	4	5	6	7	8	9	0

2. Have you ever purchased a new car?   Yes   1
                                                 No (skip to Q.3)   2

From which dealership did you buy the car?
Write name of dealership in blank_____
Why did you select _____(name of dealership)?_____

3. What do you feel are the three most important qualities of a good new car dealer?

	Service	Location	Reputation	Price	Sales Staff	Personal Attention	Other	(specify)
1st mention	1	2	3	4	5	6	7	_____
2nd mention	1	2	3	4	5	6	7	_____
3rd mention	1	2	3	4	5	6	7	_____

4. When you think of Chevrolet automobile dealers, what are the first three that come to mind?

	Capital	Henna	Peck	Other
1st mention	1	2	3	4
2nd mention	1	2	3	4
3rd mention	1	2	3	4

5. Now I'd like to know if you recall which specific new car dealer uses the following slogans?

First, what about "The Tradin' Place." Which new car dealer uses "The Tradin' Place" as its slogan?

	Capitol	Henna	Johnson	Coffey	McMorris	Peck	Other	D.K.
(McMorris Ford's Slogan)	1	2	3	4	5	6	7	8
(Henna's Slogan)	1	2	3	4	5	6	7	8
(Coffey's Slogan)	1	2	3	4	5	6	7	8
(Capitol's Slogan)	1	2	3	4	5	6	7	8
(Peck's Slogan)	1	2	3	4	5	6	7	8

6. **Have you ever heard of the Cliff Peck car dealership?**

Yes	1
No (skip to Q.10)	2

If yes, what make of new cars does Cliff Peck handle?

Chevrolet	1
Other	2
D.K.	3

Where is the Cliff Peck dealership located?

Correct ID	1
Incorrect ID	2
D.K.	3

7. **Now thinking about the service department of the three Austin Chevrolet dealers, which of the three—Capitol, Henna, or Cliff Peck—do you feel would have the best service department?**

Capitol	1
Henna	2
Cliff Peck	3
All same	4
D.K.	5

8. **Again, thinking about the three Austin Chevrolet Dealers, which one of the three do you feel would have the lowest prices on new cars?**

Capitol	1
Henna	2
Cliff Peck	3
All same	4
D.K.	5

9. **Now thinking about the selection of cars on hand at the three Austin Chevrolet dealers, which one of the three do you feel would have the largest selection of cars on hand?**

Capitol	1
Henna	2
Cliff Peck	3
All same	4
D.K.	5

Now, a few questions to help classify this questionnaire.

10. **Do you own or rent your home?**

Own	1
Rent	2

11. **How long have you lived at your present address?**	Less than 1 year	1
	1–2 years	2
	3–4 years	3
	5–9 years	4
	10 years or more	5
	D.K., unsure	6

12. **Counting yourself, how many persons now live in your household, including babies?**

Number_____

13. **What is your age?**	Under 18	1
	18–24	2
	25–34	3
	35–49	4
	50–64	5
	65 and over	6
	Refused	7

14. **What was the approximate annual income for all members of your household before taxes last year . . . would it be $15,000 or more or would it be less than that?**

$15,000 or more, Ask:		Less than $15,000, Ask:	
would it be		would it be	
Under $25,000 or	3	Over $10,000 or	2
Over $25,000	4	Under $10,000	1
Don't know	5		
Refused	6		

15. **Finally, would you please tell me your race?**	White	1
	Black	2
	Mexican-American	3
	Other	4

May I have your name, please, in case my office wants to check my work?

Name_____

Note Sex:

| | Male | 1 |
| | Female | 2 |

Thank you very much!

Verification: By_____Date_____

Wilderness Supply is a specialty retail sporting goods store located in a midwestern community of 300,000 people. Wilderness Supply, as the name implies, specializes in equipment for the outdoorsperson: the backpacker, the climber, and the canoeist. The store was opened some five years ago as a one-person operation and has grown to the point where the current store, located in the downtown area of Madison, Wisconsin, includes approximately 2,200 square feet of selling space.

General Market Outlook

Since the very nature of individual outdoor sports such as backpacking precludes accurate estimates of the number of participants, it is difficult to arrive at size estimates for national or local markets. Similarly, because of the large number of fairly small manufacturers of specialized equipment, their sales figures provide little insight into market potential. There can be little doubt however, that interest in these activities is growing and probably increasing even faster than the boom in active participation sports in general. The use of the Cascade trail system in Oregon and Washington has grown 1000 percent between 1940 and 1980, a period in which the U.S. population grew by 72 percent. A Forest Service research paper indicated that much of the increase in hiking and backpacking seems to come from children of the postwar boom introduced to outdoor activities through car camping. By 1984 the population is expected to increase by 21 million, with "89% of the growth in the 20–49 age category that does the most backpacking."[1]

A small part of the potential sales story is told

This case was prepared by Professor Charles Frazer, University of Colorado.

by the success of Recreational Equipment, Inc., in Seattle. REI is a membership cooperative with stores in Seattle and Berkeley, California, as well as a national mail-order business. It currently counts over 500,000 members with sales to them of over $60 million during the past five-year period.

COMPETITIVE CONDITIONS

Though Madison is relatively small, it includes the main campus of the major state university, which enrolls about 34,000 per semester. Since many of the students in Madison come from Minneapolis–St. Paul and make frequent trips home during the school year, the outlets located there are of some significance in limiting Wilderness Supply's potential market.

Direct competition also comes from the many mail-order outdoor suppliers. Such outlets as Recreational Equipment, Inc., in Seattle, the somewhat better known Eastern Mountain Sports in Boston and L.L. Bean of Freeport, Maine, are able to offer a larger array of equipment, though prices are about the same, especially when mailing charges are added. Despite the problem of the necessary wait involved for mail-order equipment, the mail-order suppliers remain competitive, especially for highly specialized gear or when the desired model or color is not in stock at Wilderness Supply.

Local competition also exists. A similar specialty store, though somewhat narrower in scope and smaller in size (less than half the selling space), is located on the east side of town, about three miles from Wilderness Supply. The lines of goods carried by this store are generally not as widely known as those carried by Wilderness Supply and are often priced somewhat lower.

The other local competitor is Madison Surplus. Though in part an outlet dealing in government surplus items, the store devotes about half its approximately 4,200 square feet to inexpensive camping equipment. These items include Coleman products; other coolers, stoves, lanterns, and heaters; inexpensive nylon and canvas tents in the $20–100 range; and synthetic-fill sleeping bags priced from $10 to $50. Also included are a line of inexpensive backpacks and lightweight boots.

MANAGEMENT ORIENTATION

Wilderness Supply is currently a three-way partnership organization with one partner designated as business manager. Most executive responsibilities fall to him. Primary concerns are inventory and cash flow control. Each of the three partners is responsible for various product categories and writes the orders to all suppliers for a particular class of item, such as down jackets.

Each of the three was drawn to the business out of an interest in the activities the store represents; all spend their off hours doing the related activities and using the equipment they sell during working hours. The partners all do full-time sales work with an additional staff of one full-time secretary, one full-time salesman, and six to ten part-time sales people, depending on the season. The full- and part-timers all share an interest in outdoor activities, a sense of "wilderness ethics" that precludes the expansion of the store into such areas as firearms, snowmobiles, trailbikes, and the like, and a sense of esthetics about the equipment carried by the store. Few gadgets and gimmicks are stocked; equipment must be functionally and attractively designed for a specific purpose. Members of the staff are encouraged to purchase equipment at discounted prices and use and evaluate lines carried as well as innovations in their areas of interest.

Salespeople are encouraged to speak from personal knowledge about the features of the equipment being sold and to demonstrate and explain the specific applications of the gear rather than pressure for a sale. The partners encourage an open, friendly atmosphere and those who are "just looking" are encouraged to do so and to ask questions. Wilderness Supply stands behind the products it sells and is willing, even anxious to replace any equipment that fails under reasonable conditions of use. They are supported in this policy by the major manufacturers of their equipment lines, several of whom offer lifetime guarantees against workmanship defects.

RANGE OF GOODS

The goods carried are primarily of use in self-propelled outdoor activities. While much of the backpacking equipment, for example, might also be used by the car camper, it is unlikely that he or she would be interested at the premium price commanded by the extremely sophisticated, durable, compact, and lightweight equipment designed for specialized application. While the range of models in most equipment categories is broad, it is highly sophisticated and supplied by top manufacturers in the industry, often at premium prices. Main equipment categories, suppliers, and price ranges are listed below:

CATEGORY	SUPPLIERS	PRICE RANGE

Tents
  lightweight designs
  for summer and
  winter; one to
  six people
	North Face
	Sierra Designs
	Jan Sport
	Gerry
		$125–400

Sleeping Bags
  synthetic and
  down fill
	North Face
	Sierra Designs
	Jan Sport
	Gerry
		$75–200

Boats
  canoes and kayaks,
  paddles, PFDs,
  etc.
	Old Town
	Moore
	Hyperform
	Phoenix
		$50–1000

Boots	Vasque	$40–100	
hiking and	Galibier		
climbing			
Packs	North Face	$20–150	
day packs, ruck-	Sierra Designs		
sacks, and frame	Jan Sport		
packs	Gerry		
	Kelty		
Cross-country skis	Fischer	$75–200	
also: bindings,	Elite		
boots, poles,	Toppen		
waxes, etc.	Kneissl		
Clothing	North Face	$20–100	
down jackets and	Sierra Designs		
vests, wool shirts,	Gerry		
pants and	Woolrich		
sweaters, etc.	Icelandic Sweaters		

Miscellaneous: stoves, guide and instructional books, freeze-dried foods, knives, cooking gear, storage containers, and replacement parts.

Wilderness Supply does approximately $257,000 in retail sales per year. The annual sales pattern is represented in Exhibit 1.

Each equipment category accounts for the percentage of gross income as shown in Table 1.

PROBLEMS AND OPPORTUNITIES

While Wilderness Supply has been and continues to be profitable even in view of its tremendous expansion and merchandise investment over the past five years, the partners sense some problems. Among the most basic of these is the market: Who composes it now and what other potential segments exist? Salespeople perceive the customers to be much like themselves—young, active, many with ties to the university community. Whether this is a valid perception has not been confirmed. Business Manager Huck Hooper expresses the following concern:

If our ideas of who's buying our goods are wrong, then we're wasting our efforts in trying to reach the university community. On the other hand, if we're right, it raises the

EXHIBIT 1
Wilderness Supply Sales Data

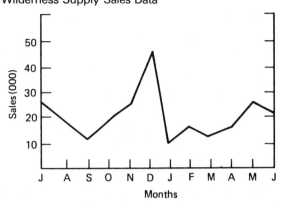

July	$24.5	Jan.	$12.7
Aug.	18.0	Feb.	21.4
Sept.	12.5	March	15.5
Oct.	19.2	April	16.5
Nov.	26.2	May	26.0
Dec.	43.3	June	21.0

question of some sort of limitations on our part. Are we reaching just people in our own age range and what should we be doing to broaden our appeal? The age range of the partners and the sales staff is from around 25 to just over 30 and I'm afraid we all think pretty much alike.

A second problem is also market related. In a store of this variety there are a great number of shoppers who simply come to look, ask advice, or comparison shop among the local outdoor outfitters. However, a large percentage of the *purchasers* tend to be a rather small nucleus which calls over and over. The indication here according to Hooper may be that the store is not widely known in the community or perhaps understood only as a high-priced purveyor of esoteric equipment for which many outdoorspeople have little use.

Advertising and promotion have been seen as at least a partial solution to the second problem

TABLE 1
Percent of Income from Product
Category

Tents	4.7
Sleeping bags	10.9
Boats	4.2
Boots	18.2
Packs	8.7
Cross-country equipment	8.2
Clothing	29.0
Miscellaneous	16.1
	100.0

noted above, but Hooper notes his frustration with advertising and its effectiveness. "We've had months when we spent $1,000 on advertising with no results and months when we've spent nothing and done very well." Expenditures have varied considerably from month to month, but approximately $14,000 was spent last year. The tendency has been to remain very flexible, taking advantage of whatever special opportunities seemed to present themselves, with special attention to anything that offered coverage in the university community. Examples of special advertising projects include ads on desk blotters distributed free to all dormitory students, similar ads on plastic phone directory covers circulated to the same audience, small space (approximately 3 by 4 inches) in basketball programs, sponsorship of couples in an annual university dance marathon to raise charity money, and quarter-page ads in a special issue of the campus paper sent to new students at the university before they arrive on campus. These activities were supplemented by irregular insertions of one of a series of standing ads (usually manufacturers' mattes) in the student paper, *The Daily*, or the *Madison Advertiser*.

Hooper feels that advertising is probably not being employed as effectively as it could be:

The problem is, we just don't have anyone on the staff with the time or the interest to help out in this area. We had a local agency for a while but they didn't understand our products and charged us too much for what little work they did. We ended up rewriting all their copy. Maybe the answer is finding a consultant.

We are now ready to launch marketing efforts to market beyond those young, active, outdoor-oriented types. We feel that it's time to extend our efforts to the greater Madison, Wisconsin, market area.

Hooper feels the most immediate questions for an advertising consultant are:

1. What should our advertising objectives be for the next campaign year?
2. How much money should we invest in advertising?
3. What creative strategy would be appropriate for our target markets?
4. How do we develop a media plan for our store?
5. How should we measure the effectiveness of our advertising efforts?

ENDNOTE

1. Harvey Manning, "Where Did All These Damn Hikers Come From?" *Backpacker-10*, 3, No 5 (Summer, 1975), 36.

QUESTION FOR DISCUSSION

1. Although Huck Hooper has a number of questions for an advertising consultant, it would seem that the first question—"What should our advertising objectives be for the next campaign year?"—is the most important. What recommendations would you make to Wilderness Supply?

SOUTH EL PASO COMMUNITY MENTAL HEALTH CENTER (B)

South El Paso Community Mental Health Center is a not-for-profit community service organization whose purpose is to provide a comprehensive program to deal with the mental, emotional, and behavioral problems of residents living in the south area of El Paso. The center offers professional help to individuals, families, community agencies, and other professionals through its inpatient and outpatient, emergency, partial hospitalization, consultation, and education services. Its annual budget is $2.1 million, which is funded in part by the National Institute of Mental Health, the Texas State Department of Behavioral Health Services, contracts with other agencies, and some fee for service (the fee being based on ability to pay). Over 80 percent of the patients are treated free of charge.

Although originating as a cooperative effort between Elizabeth Varney Child Center and St. John's Hospital, South El Paso Community Mental Health Center negotiated to become a free agent as of July 1, 1974. It is decentralized with the following services presently being provided: three outpatient clinics, crisis clinic, day treatment, outreach, children preventive services, and El Paso County Hospital inpatient unit. There are about 80 staff members consisting largely of psychiatrists, psychologists, psychiatric social workers, community mental health workers, occupational therapists, and secretarial and administrative support.

This case was prepared by Charles H. Patti. The original South El Paso Community Mental Health Center case was prepared by Professors Dorothy M. Hai, St. John's University, and Charles H. Patti, and appeared in *Advertising Management: Cases & Concepts,* by Charles H. Patti and John H. Murphy, Grid Publishing, Inc., 1978.

MENTAL HEALTH PATIENTS

The South El Paso Community Mental Health Center has a large responsibility to provide mental health services[1] to the working and dependent poor. Because it is an agency receiving substantial portions of its funding from the federal government with the purpose of serving an area marked by poverty and low-income families, it is obliged to direct a substantial portion of its effort toward the mental health needs of a population of which only 18 percent can pay even a portion of their mental health services costs.

CHARACTERISTICS OF POPULATION RECEIVING SERVICES

The South El Paso cachement area (population 202,486 in 1980) is located in the southeastern part of the city and includes an old central business district, a skid row, a state hospital, a concentration of inexpensive motels, trailer parks, and extensive black and Mexican-American neighborhoods. Age and ethnic characteristics are as shown below:

Total population of the area	202,486	(100%)
Over 18 years	103,268	(51%)
Under 18 years	99,218	(49%)
Ethnic distribution		
Negro	34,625	(17%)
Mexican-American	56,696	(28%)
Caucasian	105,090	(52%)
Other	6,075	(3%)
	202,486	(100%)

Last year the South El Paso Community Mental Health Center served 3,719 adult clients.

EXHIBIT 1
South El Paso Community Mental Health Center
Caseload

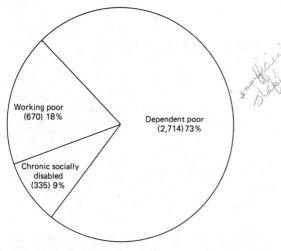

About 670 of these clients (the 18 percent who pay part of their fees) are classified as working poor. The remaining nonchronic patients are dependent poor. The entire case load of the mental health center is broken down in Exhibit 1.

The mental health needs of the 670 working poor clients differ from those of other clients. These needs relate to problems of marriage, child rearing, and personal development within the framework of the larger community. The working poor clients are not alienated; in fact, they strive to get ahead. In contrast with so many of the poor, they have energy and hope.

Dr. Richard Edelman, executive director of the center, has stated:

The problems confronting the working poor are particularly amenable to treatment by the programs of a community mental health center. We at the South El Paso Community Mental Health Center feel the need to enlarge our services to this class of residents in the area. The fruits of this work will appear not only in the lives of our clients, but also in improved social environments thoughout the South El Paso community.

COMMUNICATION AND CHALLENGES

Prevention of psychological and emotional problems has been a goal that many mental health professionals have lauded. However, the problem persists of providing enough personnel to reach all of the individuals in a community with problems or a high potential for developing problems. One alternative is to use the media to influence the perceptions and attitudes of the sizable audience that they reach, thus greatly facilitating the improvement of the mental health of a community.

In Louisville, Kentucky, the regional mental health and mental retardation agency responded to this challenge. It was one of the first agencies to try to create community awareness toward ways that individuals assess and deal with their own problems of living. Mass media were innovatively used in presenting over twenty mental health messages though 30- and 60-second television and radio public service announcements, newspaper ads, and billboard and buscard announcements. Since there were few, if any, precedents for this type of outreach, it was considered important to attempt a systematic evaluation of the effectiveness of the project.

The project—*Alternatives*—was carried out by the River Region Mental Health–Mental Retardation Board over a 60-week period. The purposes of *Alternatives* were twofold: (1) to encourage the audience to evaluate and handle their own problems (primary prevention), and (2) to increase awareness of sources of help in the community by displaying a 24-hour Crisis and Information Center telephone number with each public service announcement (secondary prevention). Each *Alternatives* public service announcement also contained the phrase "Helping You Build a Life You Can Live With."[2]

The idea of self-help and partial diagnosis (in the case of determining whether professional medical treatment is required) is not particularly new. There have been, over the past few years, calls for a more educated, more responsible public in terms of health care.

Extensive research on self-care has been conducted at the University of Nottingham in England, and in the United States there is also growing concern for the proper utilization of health care.

A few years ago the South El Paso Community Mental Health Center decided to work toward the goals of better utilization of mental health services and it developed several communications objectives. To increase the effectiveness of its services it wanted to:

Create awareness of the center's existence and what services it provided.[3]

Build recognition for the center and increase credibility among leaders in other agencies.[4]

Enhance the image of the center to get more community funding.

Promote the concept of mental health versus mental illness (to assist people to function within their own environment and to provide complete services—in/outpatient care, consulting, in-service training versus hospitals).

In building awareness, the center had used television, Spanish radio and newspapers, public affairs television with people discussing the center and its services, and television talk shows in both Spanish and English.

In addition to the mass media, the South El Paso Mental Health Center also used a number of other communications tools to build credibility, enhance its image, and spread information about its services. For example, it produced bilingual brochures to describe the uniqueness of the concept of community mental health and the specific services offered by the center. Community workshops and audiovisual presentations were organized to educate the community and to increase the skills of mental health professionals and the public.

In assessing the success of its communications efforts, Executive Director of the South El Paso Mental Health Center, Dr. Richard Edelman, commented.

While we have some evidence that our attempts to increase credibility and public awareness have been successful, we are not completely satisfied. First of all, we tend to measure success by increases in patient load or the number of complimentary comments we receive from patients, other agencies, and state and local officials. We are not certain that this is an accurate measurement of success.

Secondly, we rely on publicity or free advertising and this has proven to be somewhat slow and not conducive to pinpoint timing. Actually, the media—particularly local television stations—have been very cooperative in helping us explain our programs. However, we now have reached the point where we have much to say to very specific groups of people. Furthermore, we would like to have closer control over the release of our messages.

In recognition of the increasing importance of communicating with various publics, the South El Paso Mental Health Center hired Karen Scates as Director of Communications. After several discussions with Dr. Edelman, Karen concluded that the center should launch an advertising program to augment the public relations programs. Karen argued that to accomplish the center's stated communications goals required control of both the content and timing of messages. She felt the use of certain radio stations, neighborhood newspapers, and outdoor advertisements would help the South El Paso Mental Health Center accomplish its communications objectives faster and more effectively than current procedures.

Dr. Edelman's reaction to Karen's proposal was mixed. He was very anxious to accomplish the center's communications objectives, but he questioned the wisdom of allocating public funds for an advertising campaign. He knew that public health organizations had limited experience with the use of advertising to communicate with the public and, because of the expenditure involved, he anticipated questions from directors of the center.

Although the center's directors did raise a number of questions about the proposed communications program, Dr. Edelman and Karen Scates were able to convince the board that the program was vital at this particular time and that the success of other, similar programs throughout the country should be taken as an encouraging sign of the potential success of their proposal.

As Karen selected an advertising agency to develop the campaign for the center, she insisted that a precampaign survey be taken among the relevant target audiences so that effects of the campaign could be more realistically assessed. Selected data from this survey are presented in Exhibit 2.

EXHIBIT 2
Precampaign Survey Results

1. Name five state agencies that provide public services in your area.[a]

Services Mentioned	Percent of Respondents
Unemployment office	72
Corrections department	68
Recreation center	62
Drug rehabilitation center	43
Adoption/child care center	37
Disease control center	27
Mental health clinic	14

2. Perceived importance of public concerns.[a]

Public Concern	Percent of Respondents Indicating "Very Important"
"Having jobs for everyone"	82
"Providing more police protection"	73
"Providing a recreation center for teenagers"	70
"Increasing drug control activities"	65
"Improving child care facilities"	47
"Providing a recreation center for adults"	38
"Increasing efforts toward venereal disease control"	29
"Improving community mental health"	17

3. Which of the following services do you believe are provided by the South El Paso Community Mental Health Center? Please check all that you believe are currently provided.[b]

Service	Provided	Not Provided	Don't Know
Inpatient care	92%	8%	0%
Consultation to individuals	72	18	10

Emergency care	61	20	19
Family counseling	53	9	38
Education services	33	17	50
Job retraining[c]	22	33	45
Outpatient care	21	29	50
Drug rehabilitation[c]	19	31	50
Partial hospitalization	17	58	25
Outreach programs	17	46	37
Child preventive services	10	35	55

4. Please evaluate how well you believe the following services are provided by the South El Paso Community Mental Health Center.[b]

Service	Mean Response[d]
Consultation to individuals	5.9
Inpatient care	5.6
Family counseling	4.7
Education services	4.6
Emergency care	4.3
Outpatient care	4.3
Outreach programs	3.7
Partial hospitalization	3.6
Child preventive services	3.1
Job retraining[c]	2.6
Drug rehabilitation[c]	2.4

5. Please rank order the following services in terms of your feelings about funding support—that is, which of the following do you think is most important to fund first, second, third, etc.[b]

Service	Rank
Corrections department	1
Unemployment service	2
Drug rehabilitation	3
Child care facilities	4
Disease control centers	5
Mental health facilities	6
Recreation facilities	7

[a]The responses to these two questions were generated from personal interviews with 350 adults living in the South El Paso Community Mental Health Center's cachement area.
[b]The responses to these three questions were generated from a survey of 300 public officials and key individuals in state agencies. Response rate was 74 percent.
[c]This service is not actually supplied by the South El Paso Community Mental Health Center.
[d]Responses were on a seven-point scale with 7 as the preferred response.

On the basis of the information obtained in the survey, the agency created a multimedia campaign that included radio, television, outdoor, and newspapers. In addition to the mass media, the agency also prepared a series of direct-mail pieces that were sent to public officials and key individuals in other state agencies. Essentially, the campaign focused on the positive aspects of mental health and the copy and layouts illustrated people enjoying life on the job, with family, and in a variety of other social situations. As the campaign was about to be launched, Karen and the agency were quite convinced the campaign was well conceived and they were very optimistic about its effects on the target markets.

CURRENT DEVELOPMENTS

Two effectiveness measurements were taken during the center's advertising campaign. First, after six months of advertising (and approximately 50 percent of the budget expended), Karen commissioned a study to determine the effects of the campaign. She was anxious to determine if the campaign was working and if there were aspects of the campaign that the agency could improve during the balance of the campaign period. Highlights of this survey are presented in Exhibit 3.

Finally, Karen had a third study done after the campaign had run another six months. This was the final measurement of the effects of the campaign and Karen knew it would clearly have to demonstrate success or the board would not approve funds for another campaign. Results of the third survey are shown in Exhibit 4.

As Karen examined the data in Exhibits 2, 3, and 4, she was beginning to prepare her presentation to the board.

ENDNOTES

1. Health is defined by the World Health Organization as "a state of complete physical, mental, and social well-being and not merely the absence of disease or infirmity." Definitions of mental health include (a) a positive orientation toward life, and (b) being able to deal with everyday problems. However, there is a wide range of human behavior that is considered "normal."
2. This discussion was based on Martin Sundel, Betsy Crane, B.J. Morrison, and Charles F. Shavie, "The Alternatives Project: A Mass Media Approach to Community Mental Health and Preventive Education" (presented at the Annual Meeting of the National Council of Community Mental Health Centers, Washington, D.C., 1975).
3. It had been common practice to measure awareness levels by patient load and the number of referrals from other agencies.
4. One of the specific problems the center faced was to increase conviction that it actually *did* perform the various services it offered in its literature.

QUESTIONS FOR DISCUSSION

1. On the basis of the results of the precampaign survey, create advertising objectives for South El Paso Community Mental Health Center.
2. Do the results of the first effectiveness measure (taken six months after the advertising campaign had been launched) indicate success?
3. What should advertising's role be in helping accomplish the Center's communications objectives?

EXHIBIT 3
Survey Results After Six Months of Advertising

1. Name five state agencies that provide public services in your area.[a]

Services mentioned	Percent of Respondents
Unemployment office	71
Corrections department	70
Recreation center	64
Drug rehabilitation center	41
Adoption/child care center	35
Mental health clinic	21
Disease control center	20

2. Perceived importance of public concerns.[a]

Public Concern	Percent of Respondents Indicating "Very Important"
"Having jobs for everyone"	85
"Providing more police protection"	75
"Providing a recreation center for teenagers"	74
"Improving child care facilities"	53
"Increasing drug control activities"	50
"Providing a recreation center for adults"	30
"Improving community mental health"	25
"Increasing efforts toward venereal disease control"	18

3. Which of the following services do you believe are provided by the South El Paso Community Mental Health Center? Please check all that you believe are currently provided.[b]

Service	Provided	Not Provided	Don't Know
Inpatient care	95%	4%	1%
Consultation to individuals	80	12	8
Emergency care	64	21	15
Family counseling	61	4	35
Outpatient care	41	19	40
Education services	33	19	48
Outreach programs	32	40	28
Job retraining[c]	23	37	40
partial hospitalization	21	57	22
Drug rehabilitation[c]	18	37	45
Child preventive services	12	39	49

4. Please evaluate how well you believe the following services are provided by the South El Paso Community Mental Health Center.[b]

Service	Mean Response[d]
Inpatient care	5.8
Consultation to individuals	5.7
Family counseling	5.0
Outpatient care	4.7
Education services	4.5
Emergency care	4.4
Outreach programs	3.5
Partial hospitalization	3.5
Child preventive services	3.3
Job retraining[c]	2.9
Drug rehabilitation[c]	2.0

5. Please rank order the following services in terms of your feelings about funding support—that is, which of the following do you think is most important to fund first, second, third, etc.[b]

Service	Rank
Unemployment service	1
Corrections department	2
Drug rehabilitation	3
Disease control centers	4
Child care facilities	5
Mental health facilities	6
Recreation facilities	7

[a]The responses to these two questions were generated from personal interviews with 350 adults living in the South El Paso Community Mental Health Center's cachement area.
[b]The responses to these three questions were generated from a survey of 300 public officials and key individuals in state agencies. Response rate was 72 percent.
[c]This service is not actually supplied by the South El Paso Community Mental Health Center.
[d]Responses were on a seven-point scale with 7 as the preferred response.

EXHIBIT 4
Survey Results After One Year of Advertising

1. Name five state agencies that provide public services in your area.[a]

Services Mentioned	Percent of Respondents
Unemployment office	74
Recreation center	70
Corrections department	60
Drug rehabilitation center	35
Mental health clinic	31
Adoption/child care center	30
Disease control center	22

2. Perceived importance of public concerns.[a]

Public Concern	Percent of Respondents Indicating "Very Important"
"Having jobs for everyone"	87
"Providing a recreation center for teenagers"	76
"Providing more police protection"	68
"Increasing drug control activities"	58
"Improving child care facilities"	51
"Providing a recreation center for adults"	34
"Improving community mental health"	32
"Increasing efforts toward venereal disease control"	21

3. Which of the following services do you believe are provided by the South El Paso Community Mental Health Center? Please check all that you believe are currently provided.[b]

Service	Provided	Not Provided	Don't Know
Inpatient care	96%	2%	2%
Consultation to individuals	88	10	2
Family counseling	72	4	24
Emergency care	72	17	11
Outpatient care	45	15	40
Outreach programs	37	38	25
Education services	31	20	49
Partial hospitalization	23	55	22
Job retraining[c]	20	40	40
Drug rehabilitation[c]	20	40	40
Child preventive services	19	30	51

4. Please evaluate how well you believe the following services are provided by the South El Paso Community Mental Health Center.[b]

Service	Mean Response[d]
Inpatient care	5.9
Consultation to individuals	5.9
Family counseling	5.2
Outpatient care	5.1
Education services	4.9
Emergency care	4.7
Outreach programs	4.0
Partial hospitalization	3.8
Child preventive services	3.7
Job retraining[c]	2.5
Drug rehabilitation[c]	2.4

5. Please rank order the following services in terms of your feelings about funding support—that is, which of the following do you think is most important to fund first, second, third, etc.[b]

Service	Rank
Corrections department	1
Unemployment service	2
Drug rehabilitation	3
Child care facilities	4
Mental health facilities	5
Disease control centers	6
Recreation facilities	7

[a]The responses to these two questions were generated from personal interviews with 350 adults living in the South El Paso Community Mental Health Center's cachement area.
[b]The responses to these three questions were generated from a survey of 300 public officials and key individuals in state agencies. Response rate was 77 percent.
[c]This service is not actually supplied by the South El Paso Community Mental Health Center.
[d]Responses were on a(seven-point scale with 7 as the preferred response.

Lamar Savings was founded in Austin, Texas in 1960. The institution has grown steadily since its establishment and operated a central downtown office and a number of suburban branches located throughout the Austin area.

Five major savings and loan associations compete for the Austin market, along with a large number of smaller savings and loan associations. Besides Lamar, the four other major savings and loan associations are: First Federal Savings, University Savings, Franklin Savings, and First Texas Savings. Lamar ranked fourth in terms of total deposits behind University, First Federal, and First Texas. Local savers can also choose to open their savings account in one of sixteen major commercial banks and twenty credit unions, all located in the market. To grow and maintain a prominent position in such a competitive market, Lamar Savings has had to devote a great deal of thought and effort to developing its promotional programs.

PAST PROMOTIONAL STRATEGY

Lamar Savings Association has been committed to an objective of increasing its market share and deposits steadily during the past five years. In order to continually expand its market share and deposits, Lamar invested approximately $160,000 in media advertising last year and $145,000 during the preceding year.

Lamar's basic media budget was broken down roughly as follows during the past two years:

60% television

20% radio

This case was prepared by John H. Murphy. The original Lamar Savings Association case was prepared by John H. Murphy and appeared in *Advertising Management: Cases and Concepts,* by Charles H. Patti and John H. Murphy, Grid Publishing, Inc., 1978.

10% newspaper

10% regional magazines

In addition, outdoor advertising had been used to supplement these basic media expenditures on a seasonal basis.

In buying television time, Lamar purchased both 30- and 60-second spots on Austin's three major commercial stations (KTBC, KTVV, and KVUE). Lamar ran a fairly consistent schedule of 30-second radio spots on four major stations (KLBJ, KNOW, KVET, and KASE). A number of newspaper ads of varying sizes were run in the *American Statesman,* Austin's major daily. Magazine advertising was placed in local editions of *Newsweek, U.S. News and World Report, Time,* and *Sports Illustrated.* These magazine ads were all one full page and in full color.

Lamar also utilized a number of specialty advertising items during past years. These items included matchbooks, life savers, buttons ("Think Happy with Lamar Savings"), balloons, pens, and suckers. The firm also sent out "Welcome to Austin" letters to new residents.

A central theme of Lamar's promotional program was portrayed by its logo and the motto "Lamar—your family financial center" (see Exhibit 1). Emphasis was given to the idea of using Lamar Savings to provide all the family's financial needs. Along with this central theme, several other appeals were used in Lamar's advertising program during the past two years. These were: (1) "Be Better Off Next Year Than You Are Now," accompanied by promotional gifts emphasizing the "happy" idea coupled with financial betterment; this theme was deemphasized when economic conditions declined; (2) the theme of "financial security," used as a basic selling proposition for the depressed economy situation; (3) Lamar's growth and its strong

EXHIBIT 1
Lamar Savings Logo

financial situation, made known by publicizing of its total dividends payments.

A NEW AD AGENCY EMPHASIZES RESEARCH

Lamar Savings had recently moved the responsibility for creating and placing its advertising to a local Austin ad agency. The agency that was selected, Bonner McLane Advertising, had an excellent reputation built around its ability to develop successful campaigns for its diverse clients. In securing the Lamar account, McLane Advertising had emphasized the need to base any advertising/promotional decisions in the highly competitve Austin market on a solid foundation of marketing research.

Initially the new agency developed ads that differed only slightly from past efforts believed by Lamar to have been effective. Exhibit 2 presents an example of one of these newspaper ads.

McLane Advertising planned to delay any significant change in Lamar Savings advertising until after a thorough marketing research study could be conducted. A local marketing research firm, Metropolitan Research Services (MRS), was employed to develop a research study which could serve as the basis for making strategic decisions on all aspects of Lamar Savings' advertising/promotional efforts during the upcoming fiscal year.

EXHIBIT 2
Lamar Savings Newspaper Advertisement

After several planning sessions involving the three parties, a methodology was developed for collecting the desired information. During a two-week period MRS conducted 301 personal interviews with Austin residents to gather what was believed to be the necessary information for developing Lamar's future advertising strategy.

TABLE 1
Saver Profile

Question	Response	Percent
More than one account?	Yes	55
	No	45
Among those with more than one account, with which type of institution largest amount saved?	Bank	27
	S&L	37
	Credit union	36
Who selected specific institution(s) where save?	Husband	48
	Wife	19
	Both	29
	Other	4
Ownership of bank credit cards?	Don't have	45
	Visa	12
	Master Card	20
	Both Visa & MC	22
	Other	1
Automobile or mortgage loan	Auto loan only	15
	Mortgage loan only	38
	Both	19
	Neither	28
Excluding interbranch changes, now save anywhere did not a year ago?	Yes	14
	No	86
Among those with more than one account, the average number of accounts at financial institutions?	Banks	1.50
	Savings & Loans	1.87
	Credit unions	1.45
Among those with only one savings account, where?	Banks	40
	Savings & Loans	31
	Credit unions	29
Frequency with which savers make deposits and withdrawals?	Once a week or more	12
	2 to 3 times a month	13
	Once a month	43
	Less than once a month	32

SAVINGS PREFERENCES STUDY

MRS collected the desired information using a questionnaire survey approach. After pretesting the research instrument, data were collected through personal interviews. A random sample of households was drawn from within the primary trading areas located in close proximity to the branch locations of Lamar Savings. Thus, the sample was not necessarily representative of the total Austin market. The subjects (male or female household heads) were asked to respond to a questionnaire administered by trained interviewers at the respondent's home. To qualify for an interview, the household had to presently have a savings account.

Data were gathered in five major areas of interest. First quantitative and qualitative information about savers was obtained—for example, the number and types of savings accounts held by the subject, the frequency of usage of accounts, and so on.

Second, respondents' reactions to a series of attributes that were considered to be important when making the choice of a savings institution were obtained. Third, data related to the respondents' perceived image of each of the five major Austin area savings and loan associations were collected. (Each respondent profiled Lamar and one of the other four major saving and loan associations, which was identified through a random process.)

Fourth, data were collected on respondents' top-of-the-mind awareness of savings institutions, and also the level of recall and association of selected financial institutions' symbols and slogans.

Finally, demographic information about the respondents was collected. These data included the education, age, income, employment status, and profession of the head of the household, as well as other descriptive data on respondents.

A system of verification of all data collected was employed. The verification procedure consisted of the following: (1) A random sample was selected of approximately 15 percent of the completed questionnaires. The subjects selected for verification received a telephone call thanking them for their cooperation and inquiring as to the performance of the interviewer. If any irregularities were found in the interviewing procedure, all of the questionnaires of the interviewer were verified. If appropriate, the interviewer's work would be eliminated from the sample. (2) All questionnaires were checked for completeness and logical relationships by both a verifier and a coder prior to key punching. (3) After the data were punched onto computer cards, the entire deck was cleaned.

After the information obtained from the respondents was transferred to computer cards, the data were computer analyzed. Frequency distributions and cross-tabulations were used to verify the importance of some variables, as well as the cross-classifications of subjects according to specific characteristics.

Mean values of the attitudinal variables that were used by respondents to describe their

TABLE 2
Financial Institutions Used by Savers

	Among All Savers ($n=301$) (percent)	Among S&L Savers ($n=156$) (percent)
Savings & Loan Associations		
None	55	—
University Savings	13	30
First Federal Savings	9	19
Franklin Savings	5	11
Lamar Savings	16	36
First Texas Savings	10	23
All other S&Ls	6	14
Commercial banks		
Have an account	46	31
Do not have an account	54	69
Credit unions		
Have an account	47	48
Do not have an account	53	52

TABLE 3
Determinant Attributes in the Selection of a Savings
Institution

Attributes	Mean[a]
Security	1.78
High interest rates paid	1.83
Friendly, personal service	2.03
A convenient location	2.07
Reputation of the institution	2.09
Credit reference	2.19
Interest rate compounded daily	2.26
Cash personal checks and pay checks	2.42
Single monthly statement of all accounts with institution	2.44
Ease of acquiring loan	2.46
Checking account available	2.46
Hours open	2.58
Free parking	2.92
Travelers' check service	3.03
Drive-in window	3.06
Free save-by-mail	3.17
Trust services	3.23
Credit card available	3.46
Safety deposit boxes	3.53
Recommended by a friend	3.77
24-hour automated services	3.81
Night depository	3.85

[a]Respondents evaluated each attribute on the following scale: 1 = Extremely important, 2 = Very important, 3 = Important, 4 = Slightly important, and 5 = Not important at all.

image of savings and loan associations were subjected to an analysis of variance. A factor analysis was conducted on the variables which were used to determine the important factors in the choice of a savings institution. Chi square analyses were employed to compare the distribution of savers on the demographic variables.

One of the objectives of the research was to obtain a balanced number of responses from both the male and the female heads of the households in the sample. In order to achieve this purpose, the interviewers were instructed to try to conduct an interview with the male head of the household. If the male household head was not avail-

able, the female head was interviewed. The final sample was distributed as follows:

45% respondents, male

55% respondents, female

Tables 1 to 8 present some of the major findings of the investigation conducted for Lamar Savings by MRS.

FUTURE DIRECTIONS FOR LAMAR'S ADVERTISING

After the study results were presented to McLane Advertising, the agency's task was to develop a total advertising program for Lamar for the coming fiscal year (July 1 to June 30). In developing this program the agency hoped to

TABLE 4
Factor Loading of Determinant Attributes in the
Selection of a Savings Institution

Factor #1—Financial services	
Checking account available	.73
Cash personal and payroll checks	.69
Credit reference	.69
Credit card available	.67
Single monthly statement of all accounts	.61
Ease of acquiring loans	.59
Drive-in windows	.56
Factor #2—Stability and interest	
High interest rates paid on savings	.73
Security	.70
Interest compounded daily on savings	.64
Reputation of the institution	.54
Factor #3—Convenience	
Free parking	.73
Hours open	.73
Convenient location	.70
Factor #4—After-hours convenience	
Free save-by-mail	.76
Night depository	.56
24-hour automated services	.52

Note: Attributes with a loading of less than .5 omitted.

TABLE 5

Savers' Images of Savings and Loans (Mean Values)

	Lamar Savings ($n=253$)	University Savings ($n=56$)	First Federal Savings ($n=68$)	Franklin Savings ($n=51$)	First Texas Savings ($n=45$)
Easy/hard to get loan	2.7	2.7	2.7	2.5	2.6
Family/business oriented	2.7	2.7	2.8	2.5	2.7
Low/high interest on loans	3.0	2.9	3.0	2.9	3.0
Low/high interest on savings	3.2	3.1	3.1	3.3	3.2
Much/little advertising	2.5	2.6	2.5	2.3	3.0[a]
Personal/impersonal	2.6	2.4	2.6	2.4	2.8
Cooperative/uncooperative	2.4	2.5	2.4	2.4	2.4
Progressive/backward	2.4	2.4	2.4	2.4	2.4
Reputable/disreputable	1.9	1.9	1.9	2.1	2.0
Women-oriented/not women-oriented	2.9	2.9	3.0	2.8	3.1[a]
Friendly/unfriendly personal	2.3	2.4	2.4	2.3	2.4
Well known/unknown	1.9	1.9	1.8	1.9	2.3[a]
Convenient/inconvenient hours	2.4	2.5	2.6	2.4	2.8[a]
Many/few services	2.5	2.4	2.5	2.5	2.5
Convenient/inconvenient locations	2.1	2.4	2.3	2.0	2.4[a]
Professional/non-professional	2.3	2.3	2.2	2.4	2.3
Convenient/inconvenient parking	2.3	2.5	2.3	2.4	2.5
Concerned/not concerned with local community	2.5	2.5	2.6	2.2[a]	2.6

Note: Respondents reacted to each variable by marking one of five scale positions separating the bipolar phrases.

[a] A comparison of respondents' perception of Lamar Savings against respondents' perception of each of the other four S&Ls individually on each of the 18 variables revealed six significant differences (these are indicated by an [a]).

TABLE 6
Top-of-Mind Awareness of Savings & Loans

	First Mention (percent)	Second Mention (percent)	Third Mention (percent)	Any Mention (percent)
Lamar Savings	23	21	17	47
University Savings	22	20	13	43
First Federal Savings	18	22	15	42
Franklin Savings	14	17	23	40
First Texas Savings	13	12	14	29
All Other S&Ls	10	8	18	26
	100	100	100	[a]

Note: Respondent was asked "When you think of savings and loan associations, what are the first three that come to mind?"
[a]Percentages add to more than 100% because of multiple responses.

TABLE 7
Identification of Slogans and Symbols of Financial Institutions

	Identifying with Correct Institution (percent)	Identifying with Wrong Institution (percent)	Don't Know (percent)
An S&L ad theme	1	4	95
A bank slogan	39	13	48
"Your family financial center" (Lamar slogan)	2	7	91
A bank ad theme	30	11	59
Franklin logo	78	3	19
University Saving logo	22	16	62
First Federal logo	16	8	76
Lamar logo	3	5	92
First Texas logo	7	8	85

TABLE 8
Demographic Profile of Savers

	All Savers (n = 301) (percent)	Lamar Savers (n = 48) (percent)	All Other S&Ls Combined (n = 103) (percent)	Bank Savers (n = 142) (percent)	Credit Union Savers (n = 137) (percent)
Total	100	16	34	47	46
Savings account at					
Bank	47	45	35	100	43
Credit union	46	45	43	32	100
S&L	45	100	100	31	48
Education[a]					
Graduate study	29	41	26	31	30
College grad	25	25	22	27	23
Part college	25	17	27	22	29
H.S. grad or less	21	17	25	20	18
Age (chief wage earner)[b]					
Under 25	8	2	7	8	6
25–29	21	10	16	23	20
30–34	15	15	13	17	15
35–39	14	14	13	14	14
40–44	10	16	8	9	13
45–54	17	27	19	14	16
55 and over	15	16	24	15	16
Income[c]					
Less than $10,000	14	6	13	14	10
$10–14,999	19	15	12	18	21
$15–24,999	32	42	35	25	36
$25,000 or more	27	33	32	35	26
Refused, don't know	8	4	8	8	7
Value of savings account[d]					
Less than $500	21	15	12	24	16
$500–1,999	19	10	17	18	22
$2–4,999	16	15	16	14	19
$5–9,999	12	19	10	13	11
$10–14,999	6	8	4	7	6
$15,000 or more	12	23	23	13	15
Refused, don't know	14	10	17	11	11
Tenure[e]					
Own	73	83	85	72	76
Rent	27	17	15	28	24

Time at present address[f]					
Less than 1 year	23	10	17	20	20
1–2 years	27	21	22	34	26
3–6 years	26	23	27	23	28
7 or more years	24	46	34	23	26
Marital status					
Married	87	90	90	84	91
Single	7	4	5	6	6
Divorced, widowed	6	6	5	10	3
Chief wage earner					
Male hh head	82	86	88	80	82
Female hh head	13	10	8	14	12
Other	5	4	4	6	6
Chief wage earner employed in downtown Austin					
Yes	31	33	33	30	33
No	69	67	67	70	67
Household size					
1–2	35	28	36	36	31
3	21	23	21	23	18
4	25	30	29	20	27
5 or more	19	19	14	21	24
Type dwelling					
Single unit	77	78	83	79	80
Apartment	19	20	15	18	15
Other	4	2	2	3	5

[a]Chi square comparison of "All Savers" and "Lamar Savers" significant at the $p = .12$ level.
[b]Chi square comparison of "All Savers" and "Lamar Savers" significant at the $p = .06$ level.
[c]Chi square comparison of "All Savers" and "Lamar Savers" significant at the $p = .14$ level.
[d]Chi square comparison of "All Savers" and "Lamar Savers" significant at the $p = .05$ level.
[e]Chi square comparison of "All Savers" and "Lamar Savers" significant at the $p = .13$ level.
[f]Chi square comparison of "All Savers" and "Lamar Savers" significant at the $p = .001$ level.

draw heavily on the MRS research findings. However, before an advertising program could be developed, the agency first had to interpret the results of the study.

In addition to providing data useful in planning Lamar's advertising/promotional strategy, the Savings Preferences Study would also serve as a bench mark against which the results of the new campaign would be evaluated. That is, at the end of the one-year campaign another study following the same methodology would be conducted. Many of the same questions would be asked, and changes or shifts in respondents' level of awareness, attitudes, preferences, and so forth would be used to evaluate the success of the campaign against previously established objectives.

QUESTIONS FOR DISCUSSION

1. Are the procedures followed in conducting the study sound from a methodology standpoint? What changes in the study's design would strengthen it?

2. What are some of the major conclusions that can be drawn from the data presented? Which of these conclusions are most important and useful in planning Lamar's advertising program for the coming fiscal year?
3. How can the data presented be used in establishing advertising objectives for the coming campaign period?

4. What are some realistic advertising objectives for Lamar to consider for use in guiding their advertising efforts and for use at the end of the campaign to evaluate the campaign's effectiveness? What are the strengths and weaknesses of alternative statements of advertising objectives?

SECTION 4
BUDGETING FOR ADVERTISING

There is probably no other budget in an organization that is subjected to as much guesswork as the advertising budget. Most departments within an organization can predict quite accurately the profitability of expenditures because the relationship between the expenditure and its output usually can be measured directly (production rates of machinery, for example). Unfortunately, such reliable predictions are rarely possible with advertising. Yet ultimately the objectives of the advertising expenditure are the same as they are for all other operating budgets—to contribute to the profits of the firm.

The difficulty in determining the advertising budget lies in the complexity of evaluating the effectiveness of advertising. In the absence of precise data on the relationship between advertising and sales or profits, Advertising Managers approach decisions regarding the size of the advertising investment with considerable doubt and hesitation.

Although the Advertising Manager is frequently responsible for recommending the size of the advertising expenditure, all levels of top management are concerned about this decision because of the potential impact advertising can have on the firm and because of the large investment it often represents.

Organizations invest money in advertising because they believe communicating with customers and prospects will help accomplish marketing objectives. Logically, then, the size of the budget should be directly related to the scope of the job to be done. One of the advantages of evaluating the advertising opportunity is that advertising objectives are determined out of an assessment of the environments that have the greatest impact on the firm's success. If the size of the advertising expenditure is tied more directly to advertising objectives, the danger of over- or underspending for advertising is reduced.

In the past several years there has been an increasing effort on the part of advertisers, advertising agencies, and advertising researchers to explore more scientific approaches to the problems of determining the proper level of advertising spending.[1] Essentially, these approaches try to quantify the

For a discussion of advertisers' trends to use alternative advertising budgeting methods see "Budgeting Practices of Big Advertisers" by Charles H. Patti and Vincent J. Blasko, *Journal of Advertising Research*, December 1981, vol. 21, no. 6.

variables that influence sales and then construct a model to isolate the effects of various levels of advertising spending on sales. Although specific scientific advertising budgeting techniques have had only limited success in practice, the underlying philosophy of this approach to advertising budgeting holds promise.

There are several widely used approaches and methods of determining the advertising budget, but none is completely satisfactory. Each offers certain operational advantages, but at the same time their limitations have forced the Advertising Manager to examine more closely the specific factors that form the environment in which promotional tools function. Such factors as the physical attributes of the product or service, the frequency of purchase, the profit margin available, the size of the market, competitive activities, and top management's attitudes about advertising and its abilities to help stimulate demand all strongly influence the size of the advertising investment.

Although the Advertising Manager is usually asked to recommend a budget, sometimes the budget is determined by others in the organization. Even when the size of the advertising investment is determined by others, the Advertising Manager still participates in the decision of how to allocate the investment among the various advertising activities required to produce the campaign.

The following cases in this section of the book focus on the various advertising budget decisions facing the Advertising Manager. In some situations you will be required to recommend a specific dollar amount to be invested in advertising. In others you will be asked to evaluate budgets proposed by others or to allocate the advertising investment among budget categories.

16

BARBARA'S FLORIST

Barbara's Florist, owned and operated by Greg and Barbara Berry, is a full-service florist shop which had operated in Austin, Texas, for nearly twenty years. Barbara's primarily sold cut flowers, arrangements, and plants. The store offered home delivery and was a member of the FTD national network of florists.

Barbara's stressed its ability to handle large weddings, religious celebrations, and funerals. The store employed three designers of floral arrangements (including Barbara Berry) and all of the designers plus Greg Berry and a part-time cashier performed sales duties. All of the full-time employees had considerable expertise with respect to the plants they handled.

Currently, Barbara's imports most of its fresh-cut flowers and all of its roses from California, Florida, or outside the United States. Last year Barbara's instituted a unique pricing policy of undercutting other florists. In fact, almost two-thirds of Barbara's stock sold for less than a dollar per stem. Lower prices were believed to have increased the volume of sales and helped to differentiate Barbara's from other florists.

Despite lower prices, Barbara's marketed only high-quality floral items. Since consumers perceived a strong, direct correlation between the price of flowers and their quality, Barbara's management believed it equally as important to stress quality as well as price in promotional efforts.

FLORIST INDUSTRY TRENDS

The fact that nationally most florists were small businesses was not an indication that they were struggling financially. On the contrary, the

This case was prepared by Scott P. Bennett of Needham, Harper & Steers—Chicago; Michael L. Littman of Davis, Johnson, Mogul & Colombatto—Los Angeles; and John H. Murphy.

industry was in good health despite a reasonably prolonged period of tight money, inflation, and cost-consciousness by consumers.

As an industry florists had experienced steady growth over the past five years and sales were projected to increase in the neighborhood of 15 percent during the coming year. Florists had done particularly well in the growing market for fresh-cut roses and other flowers. Twenty percent of total industry sales were roses and the growth of this segment was expected to continue to be very strong.

However, a threat of some concern to the florist industry's growth was the entrance of supermarkets, nurseries, and discount stores into the fresh-cut flower market. These new entries had in the past concentrated their efforts in the green plants market and had met relatively little success because of the overall weakness of this market. However, many of these larger retailers had begun carrying fresh-cut flowers at lower prices than florists could match. Although at the present time approximately 88 percent of the purchasers of such flowers bought from a florist, the new entries into this market introduced some uncertainty with respect to the long-run structure of the fresh-cut flower market.

Historically, florists had higher sales in the months of April, May, and December (see Table 1). Further, roughly 80 percent of all purchases of floral items were for use as gifts and 20 percent were bought for personal use. Flowers and plants were generally considered a "safe" gift in that they were emotionally appealing and the vast majority of people appreciated receiving them.

National FTD data indicated that the times or reasons for flower purchases as gifts were as follows: get well, 15 percent; funeral, 14 percent; anniversary, 13 percent; Mother's Day, 11

TABLE 1
Percentage of Retail Sales by Month

	Jan.	Feb.	Mar.	April	May	June	July	Aug.	Sept.	Oct.	Nov.	Dec.
All retail stores	7.0	6.9	8.2	8.0	8.4	8.5	8.2	8.8	8.2	8.6	8.9	10.3
Florists	6.7	8.2	7.5	10.0	13.7	6.3	6.2	5.8	6.4	6.7	7.0	15.5

Sources: U.S. Department of Commerce and Florists' Transworld Delivery Association.

percent; surprise, 10 percent; birthday, 9 percent; holiday, 8 percent, and others, 20 percent. (Note that inclusion of non-FTD sales by local FTD members would change these estimates somewhat.) Further, most flower purchases were singular in nature. That is, they were bought on a cash-and-carry basis exclusive of other flower purchases. The most frequently purchased items were arrangements, which accounted for slightly less than 50 percent of all flower purchases nationwide from florists.

TARGET MARKETS

In organizing the firm's marketing efforts Barbara's management identified two distinct target markets. The firm's primary market consisted of students attending the University of Texas. The secondary market consisted of individuals who lived or worked in close geographic proximity (within one mile) to Barbara's location. This geographic market area included downtown Austin, student neighborhoods, and some very affluent residential areas west of downtown and the university.

The University of Texas student body was a transitory market which experienced considerable turnover each year. The enrollment figures for the most recent academic year were as follows: fall, 48,000; spring, 44,000; and summer, 20,000. These students were primarily aged 18 to 22, were 50 percent female, came from middle- and upper-middle-income families, and had considerable discretionary income.

The individuals in the secondary target were primarily up-scale adults who lived near Barbara's. Past experience indicated that these adults tended to be either young professionals age 25 to 35, evenly split between men and women, or older adults, age 50+, primarily females. These adult prospects were almost all up-scale demographically in terms of income, value of home, education, employment classification, and so on.

COMPETITION

Barbara's competed in a market that was highly fragmented, with no truly dominant florist competitor. Most of the 93 local firms listed in the Yellow Pages under "Florists—Retail" could be classified as reasonably small businesses grossing under $100,000 per year. Eighty-nine percent of Austin's florists had only one location. Freytag's had the most locations with five, and another larger florist—Connely-Hillen—had three locations. The bulk of the other multiple outlet florists had two locations.

In competing for the university market, five of Barbara's competitors appeared to cater to some extent to this market. Significantly, all five were located in close proximity to the university campus. Barbara's location, approximately a half mile from the campus, put the firm at a disadvantage. To help compensate for this disadvantage, Barbara's prices were set somewhat lower than these direct competitors. In addition, Barbara's had initiated a much larger advertising effort directed toward university students than any of the other florists.

TABLE 2
Barbara's Projected Sales and Advertising
Expenditures by Month for the Present Year

	Sales	Ad Expenditures
January	$10,000	$220
February	16,000	360
March	10,000	220
April	16,000	220
May	17,000	420
June	0	0
July	11,000	700
August	11,000	800
September	8,000	850
October	14,000[a]	1,050[a]
November	18,000[a]	700[a]
December	20,000[a]	700[a]
	$151,000[a]	$6,240[a]

[a]Estimated.
Source: Company records and management forecasts.

CURRENT SALES AND ADVERTISING

During the current year Barbara's had total projected sales of $151,000 (see Table 2 for a breakdown of sales by month). It is important to note, however, that the current year was unusual in that a flood in late May had almost completely destroyed the shop and necessitated a move to a new location across the street. As a result, Barbara's had no sales in June. Sales of flowers and plants this year were projected to break down roughly as follows: individual cut flowers, 10 percent; arrangements, 75 percent; and plants, 15 percent.

Barbara's was projected to invest approximately $6,240 in advertising during the current year. This total was broken down by media vehicles as follows: *Daily Texan* (student newspaper), $1,200; *Austin American Statesman,* $1,000; radio, $2,400; television, $0; magazines, $0; circulars, $680; and Yellow Pages (quarter page), $960. A complete summary of ad spending projections by month for the current year is presented in Table 2. Exhibit 1 presents Bar-

bara's quarter-page telephone directory ad and a recent quarter-page newspaper ad.

NEXT YEAR'S ADVERTISING BUDGET

In developing an advertising plan for next year, Barbara's management wanted to make greater use of advertising to help achieve a $60,000 increase in sales over the current year. Management was convinced that this was a realistic goal based on the assumption of an effective and expanded advertising commitment. They were willing to invest a percentage of forecasted sales well beyond the florist industry-wide average percentage of advertising-to-sales ratio in order to achieve this growth and to build their consumer franchise for the future.

As a part of an increased emphasis on advertising, management had approved a new series of print ads for next year. Exhibit 2 presents three representative ads from next year's campaign. Management felt these ads were appropriate and would do much to build Barbara's image and, at the same time, help to increase sales. The new campaign's ads were viewed as appropriate for both target markets.

Management's task now was to determine an appropriate advertising appropriation for the coming year and to develop a reasonable rationale supporting the recommended amount. In addition, after identifying an appropriate total amount to invest in advertising, management would develop a budget allocation and supporting rationale.

The proposed budget, to cover January 1 through December 31, was to be allocated across each of the following categories: by media types and vehicles; by target markets; by product lines; and by months of the year. Further, the budget was to include a contingency fund to ensure some flexibility in the conduct of Barbara's advertising program.

Finally, management was convinced that next year's media schedule should include monthly

EXHIBIT 1

Current Quarter-Page Newspaper and Yellow Page Ads

EXHIBIT 2

Representative Print Ads from New Campaign

ads in *Third Coast* magazine. It was believed that this tabloid-sized magazine publication would represent a "good buy" in reaching both the primary and secondary target markets. At this point it had become clear that decisions related to both budgeting and media planning were interrelated. Representative media costs are presented in the Appendix.

QUESTIONS FOR DISCUSSION

1. In planning the advertising appropriation for the coming year, how large a role is the level of investment during the current year likely to play? What impact might the new advertising campaign (see Exhibit 2) have on deciding how much to invest in advertising?

2. How realistic is the sales increase forecasted for the coming year? How should this forecast be related to the level of advertising investment?

3. What are the major considerations that should be evaluated in establishing an amount to invest in advertising? What factors are most important in allocating the advertising investment across budget categories, such as target markets and months of the year?

APPENDIX
REPRESENTATIVE MEDIA COSTS

NEWSPAPERS

Monthly Earned Rate (per column inch—
columns wide × inches deep)

| Inches | *Austin American-Statesman*[a] | | *Daily Texan*[b] | |
	Daily	Sunday	Inches	
Open	$14.25	$15.25	Open	$5.69
1–24	11.83	12.76	20	5.13
25	10.66	11.50	50	4.40
50	9.85	10.63	100	4.22
100	9.52	10.27	200	4.01
500	9.32	10.05	300	3.82
1,000	9.20	9.93	400	3.70
2,000	9.07	9.78	500	3.58
5,000	8.93	9.63	750	3.51
7,000	8.49	9.15	1,000	3.45

[a]Additional charge for color daily or Sunday: 1 color =
$390; 2 color = $528; 3 color = $624. Minimum ad size =
70 inches.
[b]Additional charge for color: 1 color = $130; 2 color =
$170; 3 color = $205. Minimum ad size = 50 inches.

MAGAZINE

Third Coast
(published monthly, black and white only)

Ad Size	1x	3x	6x	12x
Full Page	$625	$570	$535	$495
2/3	460	420	405	390
1/2	395	360	340	315
1/3	290	265	240	215
1/4	230	205	185	170
1/6	170	150	135	120

BROADCAST (30-SECOND SPOTS)

KLBJ FM

Mornings (6–10) and evenings (3–10)

Thursday, Friday, Saturday	$44
Monday, Tuesday, Wednesday	39

KTBC Channel 7 (CBS)		KTVV Channel 36 (NBC)	
7–9 A.M.	$40	7–9 A.M.	$25
9–11:30 A.M.	50	9–12 A.M.	20
11:30–3:30 P.M.	125	12–12:30 P.M.	25
3:30–4:00 P.M.	70	12:30–1 A.M.	20
4–5 P.M.	50	1–3 P.M.	25
5–5:30 P.M.	150	3–5 P.M.	45
5:30–6 P.M.	350	5–5:30 P.M.	65
6–6:30 P.M.	400	6–7 P.M.	105
6:30–7 P.M.	300	10:30–11:30 P.M.	105
10–10:30 P.M.	450		
10:30–11 P.M.	400		

17

GRAND CANYON CORPORATION— THE DESERT PLAYGROUND

Theme parks are a relatively new phenomenon on the American scene. There are about twenty major theme parks in the United States, and eleven of these were started in the past few years. As a business enterprise they are far more important than is generally realized since these twenty parks draw more people annually than major professional sports.

THE PARK'S BACKGROUND AND ATTRACTIONS

The Grand Canyon Corporation was founded in 1966 with headquarters in Phoenix, Arizona. It is a multimillion dollar corporation with three theme parks located in various parts of the country. The newest of these, "The Desert Playground," began operation in 1976. The 200-acre theme park is located on Interstate 10 near Phoenix, Arizona.

Actually, the Playground consists of 502 acres since management recognized the need for buffer zones and for expansion. Management tries to put $2 million into the park every year, mainly into new attractions.

The new attraction this year is a superfantastic roller coaster. One could go on and on with superlatives: the highest in the world, the deepest drops in the world, the longest, the tallest, the fastest, and so on.

The history of the Southwest plays an important part in the character of The Desert Playground. The park's designers spend a great deal of time recreating the flavor of the Old Southwest in park buildings, landscaping, rides, and attractions.

This case was prepared by E. S. Lorimor, California State University–Fresno.

The first area that visitors see after entering the park is a great central plaza, called, appropriately, Plaza Central. The plaza is entered through Spanish-style arches and is surrounded by buildings in the same style of architecture.

Among the shops on the plaza is the Sells Brothers Enormous Toy Circus. This toy shop is named after one of the best-known and most loved circuses that toured the country, primarily in the West, in the 1800s. This circus at one time employed one of the most notorious outlaws of the Old West as a ticket seller—Frank James himself.

Branching off the plaza are streets which are replicas of the streets of the Old West frontier towns. One of the interesting rides at the park is a beautifully restored stagecoach, which takes visitors at a rapid pace down broad and steep trails and at a slower pace through the old-town streets.

The Lillie Langtry Music Hall, located in the Old West area, is the setting for the park's musical presentations. Talented secondary-school and university students sing and dance in a salute to the light side of the history of the Old West. The Lost Dutchman Amphitheatre presents many famous entertainers, with "Lord Darrel Duppa" as the master of ceremonies.

Another popular attraction at the park is a journey through Colossal Cave, the famed Tucson Haunt of outlaws. Visitors float on wooden rafts while viewing the exploits of the legendary robbers. Inside the cave Miss Kitty's presents a rootin', tootin' saloon show.

Last year's major addition was Oak Creek Glade. Designed especially for children three years old and up, this attraction includes four child-size rides, a playground with a miniature fort, and a little red schoolhouse. A special barnyard animal show appeals to adults as well as children. Puppet shows depicting famous historical events of the area are another attraction in this section of the park.

Among the antiquities in the park is a gorgeous carousel, built in 1915, with 68 hand-carved wooden horses and two chariots. For those with a further yearning for the past, the Bonanza Tin Type Company makes genuine turn-of-the century tintype photographs. Still another exciting ride is a tiny, narrow-gauge train of the sort attacked by outlaws in hundreds of Hollywood westerns.

Scattered throughout the park are restaurants featuring many different types of food. Naturally, there are a number of Mexican restaurants with intriguing names such as El Sombrero, La Tortilla, and La Casa del Sol. A restaurant with American Indian food bears the name Navahopi, and The Trappers' Lodge offers jerky and buffalo steaks.

This is merely a sampling of the wide variety of rides, attractions, goods, and types of foods offered by The Desert Playground for the entire family. In contrast to many theme parks, which lease concessions, the Grand Canyon Corporation manages all food and other concessions.

In keeping with the idea of family recreation, no liquor or beer is served at the Playground. The management is concerned with the image of the park as a place for clean, wholesome, family-type fun and does not wish to allow the possibility of any trouble or drunken rowdiness.

Even though Phoenix is a winter recreation area, The Desert Playground operates only from May through October since children and young people are usually in school during the winter months. This season allows for schools to use the park for group functions early and late in the school year.

The park employs 1,600 hostesses, who work during the summer vacation, and has 200 permanent employees, including those in advertising, marketing and promotion, and personnel. Simonton and Wingfield, a Phoenix advertising agency, handles the creative aspects of the park's advertising program.

THE MARKET

The Desert Playground is located near one of the fastest-growing metropolitan areas in the country. Between 1970 and 1980 the population of the Phoenix area increased 55 percent. In 1980 the population was more than 1.5 million.

Theme park planners generally consider that 3 million people must live within a 300-mile radius of a major theme park for it to be successful. Although this is not true of the Phoenix area, a number of factors made the Grand Canyon Corporation decide to go ahead with the plan for the Phoenix park. First was the extraordinary growth of the area. Second was the fact that distances mean less in the West. The roads tend to be straighter than in the East, and people drive long distances without giving it a second thought. Third, Phoenix is a popular leisure and recreation area and is host to many visitors.

Even though a family theme park is for the entire family, the bulk of the visitors are young people and families with young children. Phoenix has an ideal market profile for these requirements. The median age is 28.2 years, with about 30 percent of the household heads under 35. The under-21 group and the young marrieds, through age 29, make up 53 percent of the Phoenix metropolitan area population.

Another target market for The Desert Playground is groups. Any group of 25 or more is offered special discounts.

DESERT PLAYGROUND PROMOTION AND ADVERTISING

The Desert Playground's management does not attempt to advertise the park nationally. Management feels that it is a better policy to aim for coverage of the Southwest, including Southern California and Nevada.

Until 1976 the attendance at the park increased approximately 10 percent annually over the previous several years. Season tickets were not an important factor until July 1981, when Mr. B's Markets were enlisted to sell them. Mr. B's has 36 food stores in the Phoenix Area, the largest number owned by any company. The stores were glad to handle the passes because they felt that the large amount of advertising done by The Desert Playground would increase their store traffic. Mr. B's also included notices in their ads stressing that the passes were available at their stores. There was an increase of more than 9,000 season passes sold in 1981 over the 1980 season (see Table 1).

In 1982 the relationship with Mr. B's was continued. In an effort to increase the ease of buying passes, the sales manager also arranged with Sav-More Drug Stores (45 outlets in the area) to handle season ticket sales. With this additional promotion, the season tickets sold almost doubled over the previous year's already high total. Because of this emphasis and the pull of the new attraction, 1982 attendance increased 15 percent over that of 1981.

The Desert Playground advertising budget was a relatively generous one for the area to be covered. It increased very slowly until management virtually decided to go for broke in the 1982 promotion of the park's new attraction, called the Screaming Eagle. The money usually went into television, radio, newspapers, outdoor, and into some municipal, regional, and entertainment magazines. (See Tables 2 and 3.) About 15 percent of the budget was planned for production of ads and for promotion.

The Playground also gets a great deal of publicity through its various charitable and community activities. Chest-related diseases, a serious problem in the Southwest, are one of its particular charities. Tickets are donated to various charitable organizations with the appropriate publicity.

Another example of the park's publicity-generating activities is Fire-Fighting Weekend, which is sponsored annually. The Playground donates one dollar to the Firemen's Fund for every ticket that firemen sell. In addition, special firefighting equipment and demonstrations may be seen at the park. This is a special attraction since Phoenix has some of the most innovative firefighting equipment available.

Management of The Desert Playground is concerned with promoting the entire area, not just the park itself. Promotional booklets carry pictures and text on Grand Canyon, Oak Creek Canyon, the Painted Desert, the colorful Fourth of July celebrations in Prescott and Flagstaff, the Casa Grande ruins, Old Tucson, and the like. The management feels that anything that attracts vacationing families to the area benefits the park.

PLANNING, DEVELOPMENT, AND PROMOTION OF THE NEW ATTRACTION

In 1979 management decided that the big new attraction for 1982 would be a superior roller coaster. Research had shown that roller coasters were very popular, especially with children and young people, and if a very special one were erected, it would result in a great deal of publicity.

Working on the theory, "if you want some-

TABLE 1
Desert Playground Attendance and Season Ticket Sales

	1979	1980	1981	1982
Attendance receipts	$15,460,000	$17,006,000	$18,705,000	$21,560,750
Season tickets sold	4,390	5,123	14,200	28,146

TABLE 2
Desert Playground Advertising and Promotion Budget

	1979	1980	1981	1982
Overall	$725,000	$750,000	$775,000	$775,000
Screaming Eagle Attraction	—	—	—	$250,000
Total	$725,000	$750,000	$775,000	$1,025,000

TABLE 3
Breakdown of Desert Playground Advertising
and Promotion Budget

	General Budget			
	1979	1980	1981	1982
Newspaper	$135,000	$130,000	$130,000	$120,000
Magazines	10,000	11,000	11,000	11,000
Radio	170,000	173,000	178,000	168,000
Television	172,000	176,000	190,000	190,000
Outdoor	128,000	145,000	150,000	170,000
Miscellaneous	110,000	115,000	116,000	116,000
General total	$725,000	$750,000	$775,000	$775,000

Screaming Eagle Attraction Budget	
Film	$100,000
Promotion	100,000
Television (additional)	50,000
Screaming Eagle total	$250,000
Overall total	$1,025,000

thing good, hire the best," they coaxed the best roller coaster architect in the business out of retirement. Sixty-eight-year-old John Allen is the designer of fifteen of the roller coasters now in use. Naturally, these facts were given to the media, and since the story had human interest, it was widely covered. Allen's statement, "This is my last roller coaster," added to the drama of the affair.

The structure John Allen designed is worthy of attention. It has 3,872 feet of track for a two-minute ride. The structure rises to 110 feet and has an initial drop of 87 feet, followed by a drop of 92 feet, During the ride, the cars hit 62 miles per hour, and a force of 2½ Gs is exerted at the bottom of the drops. Built of specially treated douglas fir, the structure has ⅜ of an inch tolerance whereas the steel track has none. The 550,000-board feet are held together by 50,000 pounds of nuts and bolts, and it takes 10,000 gallons of paint to cover them.

The park and agency advertising and promotion people started their major planning for the 1982 opening of the roller coaster in 1980. One of the first publicity activities was a Name-the-Roller-Coaster Contest. Some 500 names were submitted. The Name Committee narrowed them down to 20, then to 5, and finally chose Screaming Eagle. It seemed particularly appropriate because the eagle is a bird well-known in the lore of the Southwest, and as El Águila Chilladora it fit beautifully into the Spanish promotion.

The Screaming Eagle promotion people had some fabulous luck in doing their job. In 1981 "Roller Coaster Dream" was tops on the pop music sales charts. Although they did not usually try for national coverage, it seemed too good an opportunity to miss. Getting a list of the Top 40 stations, the company sent a picture and a story of the growing roller coaster to each station. This early story was picked up by ABC radio and 158 stations, giving the park a publicity windfall.

As the roller coaster neared completion, a poster contest was started in the Phoenix area schools. A large local art gallery exhibited the winners from each school, and a local artist who had his own children's program on television was selected as head judge. The winner of the poster contest was awarded a season pass by the park and was invited to appear with his winning poster on the chief judge's program.

An artist was selected to draw a proper design to represent the roller coaster. After designing, redesigning, and refining, he came up with a marvelous drawing of the head of a fierce-looking bald eagle nestled in the deepest drop of a stylized, white-painted roller coaster with the fitting slogan, "Fly the Screaming Eagle," underneath. (The slogan is appropriate since the cars actually leave the tracks and take to the air at various times during the ride.)

The Screaming Eagle was featured in all the publicity and advertising by The Desert Playground in 1982. For example, a press kit is prepared every year for distribution to the media. The 1982 kit splashed the Eagle over the cover and carried it on most of the brochures inside. It was featured prominently in the news release as well.

Television commercials for The Desert Playground in 1982 featured the new roller coaster. Both live-action and animation techniques were used. It was difficult to show the joyous abandon of "flying" the still unfinished Eagle, so shots of happy riders of a roller coaster in another of the corporation's parks were edited into the commercials. Both the live-action and the animation commercials were given top awards by the Phoenix Advertising Club in its annual competition.

A well-known producer in Los Angeles was selected to produce a theatrical film of the recreation available in the Southwest. Naturally, The Desert Playground was given good play, and the Screaming Eagle was the featured attraction. This film will be distributed to cinemas for three or four years, about the length of time the park promotion people estimate that the Eagle will stay ahead of the competition.

The public relations staff at The Desert Playground feel it is very important that employees be sold on each new attraction. A very heavy promotional program for the Screaming Eagle was started among them. Iron-ons, T-shirts, sweat shirts, rulers, jewelry, charm bracelets, badges, and the like, all featuring the Screaming Eagle design, were distributed among the employees. Some were given to all, others served as premiums for special ideas or efforts. One of the most coveted was the heavy, silver Screaming Eagle belt buckle. Some specialties were given to the public as well, but many were for internal promotion only. In addition, a large clip-on button with the eagle design and the statement "I'm no chicken; I flew the Screaming Eagle," is handed to each daring soul who has the patience and the fortitude to survive the lines and experience the "flight."

Various promotional campaigns were run in cooperation with other suitable businesses. For example, a promotion was done with a fast-food chain and it was tied in with the television campaign. The promotion cost $60,000 for three weeks, and each business paid half.

ADVERTISING PLANNING

The Desert Playground advertising plan for 1982 was similar to that of past years except that there was an emphasis on school groups and the new attraction had a special budget of its own. The plan included:

A. Target markets
   1. Teenagers and young adults
   2. Young marrieds and their children, including preschool
   3. Groups
   4. School groups (for education as well as recreation)
   5. College students

B. Advertising theme: The Desert Playground provides history, mystery, a lot of thrills for the whole family

C. Advertising budget: $1,025,000 ($775,000 for the park generally and $250,000 for the roller coaster)

D. Advertising objectives
   1. To attract the target markets to the Desert Playground.
   2. To describe the recreational and educational values of the park.
   3. To promote the Playground as the place to bring school groups.
   4. To capitalize on the drama of the Screaming Eagle.

QUESTIONS FOR DISCUSSION

At a recent meeting of the management of The Desert Playground and its advertising agency, several important questions were raised. Among these questions were:
1. Was the advertising budget for 1982 large enough, too large, or about right?
2. If The Desert Playground wanted to launch a national advertising program, how much money would be necessary?
3. What method of determining the advertising investment would be most appropriate?

When people think of where wine is produced in the United States, California and perhaps New York quickly come to mind. Rarely does anyone think of Texas. Although this was not always true, Texas has not been a major producer of wine since Prohibition. However, beginning in the mid-1970s several individuals and a few universities began efforts to redevelop a wine industry in Texas. Initial successes caused some people to believe that one day Texas might challenge California for the dominant position in the domestic wine market.

In 1975 and 1976 a small group of the Texas grape growers and agricultural experts from The Unversity of Texas and from Texas A & M began to organize in order to share information and work toward common goals. On March 1, 1977, a meeting was held in Austin, and the Texas Grape Growers Association (TGGA) was officially formed. Since its inception, the TGGA's membership has increased to approximately 175.

Several years after the founding of the TGGA a number of the members of the Association felt that the time was ripe for the TGGA to begin to advertise and promote Texas wines to consumers. They suggested that it was logical for the Association not to attempt to move on a national basis initially, but rather to begin by advertising their wines exclusively within the state of Texas. Although funds for such advertising were presently nonexistent, it was suggested that some important objectives could be accomplished by carefully budgeting a modest advertising appropriation. The first and foremost question in examining the suggestion that the TGGA launch a generic Texas wines advertising campaign was what constituted an appropriate

This case was prepared by Ronald J. Faber, The University of Texas at Austin, and Tom O'Guinn, University of Illinois.

level of investment during the first fiscal year of such a campaign.

EARLY HISTORY OF WINE PRODUCTION IN TEXAS

Growing grapes in Texas for wine production dates back more than three centuries. Around 1662 the Franciscan Fathers in Texas planted vineyards to produce wines for religious ceremonies and medication. Their grape vines were originally brought from Spain and Mexico. Spanish settlers in Texas also planted vineyards near El Paso, and in the 1800s German immigrants started vineyards in the hill country of central Texas.

During the late 1800s Texas vineyards played an important role in wine history. At that time, Thomas Volney Munson, considered the father of the Texas wine industry, was searching for grapes adaptable to the southern United States. Munson experimented with the Vitis Vinifera grape, the variety used in many of the best European wines. Munson succeeded in crossing this grape with native Texas varieties. He also managed to develop hardier, more disease-resistant plants. These hardy hybrid vines made Munson famous.

In the 1880s much of Europe's vineyards were ravaged by a disease called phylloxera. Munson helped to save some of these vineyards by shipping thousands of his disease-resistant rootstock vines to Europe. For his effort, Munson was awarded the French Legion of Honor.

By the early 1900s Texas had become the third largest grape-producing state in the United States, with 25 wineries operating across a wide section of the state. Not only did Texas vineyards produce large quantities of grapes, they also produced high-quality wines. Among other international awards, a Texas wine won top honors at the 1890 World's Fair. However, all wine production in Texas ceased in 1920 with the enactment of Prohibition. When wine became illegal, grape growing in Texas virtually disappeared.

In 1933, with the repeal of Prohibition, many states, most notably California, quickly began growing grapes for wine once again. However, this was not the case in Texas. Wine production remained relatively dormant in the state until the early 1970s.

RECENT DEVELOPMENTS

In the late 1960s the demand for grapes in the United States far exceeded the supply. Grape growers enjoyed boom years when there were simply not enough grapes to satisfy demand. Prices rose rapidly and profits were very good. All across the nation farmers tried to cash in on the scarcity. In Texas, enterprising farmers rushed to plant vines. Unfortunately, the boom ended, prices fell, and many of the novice growers found grape production to be an exercise in frustration. A few, however, persisted.

These survivors were scattered across the state. The most successful of these growers were concentrated in west Texas. Fungal diseases such as Pierce's disease and cotton root rot limited production in all but north, northwest, and west Texas. The air in these western regions is so dry that fungal infections of the vines are rare. In addition, the soil in west Texas is particularly good for grape production; it is permeable and has good drainage. It is, in fact, very similar to the grape-growing soils of France.

Through the use of drip irrigation west Texas growers found an efficient means of watering their vineyards. Drip irrigation, a process in which water is slowly dripped from plastic pipes, is not only an efficient means of conservation, but a means by which salt can be leached from the normally saline west Texas soil as well. The growing season, although earlier in the year, was

thought by many experts to be more desirable than those of California or New York. Birds and hail were the most serious threats to production in west Texas. They have not, however, proved to be insurmountable problems. Nets have been used to frustrate hungry birds and natural topographical barriers have been used to prevent or minimize hail damage. Late rainfalls do, however, preclude raisin production.

In 1975 there were only 25 acres of Texas land being used for grape production. A few years later there were over 1,000. This growth has not come exclusively from the private sector.

The University of Texas system, which is an important member of TGGA, owns approximately 2.5 million acres of west Texas land. The university lands had for years been exploited for their rich oil reserves. Since the land's utility from oil production is finite, the university has sought alternative uses. After walnuts, almonds, olives, kiwi, jojoba, and pecans were tried, grapes were planted. UT viticulturists and winemakers have produced some very good experimental wines. It appeared the university was primarily interested in demonstrating the commercial feasibility of such an operation and then leasing its vineyards to a large commercial winery. Both Gallo and Paul Masson have expressed interest. The university estimated that it had 40,000 to 60,000 acres suited to the growing of grapes.

Other TGGA members' vineyards and wineries had also been expanding rapidly in an attempt to take advantage of steadily increased demand. For example, the vineyards of the La Buena Vida Winery will triple in acreage by 1986. Such growth is closer to the rule than the exception. As acreage increases, so does wine production.

For example, the Fall Creek Winery produced 1,100 gallons of wine in 1980 compared with only 600 in 1979. La Buena Vida estimated 1981 production at 7,000 cases or approximately 17,000 gallons compared with only 600 cases or approximately 1,400 gallons in 1978. La Buena

Vida officials estimated 1985 production to be 15,000 cases or approximately 38,000 gallons. Total statewide production for 1981 was estimated to be 50,000 gallons or approximately 21,000 cases.

It generally takes grape vines from five to seven years from the time they are planted until they are capable of producing a crop suitable for wine production. Wines produced before vine maturation lead to poor quality wines. Yet, while the vineyard owners are waiting for their vines to mature, they are losing money. This situation can result in considerable pressure to produce a wine "long before its time" just to stay in business. These pressures were sometimes too powerful to resist and some premature Texas wines have been released on the market.

In some cases this situation has resulted in Texas wines gaining a bad reputation. However, most Texas wines were produced from vines that were six to ten years old and thus capable of producing good-quality wines. The growers learned from their experience and the quality of Texas wines had improved in recent years. Also, there were indications that success may be just around the corner for many Texas growers. One vintner produced a gold medal wine at the 1979 Eastern Wine Competition. Many wine and food critics have found several Texas wines to be truly competitive with similarly priced California and French wines.

It had been only recently that Texas wines became available in retail outlets. They could, however, be found in only a few restaurants, some liquor stores, and a few specialty stores such as wine and cheese shops around the state. It was almost impossible to find Texas wines in grocery or convenience stores. For example, in Austin, the state capital, Texas wines could be found in only a few liquor stores, three or four wine and cheese shops, and one restaurant. As production increased, the Texas grape growers and wineries were well aware of the need to expand the number of distribution outlets in which their product was available.

TRENDS IN U.S. WINE CONSUMPTION

The year 1980 was a landmark year for wines in the United States. For the first time in history, consumption of wine exceeded that of liquor (465 million gallons of wine compared with 450 million gallons of distilled spirits). Additionally, wine consumption expenditures topped the $4 billion mark for the first time. Wine consumption has been on the upswing in the United States for many years; the industry has grown steadily every year since 1962. During the decade from 1970 through 1979, consumption increased 71.6 percent (see Table 1). The increase in dollar expenditures during this period was even more phenomenal, showing an increase of 173.6 percent.

Most industry experts forecasted that wine consumption in the United States will continue to enjoy healthy growth during the 1980s despite the fact that prices should continue to rise. *Impact,* a wine industry newsletter, predicted that wine consumption will show a 6 to 10 percent per year increase in the coming years. Other industry sources projected an average annual growth rate of 6 percent through 1985. The *Wine Marketing Handbook* predicted that total U.S. wine sales will increase from 154.4 million cases in 1979 to an estimated 209.3 million cases in 1984.

Most experts believe that projected increases for the 1980s will occur not because of any significant increase in the number of people drinking wine, but, rather, because of an increase in the frequency of wine drinking among current consumers. Although the per capita consumption rate in the United States has more than doubled in twenty years, it has not yet begun to approach the rate of many other countries (see Table 2).

Wines may be divided into four different classifications: table wine, dessert wine, champagne and sparkling wines, and vermouth. Table wine accounted for three-fourths (74.6 percent) of all wine consumed in the United States. Be-

TABLE 1

Changes in U.S. Wine Consumption from 1970 to 1979

Year	Gallons Consumed (in millions)	Adult per Capita Consumption (gallons)	Consumer Expenditures (in millions)
1979	439.1	2.94	$3,998
1978	418.0	2.83	3,621
1977	389.7	2.69	3,128
1976	371.8	2.59	2,919
1975	361.6	2.58	2,685
1974	341.8	2.49	2,453
1973	337.8	2.51	2,270
1972	326.9	2.49	2,020
1971	295.7	2.37	1,755
1970	255.9	2.09	1,461

TABLE 2

Approximate Per Capita Consumption of Wine in the United States and Selected European Countries

Country	Per Capita Consumption (in gallons)
France	27.2
Italy	25.2
Spain	19.4
Switzerland	12.8
Greece	11.6
Hungary	9.4
Yugoslavia	7.8
West Germany	6.6
United States	2.0

Source: The Wine Marketing Handbook, 1980.

tween 1970 and 1979, the number of cases of table wine consumed in the United States increased 156 percent (from 45 million cases in 1970 to 115.2 millions cases in 1979). Projections indicated that by 1984 consumption of table wine will increase to 171.2 million cases. This was good news for Texas grape growers since almost all the wines produced in Texas were table wines.

The market for table wine in Texas had grown even faster than the national rate. In 1979 Texas moved from eighth largest consuming state to the fifth largest. Only California, New York, Florida, and Illinois had greater sales of table wines than Texas (see Table 3). However, while Texas accounted for 3.9 percent of all sales of table wines, this was less than what might be expected on the basis of its population (5.5 percent of total United States population). Nonetheless, as wine production in Texas expands and more local wineries are started, the increase in wine consumption in Texas should escalate. Gretchen Glasscock, one of the pioneers of the Texas wine industry, stated, "Re-

TABLE 3

Top Ten States in Table Wine Consumption in 1979

State	Cases Sold	Percent of U.S. Cases Sold
California	28,266,040	24.5
New York	11,537,336	10.0
Florida	5,892,834	5.1
Illinois	5,125,769	4.4
Texas	4,438,524	3.9
New Jersey	4,412,842	3.8
Pennsylvania	4,350,487	3.8
Michigan	4,014,262	3.5
Massachusetts	3,712,212	3.2
Ohio	3,483,502	3.0
Total top ten	75,233,808	65.2
U.S. total	115,216,641	100.0

Source: The Wine Marketing Handbook, 1980.

search has proved that wherever there is a local winery, wine consumption soars."

As the quality and reputation of domestic table wines have improved, so has consumption. In 1981 less than 25 percent of table wines consumed in the United States were imported. In recent years all of the major importing countries, with the exception of Italy, have reported a decrease in United States table wine sales. Table 4 indicates the origin of table wines consumed in the United States in 1979.

The type of table wine consumed in the United States underwent a drastic change during the twenty-year period 1960–1980. In 1960, red wines represented the vast majority of table wine consumed. However, as can be seen in Table 5, by 1980 over half of the table wine purchased was white wine. Some wine marketers believe that this change may be due more to a preference for chilled wine than just a preference for white wine. The change toward white wines, for whatever reason, was viewed as advantageous to Texas growers since they have been much more successful in producing quality white wines than red wines.

TABLE 4

1979 U.S. Table Wine Consumption by Country of Origination

Country	Gallons Consumed (in millions)	Percent
Italy	43.2	12.3
France	12.9	3.7
Germany	11.7	3.3
Other foreign countries	13.4	3.8
Total imported wines	81.2	23.1
California	246.1	70.0
New York	18.0	5.1
Other states	6.3	1.8
Total domestic wines	270.4	76.9
Total	351.6	100.0

Source: The Wine Marketing Handbook, 1980.

TABLE 5

Percent of Market Share for Different Colors of Table Wines

Color	1960 (percent)	1970 (percent)	1980 (percent)
Red	73	50	26
White	17	24	54
Rosé	10	26	20

Source: Ad Age, April 20, 1981.

Along with color, table wines are also categorized by price. The cheapest wines, costing $2 or less for a 750-ml bottle in 1978–1979, were referred to as jug wines. These inexpensive wines represented about half of all table wines sold in the United States in 1979(see Table 6). There was, however, a growing trend toward the more expensive, premium table wines. Indications were that this was not due simply to inflation, but also to a growing sophistication among American wine drinkers.

Most of the Texas winemakers were interested in selling mid-premium level wines at $3 to $5 per bottle. They believed that this was the best market at which to aim since people were moving toward the higher priced wines, and they believed Texas wine quality was competitive in this range.

Cost considerations generally prevented a Texas wine priced much lower than $3 per

TABLE 6

1978–1979 Percent of Sales for Table Wines by Price Classification

Class	Price Range	1978 (percent)	1979 (percent)
Low (jug)	under $2.00	51.7	50.1
Lower mid	$2.00–$2.75	26.7	26.9
Middle	$2.76–$4.25	12.6	13.3
Upper mid	$4.26–$5.75	5.9	6.4
Upper	over $5.75	3.1	3.3
		100.0	100.0

Source: The Wine Marketing Handbook, 1980.

bottle. While most industry experts felt that very high-priced Texas wines would experience a problem with extremely tough competition, the $3 and $5 per bottle pricing strategy had the advantage of simultaneously encouraging initial purchases and legitimizing the product. It was inexpensive enough to try, but at the same time expensive enough to be good.

WINE CONSUMERS

Sixty-nine percent of all American adults drank some form of alcoholic beverage, and almost all of these people at least occasionally drank wine. Wine consumption tended to be heavier among the younger, better-educated, and wealthier segments of the population. According to a *Newsweek* report, *Spirits of '79,* 52 percent of U.S. wine consumers were between 25 and 49 years old; almost half (49 percent) had at least attended college, and 48 percent had household incomes of $20,000 or more.

Other studies indicated that women were a particularly important target market. A study of *Glamour* magazine's working women readers revealed that a majority (72 percent) preferred wine over other alcoholic beverages. They cited taste, fewer calories, and cost as the major reasons for this preference.

A study of *Family Circle* readers found that in 83 percent of the households polled, women chose the brand of table wine purchased at least some of the time. However, 80 percent of these women also said that a man in their household was a "very" or "somewhat important" source of information about wine.

Other research reported in the *Wine Marketing Handbook* indicated that women played a large role in determining how much to spend on wine. Among the respondents, 37.5 percent said the woman had a greater role in this decision, 38.5 percent said it was equally decided; and 24 percent said that the man in the household usually had a greater influence in this decision.

While most people purchased wine for their own use, or to entertain guests, buying wine as a gift had become very popular. Wine was most commonly given as a house gift, although many people gave wine for Christmas or birthdays. The influence of holiday entertaining and gifts can be seen in the sales increase during the last quarter of the typical year (see Table 7).

The vast majority of wine consumed in the state of Texas was consumed in the state's larger metropolitan areas. Approximately 80 percent of sales came from either Dallas-Fort Worth, Houston, San Antonio, or El Paso. San Antonio and El Paso taken together accounted for 15 percent of sales; 34.5 percent came from Dallas-Fort Worth; and Houston accounted for 30.5 percent of wine sales in Texas.

In addition to residing in a metropolitan area, the average wine consumer in Texas was young, most often between the ages of 21 and 40. Along most dimensions, the wine consumers of Texas appeared quite similar to the national profile.

LEGAL ISSUES

Texas is composed of both "wet" and "dry" areas. In dry areas, located primarily in east and west Texas, it is against the law to sell alcoholic

TABLE 7
U.S. Table Wine Sales by Month in 1979

Month	Cases Sold	Percent
January	8,641,248	7.5
February	8,295,598	7.2
March	9,102,115	7.9
April	11,060,798	9.6
May	8,526,031	7.4
June	8,986,898	7.8
July	8,871,681	7.7
August	8,180,382	7.1
September	7,373,865	6.4
October	10,023,848	8.7
November	11,521,664	10.0
December	14,632,513	12.7
Total	115,216,641	100.0

Source: The Wine Marketing Handbook, 1980.

beverages. Most often county lines define these areas. In a few instances, however, there are wet/dry divisions within one county; for example, Dallas County contains wet and dry precincts. Thus, people who live in a dry area who wish to purchase wine might need only to cross the street or they might have to travel a considerable distance to make a purchase. This situation created obvious distribution and advertising problems.

Several of the Texas wineries were located in dry areas. Although it was completely legal to make the wine, it was illegal to sell it within these dry areas. This eliminated one possible channel of distribution: direct sales. The tasting rooms of wineries were often the site of substantial sales and had traditionally been a very profitable distribution channel to consumers.

In an effort to eliminate some of the inequity between wineries operating in wet versus dry areas, the TGGA had successfully lobbied the state legislature into enacting laws which allowed a vintner operating in a dry area to sell his first 25,000 gallons directly to retailers. Up until the enactment of the revised laws, all vintners were required by law to sell to a wholesaler. The new law also allowed wineries located in wet areas to sell some wine directly from their tasting rooms with all remaining wine having to go through a wholesaler. While the TGGA was encouraged by this success in getting the legislature to remove the inequity between wet and dry areas, they realized that several other legislative issues could determine the likelihood of success for the Texas wine industry. Of major concern was the need for legislative assistance during the industry's formative period. On several occasions local wineries in other states had been the object of fierce price competition from the major California wineries; the Californians had not been willing to relinquish even small local markets without a fight. For example, when a million gallon winery was built in Arkansas, price competition by California growers nearly forced it to close. It was only through the enactment of protective state tariffs that the local winery was able to survive. Several TGGA members believed that similar laws would be needed in Texas.

ADVERTISING AND PROMOTION

The TGGA had never sponsored any advertising. Further, while a few individual growers had published their own newsletters, none had attempted to engage in media advertising. As the industry began to be revitalized in Texas, many newspapers and magazines in the state had run stories on Texas wines. While this publicity was helpful, it was unlikely to be sufficient for the successful promotion of Texas wine. The members of TGGA realized that they should consider using advertising and sales promotion to stimulate sales of Texas wines. As was stated earlier, the TGGA felt that their first goal should be to concentrate on the Texas market and then, when production was sufficient, to move into the national market.

Since none of the Texas growers was large enough to engage in a large-scale advertising or promotional campaign on its own, the best approach seemed to be to band together to promote Texas wines in a generic approach. However, there was considerable disagreement among members of the TGGA as to how this could best be accomplished. One of the first considerations was to whom advertising and promotions should be directed.

One group that needed to be reached through advertising and sales promotion was retailers. In 1980 there were 7,246 wine retail outlets in Texas. Approximately 1,700 of these were located in Houston. Dallas-Fort Worth and surrounding areas contained 1,020 package stores selling wines and 544 stores were located in the San Antonio area (Bexar County). These retailers needed to be convinced that it would be worthwhile for them to devote limited shelf space to stock Texas wines. Additionally, these retailers could play an important part in helping to promote Texas wines to the consumer. For example, research on readers of *Family Circle* magazine found that women rated retail stores as an important source of information concerning wine. Fifty percent rated store displays as being "very" or "somewhat" important, and 47 percent stated that store sales personnel were at least a "somewhat important" source. The only other sources receiving a greater or equal number of positive ratings were friends and relatives and television commercials.

The retailers themselves believed that the wine companies could be helpful in educating the consumer. In a survey of liquor stores, owners and managers were asked what were the most useful services provided by wine companies. Wine information (28 percent) and displays (26 percent) were the most frequently mentioned services. Some of the Texas grape growers, therefore, felt that advertising and promotion should center on the retailer outlets and utilize these stores' personnel to help educate consumers about Texas wine.

Another possible target market was, of course, the consumer. While the first consumer objective would be to make them aware of Texas wines, altering attitudes was also essential. Wine had traditionally been linked to the sophisticate; it was thought to be a sign of culture. Identification with the state of Texas had, however, not always enjoyed that same connotation. The problem of image was one with which Texas winemakers and the TGGA would have to contend. Even though Texas had within its borders three of the nation's ten largest cities, many Texas vintners still feared that their product would be tied to the image of the Wild West, a place known more for its not-so-smooth whiskey and beer than for fine wines.

Some people were also likely to view Texas wines as a novelty and not something to be taken seriously. Several growers noted that Texas wines had done very well in blind taste tests, but when people were told that the wines were from

Texas, their interest seemed to wane. It was, therefore, crucial to convince potential consumers that high-quality wines could, and did, come from Texas.

The members of the TGGA were divided on how best to reach consumers and how any limited advertising appropriation should be used. Some argued that they should forgo advertising and concentrate solely on consumer sales promotions. These promotions could be of two types. First, attractive displays could be set up in liquor stores and supermarkets. These displays would stress the high quality of Texas wines. An attractive, medium-sized in-store display would cost in the $8 to $12 per display range. The second type of consumer promotion could use tasting booths at state fairs and other large gatherings. These would encourage people to taste Texas wines and learn firsthand of their quality.

The growers who favored consumer advertising argued that the sales promotion approach would miss a large segment of potential consumers and would do little to overcome their image problem. They stressed that media advertising was the best method of promoting Texas wines.

A major drawback to consumer advertising was the fear that the TGGA's message would get lost in the huge amount of wine advertising. Budgets for advertising wine had been growing at phenomenal rates. In 1979, $136.6 million was spent on wine advertising. This was more than twice the amount spent just two years earlier. On the average, the industry had been spending just over $.31 on advertising per gallon of wine sold. Gallo alone, the industry leader, spent over $20 million in 1979, with over 75 percent of it going to network television. Although these were national figures and the TGGA planned to concentrate on just Texas, any potential advertising campaign might still look very small when compared with their competitors.

Two charcteristics stand out in terms of wine advertising. First, the majority of wine advertis-

TABLE 8
Wine Advertising Expenditures by Media in 1979

Media	Millions of Dollars	Percent
Magazine	17.0	12.5
Newspaper	4.9	3.6
Outdoor	.1	—
Total print	220	16.1
Spot TV	36.6	26.8
Network TV	66.7	48.8
Spot radio	10.1	7.4
Network radio	1.2	.9
Total broadcast	114.6	83.9
Grand total	136.6	100.0

Source: The Wine Marketing Handbook, 1980.

TABLE 9
Magazine Advertising Expenditures by Vintners by Month in 1979

Month	Thousands of Dollars	Percent
January	425.8	2.5
February	238.5	1.4
March	425.8	2.5
April	1,396.7	8.2
May	1,618.1	9.5
June	1,039.0	6.1
July	647.2	3.8
August	408.8	2.4
September	1,124.2	6.6
October	3,372.5	19.8
November	3,491.7	20.5
December	2,844.4	16.7

Source: The Wine Marketing Handbook, 1980.

ing was placed in the broadcast media. Over 75 percent of all wine advertising dollars in 1979 was spent on television and an additional 8.3 percent went to radio. Table 8 presents a breakdown of wine advertising by media.

Second, wine advertising was heavily concentrated during the last quarter of the calendar year. Over half of all the advertising dollars invested went for ads during the holiday period. Table 9 presents a breakdown of magazine advertising expenditures by month in 1979.

QUESTIONS FOR DISCUSSION

1. How sound is the TGGA's decision to concentrate initially on the Texas market? What other markets would logically be attractive? Why?

2. Should the TGGA develop an advertising campaign for the upcoming year?

3. Who should the TGGA's target market be? Which potential target groups are most critical at this point in time? What should the TGGA try to accomplish with advertising during the next year?

4. What total advertising appropriation would be most realistic for promotion and advertising of Texas wines during the coming year? How much of this allocation should be budgeted across each of the major budget categories?

SECTION 5
CREATIVE CONSIDERATIONS IN ADVERTISING

Much of the attention focused on advertising centers on the creative execution—the specific television or radio commercial, the specific full-page, four-color magazine advertisement. This emphasis is somewhat to be expected since whether or not the target market responds to the individual advertisement is largely determined by how creative the ad is. "Creativity" very likely is the most important aspect of the advertising effort because increasingly it is the promise and the presentation, rather than the product, that determines success or failure for a marketer. The widespread availability of production technology has made it difficult to introduce products that are truly innovations competitors cannot emulate. Hence, the strategy for successful marketing often becomes differentiation on a nonproduct basis—which typically requires creating brand preference through advertising.

Though advertising management is vitally interested in developing a competitive advantage through creative advertising, the direct responsibility for this task is usually assigned to a creative specialist who works for an advertising agency. Management's main contribution is to provide appropriate background information and to make certain that all advertising is consistent with the overall promotion objectives of the firm. The process of creating the advertising message begins and ends with the Advertising Manager. The agency's function is to develop a statement of advertising creative strategy (an overall plan) and the translation or execution of the plan (the actual commercials or advertisements). If the plan and advertisements are compatible with the advertiser's larger promotion objectives, the agency's work is accepted and the creative work is then delivered to the target market via the media. If, on the other hand, management finds the creative strategy and/or the execution inconsistent with objectives, the agency's efforts are either completely rejected or modified.

Advertising Managers rarely become directly involved in the creation of advertising messages, yet the effectiveness of the advertising campaign depends on their understanding of the importance of creative strategy. If an advertiser's overall creative strategy is weak or incorrect, it is highly improbable that any series of commercials or advertisements based on that strategy will be effective.

Because creative strategy should develop from an understanding of the marketing factors surrounding the organization, the most effective way to decide on creative strategy is first to make a careful evaluation of this environment. This phase, commonly known as a situation analysis, requires the systematic gathering of information about the consumer, the market, the product or service, the competition, and so on.

After the creative strategy has been agreed on, the advertising agency can create the symbols that best translate the main selling idea of that strategy into an appropriate message for the target audience. Marketers rely heavily on the creative expertise and experience of advertising agencies because there are so many alternative execution possibilities. Questions about *message structure* (one-sided versus two-sided approaches, use of fear appeals, use of humor, long versus short copy, and so on), about *visual aspects* (photography or illustration, color or black and white, layout design and the like), and about *placement* (position in the media, unit of space or time, and so forth) are all important. The advertising agency relies on past experience and research in developing what it thinks will be the most effective way of generating prospect interest and motivation. The Advertising Manager's task is to evaluate the agency's recommendations.

It is extremely difficult to determine the precise effects of a particular creative strategy and its execution before it is used. Therefore, the following cases provide you with an opportunity to develop skills and judgment in two key areas: formulating statements of creative strategy and evaluating the appropriateness of recommended strategies and executions.

19
SPRINT COMMUNICATIONS, INC.

Mr. Philip Gonsher, District Manager of Consumer Sales for Sprint Communications, sat in his office reviewing industry and company reports relating to the telephone industry.[1] As a relatively new and small competitor in the long-distance telecommunications industry, Sprint Communications is concerned with analyzing its various marketing environments as a means of discovering the best competitive advantage for Sprint in the future. Currently, Sprint's unique advantage is its ability to offer lower long-distance rates than those of AT&T. However, as both government and competitive pressures increase in the industry, Mr. Gonsher is contemplating Sprint's future reactions to likely changes in the competitive environment.

TELECOMMUNICATIONS INDUSTRY

History

Alexander Graham Bell and Thomas A. Watson were ultimately to affect the lives of all Americans and most people in the world when they invented the telephone in 1875. The original telephone invented by these two men has been reinvented many times since then by the Bell Telephone Laboratories. In July 1878 there were only 10,755 telephones in service; by 1976 there were approximately 145 million phones in the United States. Also, in 1976 the AT&T Long Lines Department handled over 12 million interstate telephone calls on an average day.

Telecommunications is a regulated industry. The primary objective of the Communications Act of 1934, which created the Federal Communications Commission, was to ensure the availability of universal, affordable telephone service. The FCC was directed to regulate with the

This case was prepared by Mary Ann Stutts, Southwest Texas State University.

"public interest" as its main consideration. Since 1934 this commitment to the public interest has caused the FCC and the courts to open markets formerly monopolized by telephone companies to competition for such items as customer premises equipment (such as telephone sets) and long-distance service.

In 1978 the Supreme Court ruled that a specialized common carrier (SCC) could provide any service that the FCC had not specifically barred it from providing. A series of Federal Court decisions in 1977 and 1978 confirmed that specialized common carriers could provide long-distance services similar to those provided by AT&T and other local telephone companies. These local telephone companies must provide the local interconnections between the specialized carrier's switch terminals and their customers' telephones. An example of a residential long-distance phone call from Phoenix to Chicago via a specialized common carrier and the Bell System long-distance network is shown in Exhibit 1.

In 1980 the FCC joined the courts in their feelings that the public interest would best be served if all interstate telecommunications services were allowed to be provided competitively. The FCC also proposed total deregulation of telecommunications services provided by competitive carriers. However, the future of total deregulation is uncertain because of the resumption of the Justice Department's AT&T antitrust trial in 1981.

Structure of the Industry

There are 23 Bell System companies that provide service to about 80 percent of the telephones in the United States with the remainder being served by approximately 1,450 independent telephone companies. AT&T's Long Lines Department provides most of the interconnec-

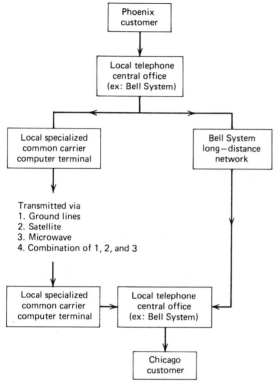

EXHIBIT 1

Long-Distance Choices—Residential Customer Call
from Phoenix to Chicago
Source: Adapted from Telecommunications, Standard &
Poor's Industry Surveys, March 26, 1981, p. T18.

tions among the Bell System and independent
exchanges and operates the AT&T long-distance network. Alternative sources of long-distance services have now emerged with specialized common carriers offering long-distance
services over their own facilities (such as satellites, microwave, and so on) and in competition
with AT&T.

Industry Growth. Even amid the uncertainties
of deregulation, the telephone industry continues to expand. Traditional telephone company[2] revenues (excluding SCC) exceeded $61
billion in 1980, compared with about $55.7

billion in 1979 (Table 1). During 1979 local
services provided approximately 44 percent of
telephone company revenues and long-distance
52 percent. Other revenues, such as fees from
directory advertising, contributed the remainder.

The telephone industry is largely recession-re-
sistant. From 1971 through 1980, industry revenues increased at a compound annual rate of
about 12 percent. AT&T's local revenues increased at an annual rate of 9.9 percent and
long-distance revenues grew by 13.4 percent a
year during 1976–1980. For other independent
telephone companies, local revenues rose by an
average of 10.4 percent a year for 1976–1979,
and long-distance revenues climbed at an 18
percent annual rate. As shown in Table 2, the
independent telephone companies' share of total
telephone revenues has been increasing while
AT&T's has declined.

Future Expansion. Steady growth is projected
for telephone revenues over the next several
years. This growth will also include an increasing
number of subscribers on the local level and a
rise in long-distance call volume (Table 3). It has
been projected that local-service revenues
should increase at an annual rate of more than
13 percent to nearly $40 billion by the end of
1985, with the long-distance market increasing
14 percent a year to more than $68 billion over
the same period. Local revenues will probably
continue to go to the regulated monopoly
carriers, and the SCCs are expected to gain an
increasing share of long-distance revenues.
Thus, it would appear that opportunities available in most markets should be sufficient to
support continued growth by both traditional
companies and the specialized common carriers.

The SCCs typically compete with AT&T's
long-distance telephone network on the basis of
lower prices[3] and similar services (that is, billing
record, away-from-home calling). According to
AT&T, SCC revenues may have reached $360
million in 1980. MCI, the largest SCC, ac-

TABLE 1
Revenues and Expenses of Large Telephone Companies (in millions)

	Operating Revenues				Total Oper. Exp.	Net Oper. Revs.	Taxes	Net Oper. Inc.	Net Inc.
Year	Local	Toll	Misc.[a]	Total					
1979	22,744	26,258	1,602	50,604	33,477	17,127	6,930	9,084	6,152
R1978	20,762	23,310	1,587	45,659	29,351	16,309	7,225	8,181	6,139
1977	19,006	20,351	1,379	40,736	26,111	14,825	6,400	7,295	5,251
1976	17,348	18,051	1,200	36,599	23,316	13,282	5,788	6,681	4,437
1975	15,493	15,530	1,047	32,070	20,665	11,405	4,806	5,790	3,631
1974	14,108	13,890	943	28,941	18,420	10,521	4,935	5,296	3,595
1973	12,619	12,541	875	23,146	14,868	8,213	3,920	4,034	2,875
1972	11,437	10,834	875	23,146	14,868	8,213	3,920	4,034	2,875
1971	10,127	9,559	724	20,410	13,253	7,158	3,324	3,487	2,537
1970	9,054	8,385	661	18,100	11,618	6,482	3,472	3,010	2,341
1969	8,369	7,804	650'	16,823	10,294	6,528	3,618	2,813	2,261

Note: Data are for Class A carriers only, representing over 90% of gross operating revenues of the telephone industry.
[a]Includes earth station revenues.
R = Revised.
Source: Telecommunications, *Standard & Poor's Industry Surveys,* March 26, 1981, p. T15.

TABLE 2
Independent's Share of Telephone Market

Year	Number of Independent Companies	Independents' Operating Revenues (thousand $)	Percent of Total Telephone Operating Revenues	Independents' Telephones in Service (thousands)	Percent of Total Telephones in Service
E1980	1,450	10,500,000	17.3	34,900	19.4
1979	1,488	9,240,000	16.9	33,226	18.9
1978	1,527	8,085,000	16.2	31,549	18.7
1977	1,556	7,115,000	16.0	29,675	18.3
1976	1,590	6,300,000	15.8	28,209	18.2
1975	1,618	5,500,000	15.7	26,823	18.0
1974	1,641	4,920,000	15.5	25,826	17.9
1973	1,695	4,316,990	15.2	24,351	17.6
1972	1,758	3,788,699	15.0	22,796	17.3
1971	1,805	3,322,679	14.9	21,444	17.1
1970	1,841	2,891,814	14.3	20,312	16.9
1965	2,421	1,638,264	12.6	15,016	16.0
1960	3,299	1,008,451	11.1	11,340	15.3
1955	4,700	684,561	9.7	8,406	14.9
1950	5,529	314,078	8.6	6,338	14.7

E = Estimated.
Source: Telecommunications, *Standards & Poor's Industry Surveys,* March 26, 1981, p. T17.

TABLE 3
Calling Volume Growth

	1975	1976	1977	1978	1979	1975–79 Growth Rate
Long-distance calls (mil.)	R10,938	11,815	13,000	R14,649	16,224	10.6
Percent year-to-year change	R5.2	R8.0	10.0	12.7	10.8	—
Customer dialed (percent)	88.0	90.3	91.9	93.5	95.0	—
Overseas calls (mil.)	190	220	253	309	372	18.3
Percent year-to-year change	11.8	15.8	15.0	22.1	20.4	—
WATS messages (mil.)	1,942	2,451	3,046	3,631	4,244	21.6
Percent year-to-year change	21.0	26.2	24.3	19.2	16.9	—

R = Revised.
Source: Telecommunications, *Standard & Poor's Industry Surveys,* March 26, 1981, p. T16.

counted for approximately $234 million of that total revenue. Revenue growth of as much as 50 percent a year through 1985 are projected for the SCCs. Even that rate of expansion would give the SCCs total 1985 revenues of about $2.7 billion or only one-tenth of the long-distance revenues AT&T reported for 1980. The SCCs would have a share of approximately 4 percent of the $68 billion long-distance market projected for 1985.

Competition

Approximately 180 million residential long-distance calls are made in the United States each month. The total market for long-distance service in 1980 was more than $30 billion. Competition in this long-distance market is now divided among five major companies: AT&T, MCI, ITT (International Telephone and Telegraph), Sprint (Southern Pacific Communications Company), and Western Union Corporation. A comparison of the rates and services of these five companies, made in January of 1981, is shown in Table 4.

In 1980 the Bell System's revenues were nearly $50.8 billion, an 11.8 percent increase over 1979. Basic monthly rates and equipment charges to businesses accounted for 37 percent of that total, and 4.3 percent came from local message charges. Long-distance calls, both intra and interstate, represented 47 percent; the remainder came from WATS, private line service for business and government, and from directory advertising.

MCI is the only one of the four SCCs that is committed solely to the communications business. Southern Pacific (Sprint) is a major railroad holding company; ITT is an international conglomerate with extensive communications expertise; and Western Union is an established communications carrier with a nationwide network. MCI was among the first to enter the deregulated long-distance market and through its advertising has maintained a highly visible image. It also has the largest market share among the SCCs (approximately 65 percent in 1980). MCI had a customer base of 40,000 in 1980; by 1981 that had jumped to 425,000, and new subscribers are joining the system at the rate of 35,000 to 40,000 a month. The MCI system currently includes more than 4,000 cities. Although all MCI advertising is directed toward residential users, a spillover effect keeps the number of business customers growing (from 40,000 to 100,000 in a little more than a year).

TABLE 4
Comparison: AT&T versus Four Alternative Phone Services

Company and Plan	Range of Costs for Calls of 100 to 3000 miles (cents per minute)			Monthly Change for Service	Minimum Monthly Charge	Initial Setup Charge	Billing Units, in Seconds (Initial/Subsequent)	Extra Charge for Away-from-Home Calls	Number of Metropolitan Areas Now Served
	Day (8 A.M.–5 P.M.)	Evening (5 P.M.–11 P.M.)	Night (11 P.M.–8 A.M.) and weekend						
AT&T (Direct dial)	30–40[a]	20–26[b]	12–16[c]	None	None	None	60/60	[d]	All
ITT city call[c]	26–40	17–26[f]	5–8	$10	None	$30	30/1	None	105
ITT city call I	Not offered	[f]	5–8	$5	None	$10	30/1	None	105
MCI Execunet[e]	26–35	11–14	11–14	$10	None	None	60/60	$5 a month[g]	86
MCI Execunet Supersaver	Not offered	11–14	11–14	$5	None	None	60/60	$5 a month[g]	86
Southern Pacific Sprint[e]	23–33[h]	9–13[i]	9–13[i]	$10	$25	None	30/30	None	138
Southern Pacific Sprint Ltd.	Not offered	9–13[i]	9–13[i]	$5	None	$15	30/30	None	138
Western Union Metro I[e]	25–35[j]	12–16[k]	9–12[l]	None	$40[m]	None	30/30	$2 a month	29
Western Union Off-Peak Metro I	Not offered	12–16[k]	9–12[l]	None	$10[m]	None	30/30	$2 a month	29

[a]First minute, 45–57 cents.
[b]First minute, 29–37 cents. Night rates apply Saturday evening.
[c]First minute, 18–22 cents. Evening rates apply from 5 P.M. to 11 P.M. on Sunday.
[d]Operator-assisted calls billed to credit card or home phone are at much higher rates.
[e]24-hour service designed primarily for business.
[f]Rate is 10–16 cents from 8 P.M. to 11 P.M. City Call I not avilable from 5 P.M. to 8 P.M.
[g]For credit card. Calls in evening and night periods for higher rates.
[h]Plus 15 cents a call.
[i]Plus 10 cents a call.
[j]Day period is 7 A.M. to 6 P.M.
[k]Evening period is 6 P.M. to 11 P.M.
[l]Night period is 11 P.M. to 7 A.M.
[m]After first month.
Source: *Consumer Reports*, March 1981, p. 166.

ITT City Call has 40,000 customers and Western Union's Metro I Service has only 5,000.

SPRINT

Background

Southern Pacific Communications Company (SPC) was originally part of Southern Pacific Railroad, whose heritage dates back to 1862. In that year the Pacific Railway Act chartered Central Pacific Railroad, SP's predecessor, to construct a railway and telegraph line. Today the railroad operates one of the largest private microwave networks in the country. When a series of Federal Court and FCC decisions dating back to 1969 opened the telecommunications industry to competition, it was only natural for Southern Pacific to form a company to become part of this dynamic and growing industry.

SPC was established in 1970, with the original network following the railroad's right-of-way from San Francisco to Dallas. Today that network has been expanded greatly and all of SPC's carrier equipment and personnel are totally independent of the railroad.

Following the critical Federal Court decisions of 1977 and 1978, which stated that specialized common carriers could provide long-distances services similar to those provided by AT&T, SPC entered the new market with the introduction of Sprint V, a low-cost business long-distance service. SPC was able to expand its customer base from 977 to more than 16,000 in 1978.

Marketing Position

In addition to Sprint V, SPC offers a residential service called Sprint LTD. (For a detailed explanation of the services offered by the Sprint System and Sprint Options available, see Exhibits 2 and 3). Sales increased 98 percent from 1978 to 1979, jumping from $49.9 million to $99 million. The number of cities served by the Sprint System in 1981 had expanded to 170.

TABLE 5
Number of Sprint System Customers

	1980	1981
Sprint V (business)	70,000	90,000
Sprint LTD (residential)	10,000	140,000
Total	80,000	230,000

Essentially, anyone with long-distance telephone bills of $15 or more a month is considered to be a potential customer for the Sprint System. Table 5 shows the number of business and residential Sprint customers in 1980 and 1981. The largest increase was in residential customers; the number of customers rose from 10,000 in 1980 to 140,000 in 1981.

Advertising and Promotional Efforts

AT&T increased its advertising expenditures 18 percent in 1980 to an estimated $259,170,000. Long-distance lines received the largest share of advertising in 1980 with a budget of $39,886,300. This amount was down from $44,365,800 in 1979. Regional Bell System ad budgets in 1980 ranged from a high of $8,316,400 for Southwestern Bell Telephone Company to a low of $75,000 for New York and New Jersey Bell Telephone Companies. Table 6 shows a media breakdown of the 1980 advertising budget allocated to long-distance lines.

Prior to entry of the SCCs into the telecommunications industry, AT&T advertisements,

TABLE 6
Media Allocation of 1980 AT&T Long-Distance Budget

Network TV	$23,015,900
Magazines	10,532,500
Other (nonspecified media)	6,337,900
Total	$39,886,300

Source: "100 Leading National Advertisers," *Advertising Age,* September 10, 1981, p. 24.

EXHIBIT 2
Sprint System

Sprint V	A 24-hour long-distance telephone service for business users, featuring rates as much as 30 percent lower than the phone company's.
	A Sprint call first travels through local phone lines to the SPC technical operating center, where it is switched by SPC equipment to the microwave relays or satellite channels for transmission to the target city. There, the call is switched back to the city's local phone lines and directed to its destination.
	Sprint is easy to use and requires only a push-button phone. By dialing a local access number, the user is connected to the Sprint switching system. Next, a confidential authorization code is entered by the user, followed by the area code and number being called.
Sprint LTD	Because the Sprint network receives only light use after business hours, in October 1979 SPC made the network available to consumers during this time. LTD residential service is available between the hours of 5:00 P.M. and 8:00 A.M. Monday through Friday, all day weekends and selected holidays. By using this service, consumers can save as much as 50 percent on their long-distance calls.
In-Sprint	This is SPC's low-cost alternative to collect calls, inward WATS, and credit card calls. Unlike inward WATS, however, the number of calls that may be received simultaneously is limited only by the number of regular local telephone lines in place. In addition, a detailed listing of each call received is provided with the monthly invoice.
	Callers from any part of the country served by the Sprint system can call in to a designated long-distance number at no charge to them. By their simply dialing the local access number followed by a special code, SPC's computerized switching equipment translates that code into the ten-digit long-distance number being called.

Source: Southern Pacific Communications Company Media Facts, SP Communications, Burlingame, CA, 1979.

both print and broadcast, were aimed primarily at creating generic demand for long-distance telephone usage. This was accomplished with warm, emotional appeals such as the "Reach Out and Touch Someone" and "Old Friends" campaigns. A variation of this theme, and a possible response to price advertising by competitors, is shown in Exhibit 4.

MCI's advertising budget for 1980–1981 was $15 million, double that of the previous year. MCI has used different media in different regions of the country, primarily spot television, radio, newspapers, and direct mail. For example, statement stuffers are often included in customers' monthly bills informing them of even lower "holiday specials" such as Halloween or Father's Day calling. Creatively, MCI has focused on a twist on AT&T's "Reach Out and Touch Someone," by adding the phrase, "But do it for half of what Bell charges" (Exhibit 5).

ITT focuses its advertising efforts on small-to-medium-sized business customers, with 30-, 60-,

EXHIBIT 3
Sprint Options

Speedial	With this abbreviated dialing option, a customer's frequently called numbers—10 digits including area code—are each replaced by a three-digit code. This simplifies the dialing process for the busy user.
Accounting Codes	Available in packages of 99, the two-digit accounting code is ideal for offices where many clients are being serviced (law firms, ad agencies, P.R. firms, etc.). All that the customer need do is dial the two digits at the end of the number called. Accounting codes facilitate record keeping and budget allocations since, when the monthly bill arrives, there is a separate itemization of numbers called for each accounting code.
Sprintdialer	This automatic dialing service with computer memory dials the local access number and the authorization code—13 digits in all—with one push of a button. The Sprintdialer can be attached to rotary dial phones and enables access to the Sprint network (which could normally not be reached via this type of phone).

Source: Southern Pacific Communications Company Media Facts, SP Communications, Burlingame, CA, 1979.

and 120-second spots on a wide range of TV shows. In print it has used *The Wall Street Journal* and business and sports sections of other newspapers. Western Union's Metro I has used only direct mail.

Sprint's advertising budget increased from $5 million in 1980 to $15 million in 1981. The budget was allocated among television, radio, regional magazines (such as *Time* and *Newsweek*), in-flight magazines, local newspapers, and direct mail. Similar to those of MCI and other SCCs, Sprint's print ads stress "cost-savings" over the Bell System (Exhibit 6). Ads tend to be of an institutional nature, implying that both business and residential users can benefit by acquiring the services of the Sprint System.

SPRINT COMMUNICATIONS CHALLENGES

Even though the market for long-distance services is expected to expand rapidly enough to accommodate moderate growth by both old and new competitors, Mr. Gonsher is wondering what the basis of a future advertising campaign for Sprint should be. What will happen to the current Sprint competitive advantage of price if AT&T lowers its long-distance rates to compete with those of Sprint? Should Sprint narrow its target market definition and concentrate more on heavy users of long-distance service? Does Sprint possess any unique service attributes that could help create a favorable company image?

Mr. Gonsher is considering these and other questions as he prepares a marketing and advertising plan for presentation to top management of the Sprint System.

ENDNOTES

1. Material for this case was taken from the following sources:
   Telecommunications, *Standard & Poor's Industry Surveys*, March 26, 1981, p. T9–T20.

EXHIBIT 4
A Bell System Print Advertisement

EXHIBIT 5
An MCI Print Advertisement

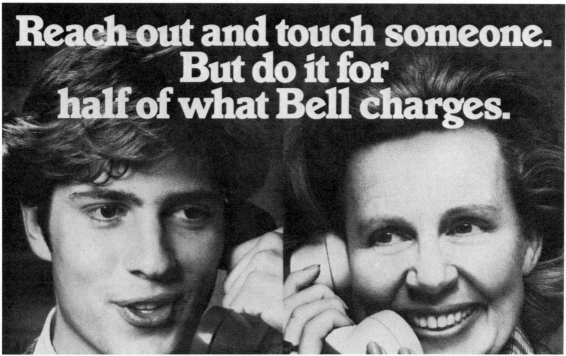

Reach out and touch someone. But do it for half of what Bell charges.

The same system that big business uses to save millions on its long distance bills is now available in your home.

For years now, more than half the Fortune 500 have been turning from Bell to MCI for their long distance calls.

In all, 40,000 companies, large and small, across the country make a million calls a day on MCI and cut the cost of their long distance calls anywhere from 30% to 60%.

But the big news is that you can now get those same MCI long distance savings on your own home phone.

LONG DISTANCE CALLS	MINUTES	BELL	MCI
Denver to Chicago	10	$2.31	$1.34
Evergreen to Phoenix	5	1.20	.64
Denver to Salt Lake City	55	12.24	6.46
Boulder to Omaha	17	3.86	2.09
Denver to New York City	10	2.44	1.40
Littleton to Cleveland	26	6.18	3.56
Denver to Indianapolis	20	4.78	2.70
Englewood to Atlanta	11	2.67	1.51
Lakewood to Dallas	6	1.43	.78
Aurora to Los Angeles	3	.76	.40
Denver to Kansas City	12	2.75	1.51
Denver to Boston	30	7.12	4.25

Rates show comparative pricing between Bell's evening rate and MCI's evening/weekend rate. Final rate authorities on all tariffed services are MCI Tariff FCC 1 and AT&T Tariff 263.

Nothing to install. All you need is a push-button phone and a desire to cut your long distance phone bills.

The way it works: You just have to punch a few extra numbers on your push-button phone.

Everything else is the same. Except for the fact that you save a lot of money.

*Pending FCC approval.

If you don't already have a push-button phone, your local phone company can put one in for a small monthly charge.

That cost can be more than made up the first time you place a long distance call on MCI. Because weekdays, MCI savings average 30%. Evenings, savings average 50%. And on Sunday evenings, MCI also saves you an average of 50% over Bell's rate cut.

Special events like free calls all day on Christmas and Mother's Day.

On top of the large savings, last year MCI gave its customers an entire day of long distance calls absolutely free on Christmas. This year, we're giving free calls on Mother's Day.*All day.

How many times have you put off calling for fear of what next month's phone bill will look like? No more.

Who should use MCI?

Look over your last few months' long distance bills. If they are running more than $25 a month, you can obviously benefit from the savings MCI can give you.

Since there is a $10-a-month fee (really a computer access charge), if you're only a light user of long distance service, it stands to reason you might not be interested. But if you're the kind of person for whom long distance call have become a necessity, nothing's come along that can be as much help to you as MCI.

For business, the savings on calls are the same.

MCI's rates can be lower than Bell's famous WATS line. And with an MCI credit card, your employees can take advantage of the MCI savings when they're out of the office, traveling on business.

Truth is, you haven't been talking too much. You've just been paying too much.

Naturally, with a new idea like this, you probably have some questions.

For a free brochure that answers every conceivable question about MCI, just fill out and send in the coupon below.

Or call us at 861-5808.

All things considered, the call should be the most profitable phone call you'll ever make.

MCI
The nation's long distance phone company.

Please send me more information on how to cut the cost of my long distance calls.

For Home ☐   For Business ☐

Name_____

Address_____

City_____ State_____ Zip Code_____

Telephone Number_____

MCI Telecommunications
1700 Broadway, Denver, CO 80290

RM-2

EXHIBIT 6
Sprint Print Ad

LONG DISTANCE CALLS CAN COST YOU HALF AS MUCH WHEN YOU'VE GOT OUR NUMBER.

(800) 521-4949

In Michigan (313) 645-6020

If you want to know how to beat the high cost of calling, give us a call.

We'll tell you all about Sprint, a unique service that saves you big money on long distance calls.

Here's how it works:

By dialing a local telephone number, you reach the Sprint network. Then you enter your personal code, the area code and number of the person you're calling. It's that simple. You are instantly in touch with a coast-to-coast network that electronically routes your calls to thousands of communities.

Here's when it works:

For many people, the best time for a good talk is in the evening. That's when Sprint saves you the most. Up to 50% on your long distance calls.

And since Sprint is part of the $5 billion Southern Pacific organization, you can rest easy, knowing you're served by a substantial, reliable company.

You can enjoy these savings during the business day as well. Just ask about Sprint V. It gives you unlimited use of the Sprint network, 24 hours a day, seven days a week. And saves you from 20 to 50% over Bell's rates, even when Bell's rates are down.

So give us a call. And get our number. We'll keep you in touch for half as much.

800/521-4949 (In Michigan (313) 645-6020)

"100 Leading National Advertisers," *Advertising Age,* September 10, 1981, p. 24.

"Bypassing Ma Bell," *Consumer Reports,* March 1981, pp. 164–67.

Roberta Reynes, "Dialing for Dollars," *Marketing Communications,* pp. 56–59.

H. M. Boettinger, *The Telephone Book* (Croton-on-Hudson, N.Y.: Riverwood Publishers Ltd., 1977).

2. Traditional telephone companies include AT&T and other independent telephone companies, excluding specialized common carriers.

3. There are various explanations for the lower rates of the SCCs. The primary reason that the SCCs are able to charge lower long-distance rates than AT&T is related to local telephone service. The SCCs do not provide any local telephone service. As a regulated monopoly, AT&T's long-distance rates have been set artifically high to subsidize the basic monthly service charge for local service provided by AT&T. Additionally, SCCs have not had to invest heavily in research and development, as did AT&T over the past hundred years. Rather, the SCCs have been able to capitalize on much newer technology in the telecommunications field such as satellites and microwave transmissions.

QUESTIONS FOR DISCUSSION

1. What should Mr. Gonsher recommend as a service positioning statement for Sprint?

2. What service attributes should be used to differentiate Sprint from competitors?

3. What should be the new advertising budget? How should this budget be allocated?

4. What should Mr. Gonsher recommend as a new creative strategy for Sprint?

One of the fastest growing industries in the United States in the past ten years has been the direct marketing of a wide variety of consumer goods and services. Today it is not unusual for most of us to "shop by mail" (or use some other form of direct marketing) for almost anything imaginable. Among the most well-known and successful direct marketers is Neiman-Marcus, a retail department store that also discovered the additional profits of selling such unusual gifts as elephants, airplanes, and $1,000 boxes of chocolate candy—all by mail.

But Neiman-Marcus is certainly not alone. There are literally thousands of companies selling via direct marketing. One of these companies is American Import Corporation. American Import was started in 1969 by Tom and Sally Struven. They started their business by importing a line of Japanese-made sports watches and selling them for $29.95 with advertisements in *The Wall Street Journal, The Rotarian, Elks Magazine,* and the *Legionnaire*. At that time comparable watches were retailing for $49.95 to $79.95. The Struvens were successful, and in the next few years they continued to expand their product lines, compiled their own customer list, and eventually issued a shopping catalog. Although the catalog was successful, they discovered that the most successful way to introduce a new item was to advertise it separately.

THE MICRORECORDER

In early 1980 Tom and Sally Struven made arrangements to purchase 50,000 microrecorders from a Korean manufacturer. These recorders measured $1 \times 2\frac{1}{2} \times 5\frac{1}{2}$ inches and were supplied with a built-in microphone, a vinyl carrying case, a wrist strap, and one

This case was prepared by Charles H. Patti.

30-minute microcassette. The microrecorder is operated by 4 AA batteries or an optional AC adapter.

This type of recorder became very popular in the past few years, particularly among businesspeople. A traveling executive or salesperson could dictate letters on the microrecorder and then have a secretary transcribe them onto letterheads. The microrecorder is also ideal as an audio note pad, substituting for paper and pencil note-taking.

PRICING THE MICRORECORDER

The first microrecorder was brought to the mass market in 1975 and it retailed for $400. Since then, several companies entered the market and today there are approximately twelve major brands available through traditional retail locations. The prices of microrecorders vary by the sophistication of the individual piece of equipment; however, the retail price range is $90 to $250.

American Import Corporation decided to offer its microrecorder for $39.95. Although American Import's product was a technically simple product, it did a very capable and reliable job of performing the basic task of recording and playing back the human voice.

PROMOTION OF THE MICRORECORDER

With several years of direct marketing experience behind them, the Struvens decided to introduce the microrecorder via direct marketing. They were planning an advertising campaign in *Barron's, The Wall Street Journal,* the *New York Times,* the *Chicago Tribune,* the *Los Angeles Times,* and a spot television campaign in selected markets.

A Completely New Microcassette Recorder... From The Originators Of Microcassette Sound Systems.

Pearlcorder X-01. It's packed with innovations that you would expect from the world leader in microcassette sound systems. We've used all electronic controls. And put them on the front where they should be for easy operation.

Naturally superb Pearlcorder quality is one of the basic components. That's what our fine reputation is built on and has been since we originated microcassette sound systems in 1969.

We call it X-01, but you'll probably call it the best microcassette recorder you've listened to.

It's at your dealer now.

EXHIBIT 1
A Print Advertisement for Pearlcorder

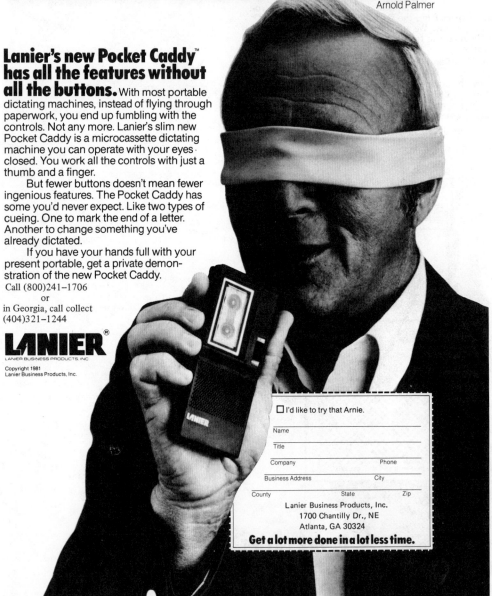

"TRY THIS WITH ANY OTHER DICTATING MACHINE."

Arnold Palmer

Lanier's new Pocket Caddy™ has all the features without all the buttons. With most portable dictating machines, instead of flying through paperwork, you end up fumbling with the controls. Not any more. Lanier's slim new Pocket Caddy is a microcassette dictating machine you can operate with your eyes closed. You work all the controls with just a thumb and a finger.

But fewer buttons doesn't mean fewer ingenious features. The Pocket Caddy has some you'd never expect. Like two types of cueing. One to mark the end of a letter. Another to change something you've already dictated.

If you have your hands full with your present portable, get a private demonstration of the new Pocket Caddy.
Call (800)241–1706
or
in Georgia, call collect
(404)321–1244

LANIER®
LANIER BUSINESS PRODUCTS, INC.

Copyright 1981
Lanier Business Products, Inc.

☐ I'd like to try that Arnie.

Name

Title

Company   Phone

Business Address   City

County   State   Zip

Lanier Business Products, Inc.
1700 Chantilly Dr., NE
Atlanta, GA 30324

Get a lot more done in a lot less time.

EXHIBIT 2
A Print Advertisement for Lanier

CREATIVE APPROACHES

The Struvens were very excited about the sales prospects of their new microrecorder, and while the media portion of their advertising campaign was rather obvious, they could not decide on the best creative approach for the product.

Several possible themes came to mind. For example, should the product be sold on the basis of its comparatively low price? Its simplicity of operation? Its flexibility of use? Its size/convenience? Perhaps they should use a competitive-comparison strategy? How about their no-risk, 30-day trial? Exhibits 1 and 2 present examples of typical print advertisements for two of the leading selling brands of microcassette recorders, the Pearlcorder and Lanier.

The products had arrived from Korea. The media schedule had been set. Shipping procedures were established. Contractual arrangements with service organizations had been made. The only obstacle between American Import Corporation and a new source of profits seemed to be the selection of the most promising creative strategy for its new microrecorder.

QUESTIONS FOR DISCUSSION

1. What creative strategy would you recommend to Mr. Struven?
2. Suggest three alternative creative executions of the recommended strategy for a print advertisement.

REPUBLIC STEEL CORPORATION

Republic Steel, a leading U.S. steel-making company headquartered in Cleveland, Ohio, annually produced millions of tons of steel mill products. Among these products were a variety of standard and structural pipe products, one of which was identified as CSR (Continous Stretch Run). Salespeople from nineteen district sales offices throughout the United States sold these pipes to plumbing, heating, and air-conditioning contractors and wholesalers, mechanical contractors, and industrial and general mill supply houses. Specifically, the market for CSR pipe consisted of:

1. Plumbing, heating, and air conditioning contractors (including mechanical contractors engaged in the special trades and involved with high-rise industrial, institutional, and multiple-unit residence construction).
2. Construction market—CSR wholesalers.
3. Plumbing and heating wholesalers (engaged in the wholesale distribution of plumbing and heating supplies including pipe, valves, fittings, and fixtures).
4. Air-conditioning and refrigeration wholesalers (wholesaler distributors of air-conditioning and refrigeration equipment and complete systems).
5. Pipe-fitting and valve specialists. (As opposed to the preceding two types of wholesalers, who handled pipe as well as various kinds of fixtures, the pipe-fitting and valve specialist handled only pipe and the component parts of piping systems.)

The pipe products were an important line upon which Republic Steel depended for a significant portion of its sales volume and profit contributions. Despite a wide variety of sizes

This case was prepared by William E. Schlender, North Texas State University, and Eleanor Brantley Schwartz, University of Missouri—Kansas City.

and specifications, the highly standardized product had strong competition for its 7 percent market share. Republic Steel had little competitive edge. However, management felt Republic did not have the market share it could have, especially with the newest mill, as many salespeople, and as much tonnage capacity as its competitors.

The vice-president of sales pointed out that a 15 percent increase in CSR standard pipe sales for the year would contribute an additional $400,000 toward fixed expenses and gross profits. Two avenues of action were decided upon to stimulate CSR sales and to increase market share: a massive advertising campaign, and a sales incentive contest.

The advertising objectives for the CSR pipe campaign were to:

1. Increase customer awareness of the product's advantages.
2. Establish a distinctive brand awareness and preference for CSR.
3. Demonstrate to wholesalers that Republic Steel supported its sales effort with effective promotional activity.

J.C. FRISBEE, SR., CAMPAIGN

Because most steel companies made about the same product with little distinctive product differentiation, Republic assigned Meldrum and Fewsmith Advertising Agency (M & F) to create a memorable, hard-hitting, attention-getting advertising campaign, something out of the ordinary and different from anyone else's in the industry. Working closely with Republic's advertising department, M & F's creative staff developed what they described as a ridiculous, fictitious family-owned company founded by a stingy, narrow guy whose biggest obsession was to save money—by using CSR pipe.

REPUBLIC

J.C. Frisbee, Sr., solves his pressure problems with CSR!

what a weld!

Freddy Fern, third assistant vice president in charge of J.C. Frisbee Co. efficiency, was under such intense pressure that he was wasting fully two-thirds of his time on trips to the water cooler.

J. C. Sr, hard man that he was, still believed that efficiency begins with a cool head. Suddenly the ideal solution struck him. Hard.

Republic CSR® steel pipe, the well-adjusted pipe! Continuous stretch reduction means perfectly adjusted roundness, straightness, and weld strength. So strong, it stands up to pressure. So free of hard spots that it bends, cuts, and threads to your every whim.

J. C. Sr. had CSR pipe installed from the water cooler to a faucet attached to Freddy's desk. Freddy can't say enough about it.

Which goes to show—when you help make an efficiency expert more efficient, he'll never forget you for it. Republic Steel Corporation, Cleveland, Ohio.

the well-adjusted pipe.

Republic steel

Arrange for our distributor pipe program. Our simple lesson training program is designed to increase your pipe sales and profits. Call your local Republic salesman or write Republic Steel Corporation, Mail Republic Building, P.O. Box 6778, Cleveland, Ohio 44101.

[This paragraph appears only in INDUSTRIAL DISTRIBUTION magazine.]

This double-page, four-color advertisement appears in INDUSTRIAL DISTRIBUTION, April; and SUPPLY HOUSE TIMES, June, 1971.

Meldrum and Fewsmith, Inc./5-1382-A

EXHIBIT 1
Frisbee Campaign Advertisement

A humorous character, J.C. Frisbee, Sr., with all kinds of characteristics attached to him—such as his being an overweight golfer—was suggested to expound the advantages of CSR pipe. The objective for Mr. Frisbee was to create an informal tone and image, humanizing and lightening the customer's concept of the product. Paternalistic, hard-hitting, but lovable, Frisbee was human—loved golf, but also loved running a company and selling CSR pipe. Exhibits 1 to 3 present examples of the four color, two-page-spread ads run during the campaign.

To reach the pipe market, the advertising agency chose the following publications to carry the Frisbee schedule: *Heating, Piping & Air Conditioning, Plant Operating Management, the Contractor, Supply House Times,* and *Industrial Distributor.* M & F was confident that by running the Frisbee campaign in these trade publications, Republic would reach almost all of the important buying influences for CSR pipe.

The Mr. Frisbee campaign was a radical departure from other well-known steel companies' industrial advertisements. Traditionally, industrial advertising was straightforward reassurance that the company and its product could provide the performance the user needed. The product was illustrated, some information was given about it, and a request for inquiries was included. Either "show-and-tell" situations, indicating the solid, respectable character of the seller, or user-satisfaction testimonials in a setting where the product was used were basic themes used to give the image of a safe, dependable, respectable company with which to do business. Many customers, wanting to be informed, not amused, liked this factual orientation.

Republic Steel's previous advertising was typical of industrial advertisements among metal producers with heavy emphasis upon quality, service, and delivery. Would a novel, but

REPUBLIC

J.C. Frisbee, Jr., invents a smooth filing system with CSR!

super smooth

Buried under a mountain of memos, J. C. Frisbee, Jr., executive vice president of J. C. Frisbee Co., woke up to the fact that something had to be done. He couldn't see the top of his desk. His office was a shambles. And besides, where could he put his feet? Suddenly he came up with a smooth solution! Republic CSR* steel pipe, the well-adjusted pipe! Continuous stretch reduction means perfectly adjusted roundness, straightness, and weld strength. So smooth, inside and out! So easy to bend, cut, and thread, it would make the perfect filing system. And it did! Papers never stuck inside the pipe. And the outside finish of CSR blended perfectly with the satin finish of J. C., Jr.'s woodwork.
Which goes to show — we'll go to any length to solve a sticky problem. With superior quality pipe. And with zippy delivery from our distributors. (They're backed by our extensive mill inventory stocks.) Republic Steel Corporation, Cleveland, OH 44101

the
well-adjusted
pipe.

Republicsteel

This double-page, four-color advertisement appears in THE CONTRACTOR, June 15, 1971.

Meldrum and Fewsmith, Inc./S-1381

EXHIBIT 2
Frisbee Campaign Advertisement

drastic, deviation from the usual advertising alienate enough of these customers to affect the campaign's effectiveness and, therefore, Republic's sales and market share? Republic Steel had decided to chance it.

CAMPAIGN RESULTS

Over a two-year period 597 inquiries were received from the publication advertising. These inquiries broke down into 78 letters which congratulated Republic on running the program,

43 requests for Frisbee sales aid items, and the remainder for product literature. Since ads did not request any direct action, Republic considered this response quite favorable.

The Pipe Sales Division believed the program generated enthusiasm among district salespeople, motivating them to spend an increased amount of time on CSR pipe accounts because the blanket solicitation required in each district to capture and maintain a larger share of the market was achieved. This was significant especially in that Republic Steel salespeople sold all of Republic's products, and the Pipe Division

The boys at J.C. Frisbee Co. love CSR pipe.

so bendable.

Nobody noticed Republic CSR® steel pipe at J. C. Frisbee Co. – until J. C. Frisbee Jr. forgot to order a keg/tap for the refreshments at the annual picnic.

Now they know – CSR saved the day, arriving like lightning from a nearby Republic distributor. And so well adjusted! Continuous stretch reduction means perfectly adjusted roundness, smoothness, and straightness. Go free of hard spots that it bends, cuts, and threads to your every whim!

After thorough field testing, the boys agreed: CSR makes for happy times. With consistent quality. And with jippy delivery from distributors who assume the cost of possession and who are backed by Republic's extensive mill inventory stocks.

Which goes to show – you do something nice for people, they'll love you for it. Republic Steel Corporation, Cleveland, OH 44101.

the well-adjusted pipe.

Republicsteel

This double-page, four color advertisement appears in THE CONTRACTOR, July 15, 1971.
Meldrum and Fewsmith, Inc./S-1284

EXHIBIT 3
Frisbee Campaign Advertisement

competed with other sales divisions for the salespeople's time and attention.

None of Republic Steel's advertising was considered a part of the sales process per se. However, the Republic sales staff's enthusiasm about Mr. Frisbee resulted in Mr. Frisbee's being used as the theme for a sales incentive campaign, "CSR Sell-A-Ton Marathon." Mr. Frisbee, as "honorary chairman" for the sales contest, was featured on scoreboards in each district sales office. A monthly memo from J.C. Frisbee gave progress reports and inspirational messages to sustain interest and motivation. Free promotion items carried the Frisbee theme to appeal to authorized wholesalers. Premiums to smaller firms that did not have a budget large enough to promote themselves were also used with the motive that if Republic helped them promote themselves, then they would think favorably of Republic Steel and give CSR pipe their warehouse "shelf space."

The Frisbee ads for Republic Steel were checked for effectiveness through publication readership reports. Results of these studies served as a barometer of success in communicating with customer groups. Nine publication readership reports were received covering ads in the Frisbee series. Meldrum and Fewsmith achieved comparability among the various readership services by translating all studies into the categories of "noted," "read some," and "read most." The Frisbee ads averaged 70 percent "noted," 20 percent "read some," and 14 percent "read most," among all ads in the magazines studies.

In addition, Republic added a direct-mail phase which consisted of two steps; (1) a mailing to a list of present and potential customers, management, and purchasing personnel at industrial wholesaler outlets in Republic's sales districts nationwide (see Exhibit 4), and (2) a mailing to individuals who returned the postal inquiry card (see Exhibit 5). No formal analysis was made of the direct-mail phase of the campaign.

The advertising campaign, along with the sales contest, was lauded as a success with increased tonnage, 77 new customers, and the 15 percent

EXHIBIT 4
Frisbee Sales Promotional Letter

increase in sales objective met. As a result, Republic decided to continue to run the Frisbee campaign in the coming fiscal year to help maintain this increase in sales and market share by reminding the industry that Republic offered the "well-adjusted" CSR pipe.

After Republic and its agency had agreed that the campaign should be continued for another year, Republic's Advertising Manager raised some issues she felt were significant. Although the Ad Manager "had good feelings" about the past effectiveness of the Frisbee campaign, she wondered how long the program would continue to be catchy.

QUESTIONS FOR DISCUSSION

1. Should the Frisbee campaign be extended into the coming year? What about beyond next year?
2. Do the results cited above actually prove the campaign had been as big a success as Republic and its agency believed?
3. What statement of creative strategy could have guided the Frisbee executions?
4. What alternative statements of creative strategy could be considered as possible replacements for the Frisbee campaign? How would executions of these strategies be handled?

Memo from the desk of
J.C. Frisbee

Dear Friend of CSR:

Thanks for requesting my own Official
Frisbee Drinking Team Mug.
I'm pleased to send you one.

It'll sure make your day go smoother. (Just
like Republic CSR, the pipe that pleases!)

So, thanks again. And in behalf of the whole
Frisbee Company family, welcome to our
drinking team!

Best wishes,

J. C. Frisbee, Sr.
President, J.C. Frisbee Company

Republicsteel

EXHIBIT 5
Frisbee Sales Promotional Letter

"Thanks for coming over," waves the familiar, rotund pizza cook on Phoenix late-night television, "to Peter Piper Pizza." That same jocular pizza cook is in reality Anthony Cavolo, the company's chairman, who in just four years has expanded his pizza empire from one to five locations in the Phoenix metropolitan area and is in the process of franchising several others.

Cavolo began in the restaurant business in New York, where he operated a delicatessen for several years. He later added tables and chairs and a take-out service selling buckets of spaghetti, until the business grew to an Italian steak and pasta restaurant. Upon retirement, Cavolo moved to the Phoenix area but eventually became bored and decided to open his own pizza restaurant after sampling the pizza there.

"I was fifty years old when I got here, and I had no intention of starting a whole brand-new career, but that's the way it worked out," reminisced Cavolo, "We looked around and did some research, nothing formal, of course, and we saw the opportunity in the fast-food business." Apparently he was right, as the first location alone sold over 200,000 pizzas last year, and Steve Herrgesell, Peter Piper Pizza's president and Cavolo's son-in-law, forecasts, "This year's sales are expected to top $3 million."

MARKETING BACKGROUND INFORMATION

In recent years Americans have spent about 30 percent of their food dollars in restaurants and about 70 percent in grocery stores. Fast-food restaurants account for about 25 percent of the restaurant sales, according to a recent survey,

This case was prepared by Richard F. Beltramini and Nancy J. Stephens, both of Arizona State University.

and the estimated total dollar amount of sales for this category was $20.4 billion in 1978.

Among the top fast-food restaurants in the United States, only one is a pizza chain (see Table 1). The broader product category of Italian food commanded approximately a 4 percent share of market in 1976 (see Table 2). In total, there are an estimated 15,000 pizza outlets across the country (7,500 chain-related and 7,500 independents).

According to industry experts, fast food will continue to be a rapidly growing sector of the economy. It is pointed out, however, that large, better-financed companies will continue to gain market share to the detriment of smaller, regional companies.

Why do people eat out? The reason given most often by respondents in a recent A.C. Nielsen survey was "for a change of routine," closely followed by "it's easier than cooking." These two explanations were given by nine out of ten people in the survey.

Consumers in the Nielsen survey also had some opinions about fast-food restaurants. For example, when asked to compare the cost of eating in a fast-food restaurant with the cost of eating at home, a third believed it costs more, a third believed it costs less, and a third believed it costs about the same. Respondents were also asked to compare the nutritional value of food eaten in a fast-food restaurant with food eaten at home. Almost 70 percent believed that food eaten in a fast-food restaurant is less nutritious, while 21 percent believed that fast food and home food are about the same. Only 3 percent felt that fast food is more nutritious. Other attitudes found in the survey are shown in Table 3.

Another study, by the Newspaper Advertising Bureau, indicated that 93 percent of the population over the age of 12 has patronized a fast-food restaurant within the past six months. During

TABLE 1
Top 25 Fast-Food Restaurants Sales and Market Share by Company

Rank	Company	Sales 1976 ($000)	Sales 1975 ($000)	Market 1976	Share 1975
1.	McDonald's	$2,730,000	$2,256,000	19.6	18.4
2.	Kentucky Fried Chicken	1,165,000	999,000	8.4	8.1
3.	Burger King	741,600	614,200	5.3	5.0
4.	International Dairy Queen	620,000	620,000	4.5	5.1
5.	Pizza Hut	374,200	270,700	2.7	2.2
6.	Howard Johnson's	358,000	355,000	2.6	2.9
7.	Sambo's Restaurants	348,443	263,170	2.5	2.1
8.	Hardee's	324,304	297,900	2.3	2.4
9.	Jack-in-the-Box	323,400	274,550	2.3	2.2
10.	Burger Chef	305,000	285,000	2.2	2.3
11.	Denny's	303,520	243,375	2.2	2.0
12.	A & W International	289,00	271,000	2.1	2.2
13.	Bonanza International	275,224[a]	222,600[a]	2.0	1.8
14.	Ponderosa	242,859[a]	128,693[a]	1.7	1.0
15.	Arby's International	208,900	153,560	1.5	1.3
16.	Dunkin' Donuts	205,350	187,714	1.5	1.5
17.	Church's Fried Chicken Inc.	195,445	156,075	1.4	1.3
18.	Wendy's	187,000	74,463	1.3	0.6
19.	Red Lobster	181,000	114,000	1.3	0.9
20.	International House of Pancakes	180,000	139,402	1.3	1.1
21.	Long John Silver	156,300	81,700	1.1	0.7
22.	Friendly Ice Cream	154,000	122,000	1.1	1.0
23.	Shoney's Big Boy	141,279	121,301	1.0	1.0
24.	Morrison's Cafeterias	129,000	96,000	0.9	0.8
25.	Sizzler	120,800	96,200	0.9	0.8
	Total	$10,258,624	$8,443,603	73.7	68.7

[a]Includes international sales.
Source: Maxwell Associates, 1977.

this period, they have visited an average of 3.4 different chains.

THE PHOENIX PIZZA MARKET

Competition

Cavolo looks at his business as "a real David and Goliath situation" in reference to the large number of chain pizza restaurants in Phoenix. Village Inn (25 outlets), Pizza Hut (31 outlets), Pizza Inn (10 outlets), Godfather's Pizza (6 outlets), Round Table Pizza (5 outlets), Straw Hat Pizza (6 outlets), Mr. Gatti's (2 outlets), and Noble Roman Pizza (4 outlets) each have restaurants in the Phoenix market. In addition, there are a number of "ma and pa stores" which Cavolo regards as less threatening competitively. "We're more concerned with our unique image being imitated," he stated, adding that his pizza ingredients were of better quality than those used in chains.

TABLE 2
Major Fast-Food Restaurant Sales by Product Category

Product Group	Number of Firms	Sales 1976 ($000)	Sales 1975 ($000)	Percent Total Industry 1976	Percent Total Industry 1975
1. Hamburger	17	$ 5,239,058	$ 4,385,337	37.7	35.7
2. Full menu	46	2,721,058	2,318,365	19.6	18.8
3. Chicken	5	1,469,150	1,254,004	10.6	10.2
4. Ice cream	3	794,000	760,000	5.7	6.2
5. Steak	12	984,715	741,226	7.1	6.0
6. Italian	4	532,615	402,900	3.8	3.3
7. Donuts	3	289,966	261,138	2.1	2.1
8. Mexican	6	200,270	153,320	1.4	1.2
9. Seafood	5	459,000	284,500	3.3	2.3
10. Other types	8	434,106	341,020	3.1	2.8
Total	109	$13,123,938	$10,901,810	94.4	88.6

Source: Maxwell Associates, 1977.

TABLE 3
Attitudes Toward Fast-Food Restaurants[a]

1. Children would rather eat at a fast-food restaurant than eat a meal cooked at home.	agree	79%
	disagree	11%
2. Children often decide which fast-food restaurant the family will go to.	agree	78%
	disagree	12%
3. People eat at fast-food restaurants like McDonald's so they don't have to bother planning and cooking a meal	agree	77%
	disagree	13%
4. When we decide to go to a fast-food restaurant, it's usually a spur-of-the-moment decison.	agree	77%
	disagree	13%

[a]Unsure and "don't know" responses are not included.
Source: A.C. Nielsen Company, 1979.

TABLE 4
Competitors' Promotions

Competitor	Promotion
Restaurant A	$2.00 off any large pizza or $1.00 off any medium pizza.
Restaurant B	Buy one pizza at regular price, and get the next smaller size for $.99.
Restaurant C	Buy any size pizza at regular price and get another pizza of the same size and value free.
Restaurant D	$3.00 off any large pizza, $2.00 off any medium pizza, and $1.00 off any small pizza.
Restaurant E	Buy any large pizza and pitcher of a soft drink and receive a free plastic pitcher which will be refilled free for the next year.
Restaurant F	Buy any pizza at regular price and receive a free pitcher of a soft drink.
Restaurant G	$1.00 off any large pizza.

Promotion

The Phoenix fast-food pizza market is gimmick-oriented. Almost all restaurants utilize coupons and "deals" offering less expensive second pizzas, beer, and plastic pitchers. In the past Cavolo tested half-price deals but quickly learned that half of his business began coming from coupon sales. He quit "trying to be all things to all people," and today Peter Piper Pizza does not use promotions such as those outlined in Table 4.

Cavolo explains, "Those other places all show the cheese and they say look at all the stuff we put on it. They all have the same message—ours is the best, ours is the best. We don't say ours is the best. We say you come in. You tell us if you like it."

Price

According to Cavolo, it is difficult to compete with the advertising of chains, who often do over $240,000 a year in business in just one location. His no-frills product is priced about 40 percent lower than the competition, with the most expensive item at $4.50. Only pizza is served, along with beer, wine, and soda in an effort to reduce expenses. He explains, "We don't have sandwiches, we don't have spaghetti—which adds to the cost of doing business because you have to add more help."

PETER PIPER PIZZA'S ADVERTISING APPROACH

Budget

Peter Piper Pizza started spending approximately $7,000 in advertising during its first year in operation in Phoenix. This amount grew rapidly to $75,000 in 1979 and is anticipated to top $150,000 in 1980 (see Exhibit 1). Cavolo's "spend as much as you can afford on advertising" budgeting approach has usually run at about 5 percent of sales but at one point

TABLE 5
Pizza Leaders' National Advertising Budgets[a] ($000)

Media	Pizza Hut	Shakey's
Network television	$6,504.6	$ —
Spot television	2,534.3	2,126.1
Network radio	—	
Spot radio	580.3	7.7
Magazines	—	—
National newspapers	—	—
Outdoor	21.1	9.0
Total	9,640.3	2,142.8

[a]Does not include local newspaper advertising.
Source: Media Decisions, December, 1978.

approached nearly 10 percent. This is substantially more than the average fast-food restaurant, which normally budgets approximately 2 percent of sales for advertising.

Media

After experimenting with several advertising agencies, Cavolo decided to move all work in-house, "Agencies write copy that's just not me." No radio is currently being utilized, some newspaper, but the largest portion of his advertising budget is devoted to television, written and produced in-house. This approach seems consistent with that of some of the nationally successful pizza chains in a recent period (see Table 5).

EXHIBIT 1
Peter Piper Pizza's Advertising Budget

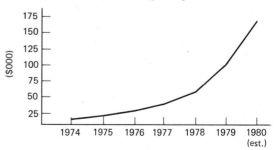

EXHIBIT 2
Sample Audio—Peter Piper Pizza 30 Second Television Spots

ADVERTISEMENT 1

Did you know that at Peter Piper Pizza you can buy a large cheese pizza for $2.75, a large sausage, mushroom, pepperoni, or any single item pizza for $3.50 and that $4.25 is the most expensive pizza on our menu? That's about half of what you'd pay elsewhere. These are our regular prices—no coupons, no gimmicks, no Tuesday night specials, just good pizza at low, low prices every day of the week. So come on over to Peter Piper Pizza.

ADVERTISEMENT 2

You tell me you missed the Tuesday night special at your local pizza parlor? You tell me you don't have a pizza coupon and funds are low? Well cheer up, friend, come on over to Peter(Piper Pizza. A large cheese pizza is only $2.75, a large sausage, mushroom, pepperoni, or any large single item pizza is $3.50. A large Peter Piper Special with the works is $4.25 and that's the most expensive pizza on our menu. Remember, no coupons, no gimmicks, just good pizza at low, low prices. So come on over to Peter Piper Pizza.

Production

"Television commercials are expensive. Even a cheap one could cost you $5,000 to produce. We make ours for an average of $150," notes Cavolo. An hour of studio time often yields Peter Piper Pizza as many as three commercials, in contrast to the approximate $50,000 needed per spot by national chain restaurants.

Creativity

Cutting expenses is the primary objective of Cavolo, a man who arrives at work at 7:00 A.M. to call New York "before the rates go up." Cavolo spends up to a day on each 30-second spot, writing and editing. This pizza cook approach is simple and straightforward—quality pizza at economy prices (see Exhibit 2).

Media

Peter Piper Pizza's advertising is placed by the in-house group, and the 15 percent discount obtained from the television stations (news-papers locally will not discount their rates) goes toward stretching the budget even further. The television spots are run in flights—heavy advertising for a three- to four-week period, then reduced to almost nothing, and back again every third month. Cavolo explains, "We feel it's better to buy advertising in bunches because you get more notice that way." His perception of the seasonal pattern of his business closely parallels that of national fast-food restaurants (see Exhibit 3).

Effectiveness

The believability of his advertising is a mystery to Cavolo, who admits, "We don't know what makes it work. Is it me? Am I that much of a personality?" Although never formally trained in advertising, he appreciates its role and is receptive to innovative techniques for communicating his unique recipe for combining quality ingredients, a matter-of-fact personality, and a limited line of inexpensive products.

EXHIBIT 3
Seasonality of Pizza Business

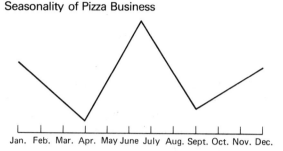

Jan. Feb. Mar. Apr. May June July Aug. Sept. Oct. Nov. Dec.

SUMMARY

Cavolo summarizes his approach: "We don't play it up because a lot of people think they're not going to get much for $2.95. A lot of people think cheap is cheap. People see it on TV and they think what are you going to get for $3.00? People tell us we ought to charge more for it, but please don't."

The 10 percent annual inflation of ingredients has caused Peter Piper Pizza to raise prices from $1.70 to $2.95, in the case of a large cheese pizza, in the last four years. Cavolo's decision to maintain high-quality ingredients remains, however, despite the current $1.50 per pound price of mozzarella cheese—the biggest and most expensive single ingredient.

Cavolo's "get something good and sell it for less" philosophy has been reasonably successful thus far, but he is concerned about what the future holds. The escalating costs of products and media have shrunk his profit margins. The cost of capital has limited expansion, although franchising seems to be a potential growth avenue. Competition continues to grow, and Cavolo's unique personal approach may begin losing its believability.

Cavolo and Herrgesell have decided to review their plans for the upcoming year's marketing communications program. In particular they are concerned about the appropriateness of their budget size, their media mix, and especially Cavolo's creative approach.

QUESTIONS FOR DISCUSSION

1. What statement of creative strategy could have provided the basis for Peter Piper Pizza's current advertising?
2. What statements of creative strategy could realistically be considered as possible extensions or replacements for Peter Piper's current strategy? How could executions of these possible strategies be handled most effectively?
3. What changes, if any, would you recommend in Peter Piper's current market communications program?

23

BRANDON FOODS COMPANY (B)[1]

Over eighty years ago Michael and Edward Brandon began the Brandon Packing Company. Michael Brandon was one of the pioneers of meat processing, and his innovative packing methods made it possible for meats to be cured year-round and transported safely to distant population centers.

Today the Brandon Foods Company is an important division of a large food conglomerate. The company employs some 3,000 people and is one of the major processors and distributors of fresh and processed beef, pork, and cheese products.

Meat manufacturing includes the slaughtering of live animals and the processing of carcasses and purchased raw meat into a full line of finished consumer beef and pork products. Brandon manufacturing operations are conducted in eight major plants: Atlanta, Denver, Independence (Iowa), Omaha, Phoenix, San Antonio, Seattle, and Wichita; and on a smaller scale at three facilities in Chattanooga, Portland (Maine), and Kansas City (Missouri).

Cheese manufacturing consists of converting whole milk and purchased bulk cheese into finished, aged, and processed American, cheddar, and Italian cheeses. Brandon cheese manufacturing operations are conducted in nine plants: four located in Kentucky, three in Wisconsin, one in Ohio, and one in Missouri.

Brandon's manufactured products are distributed by the eight major plants and by twelve wholesale distribution centers, each of which has its own sales organization. Cheese products are distributed by the nine cheese plants. This distribution system includes sales direct to food retailers as well as to other processors, wholesalers, and brokers. Brandon's products are distributed primarily on a regional basis, with concentration in the western half of the United States. Several specialized product lines, such as dry sausage products, canned meats, and cheeses, are distributed nationally. The company also operates as a major international wholesaler of natural casings used in the manufacture of sausage products.

INFLUENCES ON THE MEAT AND CHEESE MARKET

The meat and cheese industry is influenced by a number of economic factors which are beyond the control of packers and processors. During the past few years processors have been faced with the task of preserving profit margins in an environment of declining purchasing power of the dollar, continued high retail prices, high raw material prices, and rapidly increasing manufacturing costs.

Inflation, high interest rates, a slowing of real growth in the economy, and high levels of unemployment have all combined to pressure the consumers' available purchasing power. At the same time, the supply of meat has been decreasing during the past ten years. Thus, processors are faced with the problem of selling their principal product at relatively high prices to consumers who are caught in an economic squeeze and who will continue to be more selective and value conscious.

Beef, pork, and cheese products compete with lamb, poultry, seafood and frozen foods for the consumer's food expenditure dollar. Generally, as supplies of each type of live animal vary, so does consumption (see Table 1). Thus, demand must be approached in relation to the supply and price of each type of product. When one product

This case was prepared by Charles H. Patti. The original Brandon Foods case was prepared by Charles H. Patti and John H. Murphy and appeared in *Advertising Management: Cases and Concepts,* by Charles H. Patti and John H. Murphy, Grid Publishing, Inc., 1978.

TABLE 1
Per Capita Consumption of Meat, Cheese, Poultry, and Fish
(in pounds)

	1960	1965	1970	1975	1979
Beef	85.1	99.5	113.7	120.1	107.6
Veal	6.1	5.2	2.9	4.2	2.0
Lamb and mutton	4.8	3.7	3.3	2.0	1.5
Pork (excluding lard)	70.0	60.8	68.0	53.1	67.7
Total meat	166.0	169.2	187.9	179.4	178.8
Poultry (chicken and turkey)	34.0	40.9	48.5	49.2	58.6
Cheese	8.3	9.5	11.5	14.5	17.7
Fish (edible weight)	10.3	10.8	11.8	12.3	13.3

Source: Statistical Abstract of the U.S., 1980.

type is plentiful in relation to others, its relative price is lower and demand increases. This relationship holds true in the reverse situation and is modified by consumers' general preference. That is, consumers are willing to pay more per pound for beef than for pork and more for pork than for poultry.

In this difficult marketing environment, major marketers of meat products have placed increased emphasis on nutrition and product value. Most industry marketing programs attempt to build a strong consumer franchise through mass media advertising on select, high-margin products and to promote heavily in the distribution chain through allowances and deals.

COMPETITIVE ENVIRONMENT FOR BRANDON

After analyzing the competitive environment, the economic climate, and the firm's resources, Brandon Foods' marketing department developed the following product strategy:

1. Market a complete line of specialized food products of consistent quality including processed pork (ham, sliced bacon, etc.), sausage (wieners, luncheon meat, pork sausage, etc.), canned meats (refrigerated, consumer),

dry sausage (bulk and consumer size), and cheese (American, Italian, et al.).
2. Position these specialized food products so that they satisfy predetermined segments of final demand, including size, shape, color, formulation, quality, packaging, and so on.
3. Differentiate the products so that they will be distinct in the distribution channel *and* to the final consumer.
4. Develop a strong consumer franchise on these products.
5. Optimize the product mix from an overall company standpoint, favoring processed to fresh, branded to unbranded, company brands to private label.

PACKAGED LUNCHEON MEAT MARKET

Meat processors are vitally interested in the packaged luncheon meat segment of the market for several reasons:

1. The product category is highly profitable.
2. Packaged luncheon meats are branded and offer processors a product that can be advertised, thus attracting the interest of retailers and increasing the possibility of gaining market control.
3. Packaged luncheon meat can serve as a

low-risk product line introduction for consumers. That is, consumers can try a brand of packaged luncheon meat for very little financial risk. If they are satisfied with the product, they are more likely to accept more expensive product offerings (canned hams, pork sausage, bacon, weiners, etc.) of the same brand.

4. The typical retail display of packaged luncheon meats involves open facings of each variety of the product. This usually means that the thirty or so different varieties of a particular brand form an in-store display very much like a small billboard. This broad exposure is considered very beneficial to the brand's entire product line.

5. The sale of packaged luncheon meat brings about production economies by allowing processors to more fully use production equipment that is designed to process packaged luncheon meat and other meat products as well.

Relationship Between Advertising and Sales

As is indicated in Table 2, packaged luncheon meats represent about 22 percent of the estimated consumer dollar expenditures on processed meats in the Phoenix-Tucson market. In this market, total processed meat sales were estimated to be approximately $55 million in 1980. Oscar Mayer is considered the industry leader in the packaged luncheon meat market, holding large market shares in many large metropolitan areas. As is shown in Table 3, Oscar Mayer has consistently spent more on advertising than its competitors but is outspent by several firms in the Phoenix-Tucson market (see Table 4). Importantly, there is growing evidence in the industry that there is a strong positive relationship between share of market and share of advertising.

Promotional Themes

The promotional and advertising themes used to sell processed meat have centered on cash refunds and self-liquidating premium offers. In a national study covering 53 markets and including advertising in national magazines, newspapers, Sunday supplements, and point-of-purchase displays, two forms of promotion (cash refunds and self-liquidating premiums) were found to account for 49 percent of the total meat industry consumer promotions (see Table 5).

In the packaged luncheon meat category three of the four promotions found in the survey centered on cash refunds. Virtually every major national and regional brand used some form of cash refund or premium to generate interest among retailers and attract consumer attention.

TABLE 2
Estimated Market Potential for Processed Meats: 1980
(Phoenix-Tucson Markets)[a]

Product Category	Annual Market Potential ($ millions)	Percent of Total
Wieners	17.5	31.7
Bacon	16.2	29.3
Sliced luncheon meat	12.2	22.1
Canned hams	4.9	8.9
Boneless hams	4.4	8.0
Total market potential (estimated)	55.2	100.0

[a]Approximately 60 percent of this is accounted for by the Phoenix market alone.

TABLE 3
Processed Meats Estimated Advertising Volume: 1970, 1975, 1980

Manufacturer	1970 Vol. ($ 000)	1970 Percent of Total	1975 Vol. ($ 000)	1975 Percent of Total	1980 Vol. ($ 000)	1980 Percent of Total
Oscar Mayer	5,818	34	6,885	32	8,015	30
Armour	4,202	24	5,379	25	4,007	15
Hormel	2,155	12	1,721	8	1,870	7
Swift	1,574	9	1,506	7	2,939	11
Rath	974	5	1,291	6	1,068	4
Jones	840	5	861	4	802	3
Brandon	622	4	1,076	5	1,065	4
Jimmy Dean	530	3	1,070	5	2,940	11
Bob Evans	514	3	1,065	5	1,336	5
Wilson	124	1	430	2	1,870	7
Corn King	—	—	231	1	830	3
Total	17,353	100	21,515	100	26,742	100

TABLE 4
Meat Processors' Advertising Expenditures in Phoenix-Tucson: 1975 and 1980

Company	1975	Percent of Total	1980	Percent of Total
Armour	$110,200	25.2	$162,920	25.0
Brandon	47,500	10.8	83,700	12.8
Eckrich	12,750	2.9	21,300	3.3
Hormel	37,100	8.5	55,900	8.6
Jimmy Dean	8,000	1.8	14,600	2.2
Morningstar Farms	46,000	10.5	59,300	9.1
Morrell	101,200	23.1	129,700	20.0
Oscar Mayer	45,350	10.4	73,500	11.3
Plumrose	12,800	2.9	15,200	2.3
Rath	5,775	1.3	7,500	1.2
Spam	3,800	0.9	5,500	0.8
Swift	7,500	1.7	22,700	3.4
Totals	$437,975	100.0	$651,820	100.0

The meat industry has concentrated on promotional themes rather than product benefit themes for several reasons:

1. Several past research studies have shown that consumers tend to perceive five major brands as being relatively equal in quality. Therefore, brands are bought on the basis of price or some other price-related incentive.

2. Promotion—particularly cents-off coupons, contests, and premiums—tend to generate more interest among retailers in carrying the brand. Coupons redeemable in-store tend to build store traffic, which leads to increased retail sales.

3. Promotions seem to work. Evidence has shown that in the processed meat category

TABLE 5
Meat Industry Consumer Promotions by Type

Cash refunds	38%
Self-liquidating premiums	11
Free premiums	8
Contests	6
Sweepstakes	6
Mail-back store coupons	5
Store coupons	4
Misc. promotions	2
All other advertising	20
	100%

consumers *do* respond to the various promotions and sales do increase.

From a marketing point of view Brandon enjoys an enviable position in the western United States. It has an excellent distribution network, concentrating on the major chains and large independent retailers. Its brand image is very high and it holds the largest market shares in several categories of a number of important western markets. In Phoenix, for example, Brandon maintains nearly a 35 percent market share in hams, wieners, and bacon. This has been accomplished partly because consumers have come to perceive Brandon products as the "freshest" since Brandon's packaging plant is located in Phoenix. This gives the company an advantage over competitors who must ship their meats to Arizona.

Brandon Promotions During the 1970s

Despite Brandon's large market share in hams, wieners, and bacon, its share of market in packaged luncheon meat declined from about 8 percent in 1965 to 2 percent in 1975. The Phoenix market for packaged luncheon meat has been dominated by three brands: Oscar Mayer, Morrell, and Armour.

This situation was disturbing to Brandon's management, and during the mid-1970s the company concentrated on expanding and main-

taining distribution of their packaged luncheon meat products in the Phoenix and Tucson markets. To accomplish their goals, the company used a number of promotions, including the following:

Mystery Shopper. An attractive young lady was hired to punch doorbells at random daily in certain parts of town for a four-week period. If the resident could produce a package of the Brandon product (or the words "Brandon Sliced Luncheon Meat" printed on a piece of paper), she was awarded a $10 bill. If the resident could produce neither, she was given a cents-off store coupon good on Brandon sliced luncheon meat.

The promotion was advertised on middle-of-the-road radio stations, with the disc jockeys reporting the area in which the mystery shopper would do her calling each day. Winners were also announced daily.

Douglas and Waldo Contest. Brandon bought three 60-second spots a week on a popular children's show in which Waldo (a clown character) did live commercials announcing various contests for kids. Proofs of purchase were required to enter and the contest included a coloring contest, drawing Waldo eating a sandwich made with Brandon Sliced Luncheon Meat, and "write your own commercial." Prizes were always very modest.

Cents-Off Coupon Drop. Independent Mail Service, publishers of a hand-delivered weekly shopper newspaper, was used to deliver ad inserts containing cents-off coupons within a one-mile radius of stores distributing Brandon Sliced Luncheon Meat.

In-Pack Premium. Brandon developed a series of fourteen different iron-on patches featuring slang sayings from the "Nifty Fifties," packaged them in government-approved plastic pouches, and randomly in-packed them in Brandon Luncheon Meat. The objective was to get kids to collect all of the different designs. The promotion was advertised heavily on rock stations for four weeks. It was also hitchhiked on a 1,000-line, two-color newspaper ad and had rail strips support at the point of sale.

In spite of the apparent advantages of promotions, Kenneth Weiss, vice-president of marketing for Brandon, was never completely convinced that the use of promotions was the most effective way to achieve Brandon's objectives. He realized that consumers seemed to like promotions and that they were also effective in getting retailers to stock the Brandon product; however, he also knew that promotions did almost nothing to build long-term brand loyalty. Once the particular promotion ended, sales and then distribution dropped off dramatically.

By the mid-1970s Brandon was considering alternative advertising themes. After several meetings among the company advertising personnel and Brandon's advertising agency, several alternatives were identified. The alternatives included:

Continuity promotion program. This idea involved the use of advertising and point-of-purchase promotion to encourage consumers to buy the Brandon brand to collect package labels which could then be exchanged for merchandise. Items that were replaced often (such as pantyhose and film) or items that could be collected (dinnerware or flatware) were suggested. It was thought that this type of program would take advantage of the appeal of promotions and at the same time overcome the major problem—short-term results.

A product attribute advertising campaign. This idea would utilize mass media advertising to call attention to the product attributes of the Brandon product. Brandon knew that it had an excellent product (quality, variety, freshness, package, and guarantee) and at that time no other meat processor was using this advertising theme.

A brand image advertising campaign. Most of the large meat processors were using mass media advertising to attempt to communicate a positive brand image. This "image" was not based on product attributes, but simply tried to associate the brand with a pleasant scene or idea (children playing and enjoying luncheon meat, a happy family gathering where luncheon meat is being served, and the like). Brandon was considering using a similar appeal. Since it was a local company and already enjoyed a favorable reputation, the agency felt that it could be even more successful with such a campaign than its competitors.

There were, of course, some possible disadvantages to each of these three alternatives. Although the continuity promotion idea would seem to overcome the short-term problem of past promotion campaigns, it seemed unlikely that such a program would work at top effectiveness over the long term. Furthermore, any type of promotion-oriented program is essentially another form of price cutting, and Brandon felt that over the next several years it would not be able to tolerate continued discounting in a business that already was experiencing economic pressures.

The primary shortcoming of the product attribute idea was that consumers tended to perceive three to five brands as being approximately equal in product quality. Hence, the campaign might not be able to convince consumers of Brandon's product superiority.

The brand image advertising campaign would require a rather large investment in advertising—particularly when Brandon was competing against three large advertisers. If brand loyalty had not been firmly established by now, Brandon felt that they would have to invest at least as much as the industry leader to begin to make gains in consumer preference.

Brandon Advertising: 1975–1980

After evaluation of the advantages and disadvantages of the advertising alternatives available

Perceptual Multiple Dimensional Scaling ⇒ Causation

TABLE 6
Packaged Luncheon Meat Market Shares:[a] 1975, 1977, 1980 (Phoenix-Tucson market)

Brand	Market Share (percent of total)		
	1975	1977	1980
Armour	24	20	23
Brandon	2	4	2
Eckrich	3	5	8
Hormel	15	12	15
Jimmy Dean	3	4	3
Morningstar Farms	3	3	1
Morrell	18	17	16
Oscar Mayer	26	28	27
Plumrose	1	2	1
Rath	2	1	1
Spam	1	2	1
Swift	2	2	2
	100	100	100

[a]Does not include store brands.

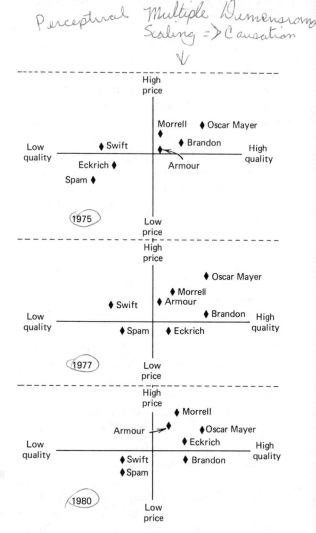

EXHIBIT 1
Consumer Images of Packaged Luncheon Meats: 1975, 1977, 1980 (Phoenix-Tucson market)

to them, Brandon's management decided to utilize the continuity promotion program. It increased its advertising budget to help generate consumer awareness of the program and in late 1975 it offered its first premium—pantyhose. As the campaign progressed, other merchandise was offered—lawn and garden tools, dishes, a ten-volume encyclopedia, and an eight-piece cutlery set. Initially, the campaign seemed to work, and market share slowly increased (see Table 6). However, by the end of 1979, Kenneth Weiss was again disappointed. After an advertising investment of more than $300,000 and promotion costs of about $400,000, Brandon's market share was again at the 2 percent level. It looked as if even a continuity promotion was effective only in the short term.

During the 1975–1980 period Brandon conducted periodic surveys among consumers to determine their attitudes and perceptions about the product category and about the Brandon brand in particular. Highlights of the results of these studies are shown in Exhibit 1 and Tables 7, 8, 9, and 10.

CURRENT SITUATION

Early next week Kenneth Weiss would meet with Brandon's advertising agency to discuss the selection of a creative strategy for their packaged luncheon meats. The product category was simply too important to abandon, yet it was too expensive to continue investing in a promotion program that did not work.

TABLE 7
Top-of-Mind Awareness (Unaided Recall) of
Packaged Luncheon Meats: 1975, 1977, 1980
(Phoenix-Tucson market)

Brand	Overall Rankings		
	1975	1977	1980
Oscar Mayer	1	1	1
Armour	2	2	2
Morrell	3	4	3
Brandon	4	3	5
Spam	5	7	7
Eckrich	6	5	4
Swift	7	6	6

TABLE 8
Preferred Brand of Packaged Luncheon Meats:
1975, 1977, 1980 (Phoenix-Tucson market)

Brand	Percent of Respondents		
	1975	1977	1980
Armour	18	15	17
Brandon	8	12	10
Eckrich	5	7	9
Morrell	12	12	14
Oscar Mayer	53	51	48
Spam	2	1	1
Swift	2	2	1
	100	100	100

TABLE 9
Consumer Concerns About Packaged Luncheon
Meats (Phoenix-Tucson market)

Concern	Percent of Respondents
Low nutrition	57
High fat, calories, and cholesterol	44
Uncertainty over ingredients	22
Poor taste	20
Poor appearance	18
Hard to keep fresh	10

TABLE 10
Major Factors that Differentiate Luncheon Meats
(Phoenix-Tucson market)

Factor	Percent of Respondents
Taste	55
General	24
Spiciness	10
Saltiness	9
Freshness	7
Smokiness	5
Amount of advertising	40
Price	31
Fat content	28
Variety of products	28
Popularity/familiarity	27
Quality	24
Ham in product line	21
Bacon in product line	17
Distribution	14

ENDNOTE

1. Some of the data in this case have been
disguised and do not necessarily reflect the
actual situation in the meat processing industry.

QUESTIONS FOR DISCUSSION

1. Based on the data presented in this case,
what creative strategy recommendations
would you make to Mr. Weiss?
2. What considerations in the case have the
greatest effect on your creative strategy
recommendations? Why?
3. What explanations would appear to hold some
promise in explaining Brandon's low share in
the packaged luncheon meat market?

SECTION 6
MEDIA PLANNING

The media portion of an advertising campaign is often considered the most important for two reasons. First, it is the media that are relied on to bring consumer and advertiser together. Despite increasing costs, mass media are still the most efficient way for advertisers to reach customers and prospects. Second, because of their efficiency in reaching millions of households, media costs account for the majority of all of the dollars invested in advertising. Advertising management has developed a strong interest in maximizing the productivity of the media investment because of the high costs involved and because of the thousands of possible media alternatives.

Like the creative portion of a campaign, a media plan consists of both strategy and tactics. Again, the involvement of the Advertising Manager is concentrated at the strategy level. The development of media strategy, like that of creative strategy, requires knowledge of all the factors in the *marketing* environment (competition, nature of product, distribution, and so on), *media* environment (availability and suitability of media alternatives), and *creative* environment (need for demonstration, color, display, and other factors). Because each organization operates in a unique environment, there is no single best media strategy. Eventually, the organization adopts a strategy and a media plan that it believes will most efficiently accomplish the stated objectives. The Advertising Manager's role is to help formulate media strategy by providing adequate background information on the marketing factors and by assisting the advertising media specialists in developing guidelines that will direct the tactical media decisions.

While media strategy essentially consists of selecting the target markets and setting media objectives, the tactics involve a series of steps that attempt to allocate funds to media in an efficient manner that will fulfill the strategy within the constraints of the budget. The tactical elements of a media plan include *evaluating media alternatives, selecting a media plan, buying and placing media,* and *evaluating the effectiveness of the plan.* Because of the specialized nature of media and the complexity of matching media with markets, most advertisers rely on media specialists (either within advertising agencies or media buying services) to perform the tactical parts of media planning.

There are wide differences among the media plans for the advertiser of consumer goods, industrial goods, and retail merchandise, and the Advertising Manager should be familiar with the problems and opportunities inherent in each of these situations. In the following cases you will be exposed to all three market settings and the two most common media tasks that face the Advertising Manager: developing media strategy and evaluating media tactics recommended by others.

24

BIG SURF, INC. (B)

William Obert sat in his office poring over promotional plans. It was his first year as owner and major stockholder of Big Surf* and it had been a very successful one. Business was 20 percent ahead of last year—particularly impressive when other amusement parks around the country had experienced a decline in attendance. Mr. Obert faced a pleasant problem—making new promotional plans which would continue Big Surf's success.

Big Surf, which was built in 1969, covers twenty acres in Tempe, a suburb of Phoenix. The main attraction is a 500,000-gallon reservoir (see Exhibit 1). From one end of the reservoir, every two minutes comes a perfect five-foot wave. Swimmers use rubber rafts and surfboards to "catch the wave" and ride it 430 feet into the shore, at the other end of the reservoir. Big Surf also offers a number of facilities including a large beach area, one seaslide, bumper boats, volleyball, locker area, snack bar, and a surf shop which rents rafts and surfboards for those who don't bring one (see Exhibit 2).

Big Surf is open seven days a week, from early March until late September, although there is some consideration by management of going to a six-day week in order to save energy costs. Spiraling energy prices in the past few years have also pushed Big Surf's admission price to $3.50 per person, a price Mr. Obert believes will probably have to be raised even further in the future. The hours of operation are 11 A.M. until 6 P.M. every day except Friday, when Big Surf stays open until 10 P.M. for the reduced rate Family Night (see Exhibit 3).

This case was prepared by Nancy J. Stephens, Arizona State University. The original Big Surf case was prepared by Charles H. Patti and was published in *Advertising Management: Cases and Concepts,* by Charles H. Patti and John H. Murphy, Grid Publishing, Inc., 1978.

*Complete corporate name is Desert Oceans, Inc., DBA, Big Surf.

THE MARKET

The market in which Big Surf operates, Phoenix, Arizona, is virtually ideal for this kind of recreational facility. The climate is sunny, warm, and dry, and a large portion of the area's 1.5 million people participate in outdoor activities, particularly water-oriented sports. For example, 107,000 Phoenix homes (or about 18 percent) have swimming pools and 12,000 own a jacuzzi. In a recent survey, one-third of Phoenix household residents indicated that they went swimming in the past 30 days (see Table 1). In another recent study of Phoenix residents, 37 percent said they consider themselves sports participants and regularly engage in swimming, tennnis, golf, or some other form of regular exercise.

The age makeup of the Phoenix population is also favorable for Big Surf. Over 30 percent of the population are under 18 years old, the age group from which Big Surf draws the majority of its customers (see Table 2). Phoenix's relatively affluent households are reflected in visitors to Big Surf (see Table 3).

TABLE 1
Activities of Phoenix Residents

Activity	Percent of Households Engaging In Activity in Past 30 Days (Total Households = 595,000)
Camped out	40.0
Gone fishing	38.9
Gone swimming	33.9
Gone bicycling	33.9
Gone boating	24.0
Gone hunting	14.9
Played golf	12.9
Played tennis	10.0

Note: Percentages total exceeds 100 because of multiple responses.
Source: Arizona Republic/Gazette Consumer Survey, 1981.

EXHIBIT 1
The 20-acre Big Surf facility includes over 600 feet of sandy beach, a 500,000-gallon reservoir that produces waves, a 300-foot water slide, and facilities for food and drink.

Phoenix also attracts a large number of tourists and vacationers, which Mr. Obert considers a secondary target market (see Tables 4–9). Another secondary target market, accounting for about 30 percent of Big Surf's business, is businesses, groups, and organizations (see Table 10). Big Surf can accommodate groups of 25 to 7,000 people with its normal swimming and surfing activities, as well as with catered food service. Groups who wish to hire bands for entertainment can use one or both of Big Surf's two fully equipped stages and spacious patios for dancing.

PROMOTION

Because of its uniqueness as a recreational facility, Big Surf has enjoyed a great deal of publicity throughout its twelve years of existence. Numerous articles and features have appeared in local as well as national print and broadcast media. Mr. Obert feels that Big Surf's high profile, created by all the publicity, has been helpful in generating business.

Big Surf has also used mass media advertising to promote attendance. During Mr. Obert's first

EXHIBIT 2
Big Surf Facilities

TABLE 2
Phoenix Residents by Age

Age Group	Number of Persons	Percent
Under 2	55,000	3.5
2–5	107,000	6.8
6–11	157,000	10.0
12–13	52,000	3.3
14–17	105,000	6.7
18–24	192,000	12.2
25–29	119,000	7.6
30–34	116,000	7.4
35–39	99,000	6.3
40–44	83,000	5.3
45–49	72,000	4.6
50–54	77,000	4.9
55–59	80,000	5.1
60–64	80,000	5.1
65–74	123,000	7.8
75 and over	53,000	3.4
Total	1,570,000	100.0

Source: Arizona Republic/Gazette Consumer Survey, 1981.

year as owner, the advertising budget was $80,000, all spent locally (see Table 11). Television received more than half of the money, with the remainder split between newspapers and radio. All the advertising is targeted at local Phoenix residents, and no special effort is made to reach tourists, groups, or organizations.

For the most part, Big Surf advertising is

TABLE 3
Big Surf Visitors by Income

Annual Income	Percent of Big Surf Visitors (Based on 71,000 households)
Under $10,000	8
$10,000–$19,999	19
$20,000–$29,999	30
$30,000–$39,999	18
$40,000–$49,999	10
$50,000 and over	15

Source: Arizona Republic/Gazette Consumer Survey, 1981.

EXHIBIT 3
Family Night Ad for Big Surf

TABLE 4
Major Expenditures of Arizona Tourists

	Method of Travel to Arizona	
	Highway	Airline
Number of tourists annually	12,903,683	1,812,986
Total expenditures ($000)	2,025,363.9	1,018,049.9
Lodging	420,669.8	345,513.2
Food	491,507.4	273,302.7
Gasoline	448,697.2	38,462.4
Entertainment	91,102.2	58,740.2

Source: Tourism and Travel in Arizona, Bureau of Business and Economic Research, College of Business Administration, Arizona State University, 1981.

TABLE 5
Entertainment Expenditures of Arizona Tourists by Quarter

Quarter	Expenditure ($000)
1st (January–March)	49,095.3
2nd (April–June)	31,297.2
3rd (July–September)	26,869.2
4th (October–December)	42,580.7

Source: Tourism and Travel in Arizona, Bureau of Business and Economic Research, College of Business Administration, Arizona State University, 1981.

TABLE 6
Geographic Distribution of Arizona Tourists

Highway Travelers		Airline Travelers	
State	Percent of Tourists	State	Percent of Tourists
California	43.8	California	23.1
Texas	8.2	Illinois	8.2
New Mexico	5.1	Texas	6.3
Colorado	4.2	New York	5.0
Nevada	3.4	Ohio	4.0
Illinois	2.7	Michigan	3.6
Michigan	2.3	Pennsylvania	2.9
All other	30.3	All others	46.9
Total	100.0	Total	100.0

Source: Tourism and Travel in Arizona, Bureau of Business and Economic Research, College of Business Administration, Arizona State University, 1981.

timed to coincide with its March to September season. Monthly attendance patterns have remained fairly stable from year to year, varying only with the weather (see Table 12). The majority of attendance, 60 percent, occurs during June, July, and August, the months school is not in session. The first three months of the season account for about 30 percent. In September, attendance normally falls off sharply, accounting for only a small percentage of the season total.

Although consumer research was done during Big Surf's early years, Mr. Obert has not yet used any research. Instead, he relies on his personal "reading" of the market to plan pro-

TABLE 7
Purpose of Visit to Arizona (Percent)

Highway Travelers	Time of Year of Visit		
	Summer	Winter	Spring
Vacation/touring	49.3	20.3	40.8
Visiting friends/relatives	21.4	34.5	36.3
Passing through	21.6	11.1	20.2
Business	12.2	17.4	6.7
Seasonal resident	3.2	25.4	4.2
Convention	2.0	4.6	1.7
Other	5.8	23.4	9.6

Note: Percentages may exceed 100 because of multiple responses.

Airline Travelers	Time of Year of Visit		
	Summer	Winter	Spring
Business	41.2	38.2	25.8
Visiting friends/relatives	37.1	24.8	43.5
Vacation/touring	17.2	6.4	14.0
Convention	6.8	28.3	22.0
Seasonal resident	0.8	3.2	1.1
Other	4.5	4.1	3.8

Note: Percentages may exceed 100 because of multiple responses.

Source: Tourism and Travel in Arizona, Bureau of Business and Economic Research, College of Business Administration, Arizona State University, 1981.

motional activities. He also employs an advertising agency to help him.

In formulating his plans for his second year in the "desert surfing" business, William Obert has made the following decisions:

A. Target markets
   1. Local residents (teenagers and preteens)
   2. Tourists and vacationers
   3. Groups and organizations

B. Advertising budget: $100,000

C. Advertising objectives
   1. To build preference for Big Surf as a recreational alternative among Phoenix teenagers and preteens

TABLE 8
Information Sources Influencing Decision to Vacation in Arizona (Percent)

Highway Travelers	Time of Year of Visit		
	Summer	Winter	Spring
Friends/relatives	61.2	77.8	67.9
Previous visits	52.3	53.3	48.8
Travel literature	24.5	21.1	16.9
Magazines	17.1	14.1	14.2
Auto club	12.1	5.9	9.3
Television	5.6	3.3	3.9
Newspapers	4.2	3.0	3.3
Radio	1.4	1.9	1.2
Other	9.5	10.0	6.7

Note: Percentages may exceed 100 because of multiple responses.

Airline Travelers	Time of Year of Visit		
	Summer	Winter	Spring
Friends/relatives	82.4	74.1	89.4
Previous visits	31.7	30.2	9.6
Travel literature	9.3	10.8	9.6
Magazines	7.3	4.3	9.6
Television	4.4	2.2	—
Travel agent	2.1	3.8	2.7
Newspapers	1.0	1.4	1.0
Radio	—	—	—
Other	3.3	14.3	14.8

Note: Percentages may exceed 100 because of multiple responses.

Source: Tourism and Travel in Arizona, Bureau of Business and Economic Research, College of Business Administration, Arizona State University, 1981.

   2. To build awareness of Big Surf among tourists and vacationers
   3. To increase awareness among local groups and organizations of Big Surf as a group activity facility

QUESTIONS FOR DISCUSSION

1. Given the target markets, advertising budget, and advertising objectives established by Mr. Obert, what media plan that will best contribute to the success of Big Surf?
2. What considerations most strongly influence media planning in this case? Why?

TABLE 9
Tourist Activities While in Arizona (Percent)

	Time of Year of Visit		
Highway Travelers	Summer	Winter	Spring
Sightseeing	90.2	87.4	84.4
Historical sites	62.6	58.7	56.5
Swimming	43.2	20.6	25.8
Camping	27.6	19.2	18.8
Hiking/backpacking	15.8	17.1	16.9
Golfing	5.3	24.1	10.2
Tennis	7.7	6.6	6.3

Note: Percentages may exceed 100 because of multiple responses.

	Time of Year of Visit		
Airline Travelers	Summer	Winter	Spring
Sightseeing	74.6	82.5	82.8
Swimming	51.7	24.5	43.4
Historical sites	37.9	28.0	38.6
Golfing	10.0	27.0	17.9
Tennis	10.0	15.5	15.9
Hiking/backpacking	8.7	5.5	10.3
Camping	4.2	1.5	3.4

Note: Percentages may exceed 100 because of multiple responses.

Source: Tourism and Travel in Arizona, Bureau of Business and Economic Research, College of Business Administration, Arizona State University, 1981.

TABLE 10
Major Phoenix Businesses by Number of Employees

Number of Employees	Number of Businesses
5,000 and over	4
2,500–4,999	3
1,000–2,499	7
500– 999	10
250– 499	35
100– 249	51
Under 100	69

Source: Arizona Republic/Gazette Consumer Survey, 1981.

TABLE 11
Big Surf Advertising Expenditures by Medium

	1980	1981
Television	$40,000	$45,000
Newspaper	18,000	20,000
Radio	12,000	15,000
Total	$70,000	$80,000

TABLE 12
Big Surf Attendance by Month

	1980	1981
March	18,756	26,400
April	24,320	31,353
May	40,924	37,952
June	55,917	61,710
July	53,658	78,569
August	58,425	58,000
September	28,113	11,000
Total	280,113	304,984

25

MODERN MACHINERY COMPANY (B)[1]

The Modern Machinery Company was founded in Chicago in 1936. The company engineers, builds, markets, and installs large metal-forming and plastic-forming presses which weigh from 2,000 to 2 million pounds. Principal users of this type of equipment are manufacturers of automobiles, automotive parts, household appliances, aircraft, electronics, furniture, and other miscellaneous metal and plastic parts (see Table 1). The company also builds presses that manufacture bowling balls, stamp out panels for men's dress shirts, make synthetic diamonds, and compact powdered materials for the atomic energy industry.

Although the machine tool business has undergone a number of severe recessions over the years, Modern has grown from a small (six employees) machinery builder to one of the world's largest manufacturers of sophisticated production equipment systems. In 1982 Modern's main manufacturing facility covered over 400,000 square feet and employed over 1,000 skilled technicians. In addition to the U.S. manufacturing facility, Modern has manufacturing agreements in five foreign countries. The company's worldwide sales effort is controlled from seven sales offices in the United States and four abroad. Supplementing the direct sales personnel are 19 domestic distributor organizations and 22 foreign distributors.

MARKETING MACHINE TOOLS

The Market

The demand for machine tools is tied directly to the demand for the end products manufactured by the equipment. The automotive industry, for example, is simply not interested in investing

This case was prepared by Charles H. Patti. The original Modern Machinery case was prepared by Charles H. Patti and appeared in *Advertising Management: Cases and Concepts*, by Charles H. Patti and John H. Murphy, Grid Publishing, Inc., 1978.

TABLE 1
Consumption of Machine Tools by S.I.C.

Standard Industrial Classification (S.I.C.)	Category Description	Percent of Total Machine Tools in Use
34	Machinery, except electrical	31.8
35	Fabricated metal products	22.9
36	Electrical machinery	13.9
37	Transportation	12.7
33/39/38/25/19	All others	18.7
Totals		100.0

large amounts of capital for machine tools when consumer demand for automobiles is soft.

Although the machine tool industry is often used as an economic indicator, it is highly cyclical (see Table 2). The last four years of the 1970s were generally quite good for machine tool builder, yet net new orders declined nearly 16 percent in 1980. High interest rates and a general decline in economic activity caused postponements and cancellations of machine tool orders throughout 1980. This trend continued in 1981 and a further slump is likely to be caused by the problems experienced by the auto industry. Although tax credits for capital investment could spur a recovery, machine tool builders prepared themselves for another trough in the cycle.

The Product

According to the National Machine Tool Builders' Association, machine tools are ". . . power-driven machines, not portable by hand, used to shape or form metal by cutting, impact, pressure, electrical techniques, or a combination of these processes" (see Exhibits 1 and 2). Essentially, machine tools are classified into two categories:

TABLE 2
Machine Tool Net New Order:1956–1980 (expressed in $ millions)

Year	Metal-Cutting Machine Tools	Metal-Forming Machine Tools	Total	Percent Change from Prior Years
1956	$ 983	$315	$1,298	—
1957	552	170	722	−44.4
1958	299	128	427	−40.9
1959	541	207	748	+75.2
1960	535	209	744	− 0.05
1961	591	181	772	+ 3.8
1962	571	244	815	+ 5.6
1963	760	301	1,061	+30.2
1964	1,038	539	1,577	+48.6
1965	1,251	441	1,692	+ 7.3
1966	1,629	445	2,074	+22.6
1967	1,134	286	1,420	−31.5
1968	1,080	394	1,474	+3.8
1969	1,195	533	1,728	+17.2
1970	651	261	912	−47.2
1971	609	252	861	− 5.6
1972	1,009	403	1,412	+64.0
1973	1,825	787	2,613	+85.1
1974	2,017	486	2,502	− 4.3
1975	916	270	1,186	−52.6
1976	1,662	568	2,230	+88.0
1977	2,202	795	2,997	+34.4
1978	3,375	969	4,344	+44.9
1979	4,495	1,048	5,543	+27.6
1980	3,885	777	4,662	−15.9

1. Metal-cutting machine tools (S.I.C. 3541): boring mills, lathes, grinders, polishers, drilling machines, gear-cutting machines.
2. Metal-forming machine tools (S.I.C. 3541): punching and shearing machines, bending and forming machines, hydraulic, mechanical, and forging presses (see Exhibits 3 and 4).

Nearly all large metal-forming and plastic-forming equipment is built to customer specifications. Although each of the major press builders holds hundreds of patents on various press components and/or systems, none of these features is felt to be clearly superior to competitive features. Press builders therefore compete primarily on the basis of price, delivery, service, and overall engineering and production capability. Modern enjoys a reputation as an industry leader because of its research and development efforts, its capability to build the largest and most sophisticated machinery, and its worldwide manufacturing, service, and sales facilities.

Price

Modern's prices are typically 10 to 15 percent higher than competition but consistent with their high quality. The average price for a single piece of forming equipment is approximately $50,000.

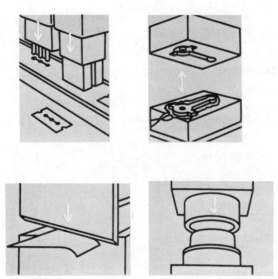

EXHIBIT 1
Basic Machine Tool-Forming Operations

The smallest machine costs about $15,000. However, Modern has sold single machines costing more than $1 million and sales of $200,000 to $300,000 are not uncommon.

Distribution

Common industry practice is to sell the product through a direct sales staff and machinery distributors. Modern employs 21 direct salespeople in seven U.S. sales offices and also uses 19 domestic distributor organizations. Personal selling is considered very important by Modern's management because of the technical nature of the product and the size and importance of each order. The sales staff concentrates its efforts on calling on the major purchasing influences, from production personnel to engineering to purchasing to top management. Company salespeople direct most of their efforts to the geographic area of machine tool concentration. Specifically, Modern has concentrated on the large but highly cyclical automotive market that is concentrated in the Detroit area (see Tables 3 and 4).

TABLE 3
Geographic Distribution of All Machine Tools

Area	Percent of Total Machine Tools in Use
Chicago	13.2
New York-Newark	10.5
Los Angeles	8.0
Detroit	7.3
Boston	6.2
All other areas	54.8
Totals	100.0

TABLE 4
Modern Machinery Sales by Market: 1965–1980

Market	1965	1970	1975	1980
Automotive	40%	47%	40%	35%
Automotive parts	22	24	19	19
Appliance	15	12	17	20
Aircraft	7	6	9	7
Electronics	6	3	9	10
Furniture	4	7	5	5
All others	6	1	1	4

Note: Expressed as percentage of sales.

Promotion

The only consistent aspect of the advertising expenditure patterns in this industry is the low advertising/sales ratio. All of the leading firms spend less than .5 percent of sales on advertising. Modern has spent as much as $450,000 per year for advertising (including direct mail, product publicity, and various other forms of sales promotion). In addition to advertising, Modern issues several product catalogs and periodically exhibits at trade shows and exhibits.

Advertising

Modern has a history of allocating a comparatively large percentage of its total sales to media advertising (see Table 5). While studies have shown that industrial firms allocate about 30

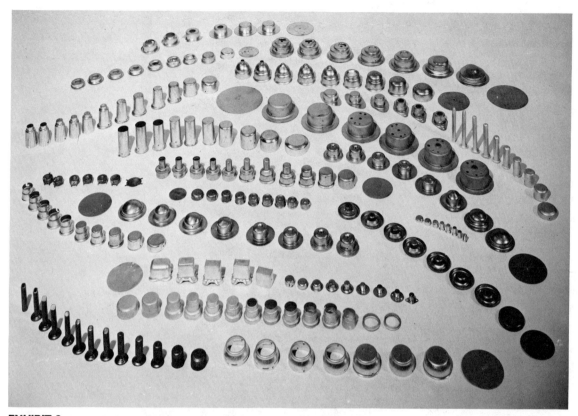

EXHIBIT 2
A variety of metal parts are made on metal-forming machine tools. Here is an
assortment of fabricated metal products formed by machine tool operations.

percent of their budgets to business publication space (see Table 6), Modern has consistently spent about 50–65 percent of its budget in the business press. The major reason for this is that Modern's management recognizes the wide range of buying influences on the purchase of a machine tool and feels that a large percentage of these influences can be reached efficiently through space advertising.

Target Markets

Modern's advertising media program is directed to three primary markets:

Domestic Metalworking Market. This industry has traditionally accounted for the largest percentage of Modern's sales and it continues to be the most important segment today. It is estimated that there are 40,000 metalworking plants in the United States. (with twenty or more employees) and over 400,000 buying influences in these plants. Modern has identified four major job functions that are most important in the decision to buy a machine tool:

1. Administrative
2. Production
3. Engineering
4. Purchasing

EXHIBIT 3
Often machine tools are custom-designed to meet the manufacturing requirements of an individual metal former. This is a custom-made metal-forming press under inspection during assembly.

The relative importance of each of these functions varies widely by size and organizational structure of customer (see Table 7); therefore, it has been nearly impossible for Modern to concentrate its advertising effort on any one particular job function. Consequently, Modern uses a rather large number of business publications (both horizontals and verticals) to

EXHIBIT 4
Metal-forming presses are also available in standard models. This is a standard OBI (open back, inclinable) press ready for delivery.

reach the largest number of prospects. The objectives of advertising to this market are to maintain a favorable company image, to inform customers and prospects of new product developments, and to generate inquiries (sales leads) for the sales staff.

International Metalworking Market. Because Modern also manufactures and markets its products outside the United States, a portion of the advertising budget is allocated to "foreign" publications. In the past, Modern has used publications whose circulation is worldwide (excluding the United States) and those that concentrate in one country or one geographic area, that is, Latin America, Europe, Far East. It is generally felt that the administrative function is far more important among foreign firms in the selection of a machine press supplier. Modern's creative aproach in international media has been "top management" oriented, emphasizing the worldwide reputation of Modern and the prestige of buying Modern equipment.

Domestic Plastic-Forming Market. This is a growth area for Modern and at this time it is not certain who the major users of large plastic-forming presses will be. Clearly, the automotive industry is the prime target. However, furniture, appliance, and aircraft manufacturers are also seen as excellent prospects. Although the relative importance of these industries is unknown at this time, Modern's management feels that it is important to communicate regularly with these potential customers. To accomplish this communications goal, a modest business press advertising program has been launched to build awareness of the Modern company name and to explain new product technologies as they are developed.

CURRENT SITUATION

Until 1945 Modern controlled 50 to 75 percent of the metal-forming press market. Its sales and engineering staffs worked closely with the major automobile manufacturers to help develop many of the mass-production systems still used today. However, the marketplace changed. Several firms (including several very capable foreign manufacturers) produce high-quality presses, and in recent years Modern had difficulty regaining even 15 percent of the market. As is shown in Table 8, Modern held about 14 percent of the market since 1965. Their two major competitors, Formco and Johnson, successfully

TABLE 5
Advertising Media Expenditures for Modern, Formco, and Johnson:
1965, 1970, 1975, 1980

	Modern		Formco		Johnson	
Year	Sales[a]	Advertising Media Expenditures[b]	Sales[a]	Advertising Media Expenditures[b]	Sales[a]	Advertising Media Expenditures[b]
1965	$45.9	$272	$41.8	$167	$35.2	$123
1970	30.7	181	45.6	173	39.8	149
1975	38.1	266	37.3	149	41.6	166
1980	100.9	450	119.4	220	107.0	246

[a]Expressed in $ millions of annual net new orders.
[b]Expressed in $ thousands.

challenged Modern's position as the industry leader, and recently these two companies surpassed Modern's sales.

Modern's management realized that many of the factors that contributed to their loss of market share were beyond their control. Certainly, Modern could have done nothing about declining economic conditions and the weak automotive market. Also, there seemed little they could have done about foreign competition. Machine tool production technology reached the

TABLE 6
Distribution of the Typical
Industrial Advertising Budget

Share of Budget Spent on:	Percent of Advertising Budget
Business publication space	31
Business publication production costs	6
Other media production costs	6
Direct mail	8
Company catalogs	17
Trade shows and exhibits	9
Dealer and distributor aids	4
Advertising department administrative costs	9
All other budget items	10

Source: McGraw-Hill Laboratory of Advertising Performance #8009.4.

mature stage long ago and the technological advantages once held almost exclusively by Modern were now widely available to any builder.

In developing their marketing strategy for the future, Modern's management made several key decisions:

- They would continue to strive for engineering superiority. Although production technology was no longer a differential advantage for Modern, they still had an outstanding reputation for engineering design and problem solving.
- They would continue to price their equipment above that of competitors. First, Modern believed that the slightly higher prices were justified because of superiority of design, and second, they believed that there would be minimal customer resistance because of the perceived value.
- Finally, Modern decided to maintain its "high profile" via advertising and promotion. The company was committed to outspending competitors in advertising, in company literature, and in trade shows and exhibits.

In a recent meeting with its advertising agency, Modern again agreed to allocate a substantial amount of money to an advertising program. The company spent $450,000 on ad-

TABLE 7
The Buying Influences on the Purchase of Machine Tools

Phase of Buying Process	Job Function			
	Administrative	Production	Engineering	Purchasing
In Plants with 20–99 Employees				
(accounts for 42% of machine tools)				
Initiating purchase	33%	48%	11%	8%
Determining type of equipment	36	44	13	7
Drawing up specifications	30	48	15	7
Determining expenditure	47	40	6	7
Selecting suppliers	41	40	10	9
Final authorization to buy	49	33	9	9
In Plants of 100 or More Employees				
(accounts for 58% of machine tools)				
Initiating purchase	7%	68%	20%	5%
Determining type of equipment	8	65	21	7
Drawing up specifications	6	58	31	3
Determining expenditure	15	64	14	8
Selecting suppliers	8	58	20	14
Final authorization to buy	18	56	15	11

Source: Metalworking Data Bank, *Iron Age Magazine.*

TABLE 8
Market Shares of Leading Builders of Metal-Forming Machine Tools: 1965, 1970, 1975, 1980

Year	Total Industry Sales[a]	Modern	Market Share (percent)	Formco	Market Share (percent)	Johnson	Market Share (percent)
1965	$275	$ 45.9	16.7	$ 41.8	15.2	$ 35.2	12.8
1970	252	30.7	12.2	45.6	18.1	39.8	15.8
1975	270	38.1	14.1	37.3	13.8	41.6	15.4
1980	770	100.9	13.1	119.4	15.5	107.0	13.9

[a]Expressed in $ millions of annual net new orders.

vertising in 1980 and, despite the industry's cloudy outlook for the immediate future, Modern was willing to invest $475,000 for an advertising program in 1981. This budget was to include all advertising and promotion items except salaries and administrative costs. Modern was particularly interested in the agency's media recommendations, for two reasons. First, it wanted to expand its efforts in both the plastic-forming market and the international metalworking market and it knew relatively little about the appropriate media to reach these markets. Second, there was growing concern about the cost per inquiry received from print advertising and Modern was eager to explore new and it hoped, more efficient, alternatives.

ENDNOTE

1. Some of the data presented in this case were taken from *Industry Surveys,* the National Machine Tool Builders' Association, *American Machinist's* Inventory of Metalworking Equipment, McGraw-Hill's *Laboratory of Advertising Performance,* and *Iron Age*'s Metalworking Data Bank. Some of the data have been disguised and do not describe the actual situation in the machine tool industry.

QUESTIONS FOR DISCUSSION

1. What is an apropriate set of media objectives for Modern Machinery? How do your media objectives relate to the company's advertising objectives?
2. What media alternatives do you suggest? Why?

When Elizabeth Roberts introduced her line of English smocking kits, she had no idea that sales would be so brisk and customers so enthusiastic about her products. Creative Smocking is the brand name of the line, which included complete kits for making children's pinafores, bonnets, and a sampler; two books on smocking; and a mechanical smocking pleater. Exhibit 1 illustrates one of the techniques used in smocking and two examples of the finished effect.

Genuine English smocking was undergoing a revival of interest in the United States. It is a method of making accordian-like pleats in fabric and applying decorative stitching to the pleats. The art can be traced back to sixth- and seventh-century garments created by the Britons and Gauls. Various forms appeared during Roman and Elizabethan eras. Originally used as a means of adding shape to clothing, in the last century it has been used primarily to make clothing more attractive. The technique can be adapted to dresses, blouses, lingerie, coats, bonnets, and other articles of clothing.

At first glance, smocking appears very complicated; however, after mastering a few basic stitches, the beginner discovers it to be one of the simplest forms of stitchery. Because of its versatility and decorative qualities, smocking can be a very creative needlecraft.

THE NEEDLEWORK INDUSTRY

Creative Smocking operated in an industry consisting of several large firms, such as Bucilla and Columbia Minerva, and numerous small, undercapitalized companies that supply thread, floss, canvas, special fabrics, and patterns. English smocking faced competition from crewel

This case was prepared by Alan D. Fletcher, University of Tennessee.

embroidery, needlepoint, cross-stitch, and other needlework techniques.

Except for a few large firms, most of the companies engaged in little or no consumer advertising. Instead, industry practice was to promote solely to the retail trade and to rely on retailer promotion of the products. Mrs. Roberts had followed the industry practice.

THE MARKET FOR SMOCKING MATERIALS

Because of the highly specialized nature of the product line, the market was small compared with those for many consumer goods. It consisted mostly of upper-middle-class women 25 years and older. Generally, the purchaser of smocking materials was a heavy user of other handwork products, such as needlepoint, cross-stitch, and embroidery. The market was national, with heaviest usage in the northeastern states and relatively light but increasing use in other areas of the United States. The consumer market was seasonal, with highest sales in the fall months of September, October, and November and the winter months of December, January, and February. Generally, the wholesale market sales led the retail market by approximately three months.

CREATIVE SMOCKING'S FIRST YEAR ON THE MARKET

Because very little had been written on English smocking, Elizabeth Roberts began her venture by writing two books, which she referred to as her "educational materials." *The Art of English Smocking* and *Smocking Designs* were intended to explain the twelve basic stitches and to show ways in which the stitches can be combined to make designs. Profusely illustrated with large pictures and diagrams, they were well written

EXHIBIT 1
Examples of Smocking

Parallel threads are used to make accordion-like pleats in the fabric to be smocked.

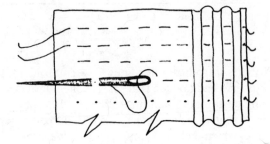

English smocking is often used around sleeves.

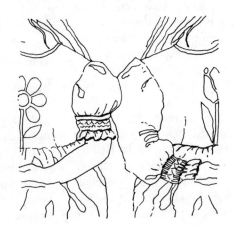

The most common application is on children's clothing.

and expertly designed. They were printed on heavy stock and had none of the amateurish appearance frequently encountered in needlework and related crafts booklets.

The books were a key to Mrs. Roberts' marketing strategy. "I felt that people would be interested in smocking if they understood something about it. It's a fascinating art, but if people don't know about it they won't try it. That's why I believe my two educational books are an indispensable part of my product line," said Mrs. Roberts.

The major items in the product line were:

	Retail Price
The Art of English Smocking	$ 2.25
Smocking Designs	1.50
Kits	
Smocking sampler	3.00
Sunbonnet	14.00
French bonnet	16.95
Pinafore	18.95
Boy's romper	19.95
Girl's romper	19.95
Blouse	25.00
Smocking pleater	79.50

Wholesale prices were 50 percent of retail. During the first year, monthly wholesale sales were as follows:

Month	Percent
January	4.0
February	5.2
March	4.4
April	2.6
May	3.0
June	12.1
July	11.8
August	11.0
September	15.8
October	15.0
November	10.4
December	4.7
	100.0

Creative Smocking products were distributed nationally, albeit thinly. Nearly all the dealers were small shop owners. Mrs. Roberts tried distributing through several large department stores in the East but decided not to continue. "They always slow paid me, and I couldn't afford a 90-day wait to receive payment," she said.

The promotional program for Creative Smocking consisted of a mix of trade advertising, and participation in trade shows. Over the first year Mrs. Roberts ran quarter-page advertisements in *National Needlework News,* a trade publication, and *Sew Business,* another trade journal. One ad appeared in *Fabric News.* Other advertisements appeared in the Counted Thread Society *Newsletter,* The National Standards Council's *The Flying Needle,* and The Embroiderers' Guild's *Needle Arts.* Total advertising expenditure during the first year was $2,200, which was approximately 10 percent of sales at wholesale.

By far the greatest promotional expenditure was for participation in national and regional trade shows, which Mrs. Roberts believed was the most productive form of promotion for her product line. "Because buyers—the retailers themselves—need to be educated about English smocking, personal contact is essential," she said. "It is difficult to communicate that kind of information in an ad."

Mrs. Roberts attended seven trade shows during the first year and incurred travel and related costs of approximately $7,000. Her belief was that such large expenditures were necessary to establish the Creative Smocking name in the trade. She noted that her display generated great interest in her merchandise. Numerous retailers attending the trade shows mentioned having seen the display at previous shows.

Fortunately for Creative Smocking, the trade press and consumer press had devoted considerable space to the product line. Although not planned as a part of the promotional program, this attention had undoubtedly been instrumental in the increased market interest in the products.

Nationally syndicated newspaper columnist Lucille Rivers featured the line in two columns. *Women's Wear Daily* ran an illustrated article by Maryann Ondovscik. *Homesewing News* also had given extensive coverage to the line. Other publications had exhibited the desire to run articles. From the press's viewpoint, English smocking as offered by Elizabeth Roberts was an important art form as well as a significant new marketing venture.

Mrs. Roberts had learned that during the coming year English smocking would be featured in stories in *Good Housekeeping*'s semiannual needlework book. Also during the coming year *Ladies' Home Journal* planned to promote mail-order sales of Creative Smocking products. The firm would be carried as the subject of a feature article that would also include an order blank for the kit. Under this arrangement, Elizabeth Roberts could fill the bulk order and split the profit equally with the magazine. *Family Circle* and *Better Homes and Gardens* also planned to feature a mail-order deal without any initial outlay of funds by Mrs. Roberts.

FUTURE ADVERTISING

Gratifying as the trade attention had been during the first year of operation, Mrs. Roberts felt that it could not be expected to continue. As the product gained a stronger foothold in the marketplace and its novelty waned with the press, Elizabeth Roberts believed that she would have to rely increasingly on her own efforts in promoting the products. She was concerned with how, on a severely limited promotion budget, she could reach her consumer market with an effective selling message through advertising. Nevertheless, she was convinced that all or at least a major portion of her advertising efforts during the year should be placed in media directed to consumers rather than retailers.

QUESTIONS FOR DISCUSSION

1. What major factors should be considered in developing a media plan for Creative Smocking? In particular, how will the other elements in the marketing mix affect media planning?
2. What alternative media strategies should Creative Smocking consider in developing a media plan?
3. How might Mrs. Roberts coordinate any nonadvertising promotional activities with media advertising?

Problem: Who Roberts should advertise to, and how, with her limited budget.

SECTION 7
ADVERTISING RESEARCH

Advertising research is one of the most controversial areas in advertising and promotion management. Much of the controversy is essentially centered around questions of its usefulness. Some regard research as an expensive, time-consuming activity that produces obvious or invalid results. Others see it as a management tool that can provide important guidance to the decision maker.

Those who either ignore or diminish the importance of advertising reseach do so for some valid reasons. Despite the potential benefits of research, advertising and promotion management should be equally aware of its major drawbacks.

Research is expensive and time-consuming. The cost and amount of time required vary according to the scope of the research project; however, any research project that collects empirical data requires a considerable investment of both funds and time. Further, a poorly conceived or executed research study can confuse rather than help to clarify the issues under study.

Perhaps the most widespread misunderstanding of the research activity is the notion that research results can make decisions. Whenever management views research in this way, it is usually frustrated because results can be "inconclusive." At best, research describes an environment and indicates relationships within that environment that can reduce uncertainty regarding a decision. Ultimately management must interpret the data and then apply the results to the particular problem at hand. Skill and creativity are required in using research as a guide in decision making.

Although advertising is closely related to marketing, there are a number of issues that are most often classified as the focus of advertising research. As we suggested earlier, the fundamental advertising question is: "What is the proper role of advertising in the stimulation of demand?" This is technically a promotion question because it indirectly requires an assessment of the role of each promotional tool. However, until the role of advertising is specified, conducting research that focuses on other advertising variables is premature.

The specific research techniques used to explore budgeting, creativity, and media decisions range from a search of secondary data, direct observations, focus group interviews, consumer panel data, large-scale surveys, and field or laboratory experiments. Such constraints as cost, time, and availability of research skills determine the appropriate techniques to employ.

Ultimately, the Advertising or Promotion Manager is responsible for planning all aspects of the advertising program and for assessing the total effectiveness of the advertising effort. Although collection of data is most often done by commercial research firms or by research departments of advertising agencies, there are several ways the Advertising or Promotion Manager can improve the productivity of the research effort. Therefore, we have created a set of cases that will allow you to gain experience in:

1. *Encouraging a research orientation.* The possibility of errors in judgment is reduced when decisions are made with the assistance of pertinent information. By developing an appreciation of research, the Advertising or Promotion Manager creates an atmosphere in which analytical problem solving predominates.
2. *Initiating a research project.* Regardless of who collects the data, the research effort is usually initiated by the Advertising or Promotion Manager. The high costs and potential impact of research results emphasize the importance of three basic research questions: what to test, when to test, and how to test.
3. *Interpreting research results.* Data alone, of course, are of little value. The results of a research project must be interpreted before they can be used. Familiarity with the skills of research design, data collection methods, and statistical analyses is essential in the intelligent use of research by management.
4. *Applying research results.* Perhaps the most critical phase of the research process is the application of results to a specific problem. Sometimes the results of a research project are inconclusive, yet because of the investment in capital, time, and effort, management can be tempted to use the results as justification for a decision. At other times, research results might indicate a course of action that is totally incompatible with industry norms. Knowing when and how to use research requires considerable experience and knowledge of both research skills and the practicalities of the marketplace.

MORNING TREAT COFFEE BAGS

The petite Morning Treat Company based in Baton Rouge, Louisiana, was attempting to battle the giants of the coffee industry by building a national market and franchise for the coffee bag. Although the company had sold over one million bags per month during the previous year in foreign markets such as Japan and through specialty retailers like Neiman-Marcus, management was keenly interested in expanding distribution and sales through supermarkets.

The company's product was marketed under the name "Morning Treat Coffee Bags." Like the familiar tea bag, the coffee bag allowed an individual to brew a single serving of fresh-ground coffee with the ease of using instant coffee. The bags were available in ten roasts including dark, coffee with chicory, regular, and decaffeinated. Each bag was sealed in a foil pouch (see Exhibit 1) which permitted maximum freshness for nine months. Designed for convenience, the coffee bag seemed especially suited for the traveler, office worker, student, and generally the one to three cups per day coffee drinker, although the retail price was almost a third more than regular coffee on a per cup basis.

According to Mr. Sam Gallo, a developer and president of the Morning Treat Coffee Company, the coffee bag concept was not new. Almost 75 years ago, tea merchants invented the tea bag. These bags consisted of silk sachets full of tea leaves. Naturally, coffee was also put into the sachets, but the bags went stale and rancid since the oils and acid contained in the ground coffee spoiled the bags.

For decades various individuals tried unsuccessfully to make a coffee bag. Then in 1960 an America engineer, Mr. Earl Hiscock, began working to solve the coffee bag enigma. He tried

This case was prepared by Marshall Taylor of J. Walter Thompson, New York; and John H. Murphy.

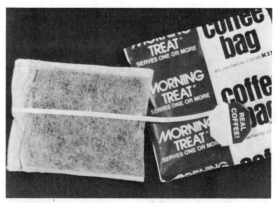

EXHIBIT 1
Morning Treat Coffee Bag and Individual Foil Package

sealing the bag in a vacuumed container. This kept the coffee from going stale, but the bag still discolored and spoiled. Mr. Hiscock discovered that the cellulosic structure of the bags was responsible for the spoilage. Seven years later he patented an inert, noncellulosic filter-like material and the pouch design to hold the coffee. However, these were only theoretical patents since Mr. Hiscock never produced coffee bags.

That task was left to Mr. Gallo. He obtained the patents from Mr. Hiscock and made the coffee bag practical by patenting several processes that made mass production feasible. Although the coffee bag became a practical and workable reality, General Foods and Proctor and Gamble, the nation's largest coffee manufacturers, had chosen not to venture into this product line extension.

Mr. Gallo approached some of these coffee marketers but found that they were not interested in coffee bags. Mr. Gallo felt that because these companies had a virtual monopoly over the coffee industry, there was no reason why they should produce a coffee bag unless a competitor threatened a significant share of their market. At the same time, Mr. Gallo believed that if General Foods were to market a coffee bag, Procter and Gamble would have one on the market within 90 days. However, unless Mr. Gallo's company gained a significant share of the coffee market, the giant companies would probably ignore him and the coffee bag.

THE COFFEE MARKET AND THE PRODUCT'S POSITIONING

More coffee is consumed in the United States than in any other country in the world. Industry sources estimated that more than seven out of ten adults in the United States drink coffee. Further, on a typical winter day Americans consume approximately 400 million cups of coffee. Retail sales of coffee in supermarkets is a multibillion dollar business.

The light and medium users (one to three cups per day) accounted for roughly three-fourths of all coffee consumption. Coffee consumption was spread fairly evenly among various age groups. The south and north-central parts of the United States accounted for almost 60 percent of coffee usage.

Mr. Gallo realized that in order for him to garner even a fraction of the huge potential market for his firm's coffee bags, Morning Treat would most likely have to rely on an effective introductory advertising compaign. In considering the use of advertising, he also was aware that Morning Treat faced the very difficult task of convincing consumers not only to break with traditional means of preparing coffee and try a new concept but also to buy an unfamiliar brand.

On the other hand, Mr. Gallo felt Morning Treat was fortunate in that it was significantly different from the other products in its category. Thus, he believed it could potentially carve a niche for itself in the coffee market. Its competitors were regular and instant coffee marketers, not other coffee bag manufacturers.

Morning Treat's main benefit was convenience; therefore, Mr. Gallo believed it should be marketed to those consumers who did not like or need to make a pot of coffee but who would rather drink fresh-brewed coffee than instant. This uniquely positioned Morning Treat somewhere between regular ground coffee and instant. Mr. Gallo was convinced that this positioning should apply only to its common coffee types: regular and decaffeinated. Other types and roasts of coffee, such as Louisiana dark, Columbian, and Santos, were products that were specialty items. Morning Treat's efforts should focus on the regular and decaffeinated coffee markets.

In order to develop an effective advertising campaign for the coffee bag, Mr. Gallo hired an advertising agency. The agency developed a number of recommendations, which are described in the following section.

THE AGENCY'S RECOMMENDATIONS

First, the agency recommended a new name for the product—"Java." The agency pointed out that a simple and short name was preferable to Morning Treat (which in itself was limiting). Java was descriptive and suggested exotic, romantic experiences.

Most important, Java was a slang term for coffee. According to the dictionary, Java could also refer to the main island of Indonesia where a large amount of coffee was grown or to the coffee bean or plant. Therefore, Java should make the product instantly recognizable as some sort of coffee product.

To specify the product even more, the agency recommended that the words "coffee bags" be used in conjunction with the new name Java to produce immediate recognition that the product was more than a new brand of coffee. Thus, the new name under which the product would be advertised was "Java Coffee Bags."

Before designing a package or advertising, the agency designed a logo for the product (see Exhibit 2). The typeface Korinna Heavy was chosen because it is bold and easy to read. The use of serif type helped to create a pleasing visual effect. The upper case "J" was elongated

EXHIBIT 2
Proposed Java Logo

EXHIBIT 3
Proposed Java Package Design

to increase the uniqueness of the logo. The letters were spaced closely together to reflect the current style of setting type. The coffee bag was hung from the "J" to allow the product to be visible every time that the logo was displayed. This mnemonic device created an intriguing effect. The agency believed that the logo had a simple poster-like quality that would easily stand out against the clutter and competition on the grocery store shelf.

Following the development of a logo, the agency created a new package design (see Exhibit 3). The agency stressed the importance of having an esthetically pleasing package since the visual impression the brand made on the consumer through advertisements and in the store was a crucial factor in determining consumer acceptance.

The package for Java Coffee Bags was designed to give the product specific identity and color as well as a quick description of the contents. The colors used were light and dark brown tones that conveyed a feeling of richness—a very important attribute for a coffee. The package design consisted of the logo over a photograph of coffee beans spread over a neutral colored wooden butcher's block. The white letters and coffee bag showed up very well against the dark brown coffee beans. The butcher's block added an appropriate texture and contrast to the photograph.

In addition to a new name, logo, and package design, the agency proposed a campaign series of print, outdoor, and broadcast ads. Example roughs from the introductory print campaign are presented in Exhibits 4 and 5 (visuals are indications of photographs). All the headlines for the introductory print ads were written to

EXHIBIT 4
Layout for Introductory Print Advertisement

EXHIBIT 5
Layout for Introductory Print Advertisement

announce news to the consumer. Each headline offered a distinct benefit: the coffee bag is small, quick, convenient, easy, and neat. Each headline positioned the coffee bag against brewing regular coffee and also offered the instant coffee drinker an alternative. Copy in these introductory ads told lovers of the taste of brewed coffee that they could have brewed flavor with the convenience of instant. It also told those who drank instant that fresh brewed coffee was now just as easy. Phrases like "Meet the world's smallest coffee maker," implied that the product was "new" without employing the overused word itself.

The tag line "Fresh ground coffee by the cup" was used throughout the entire campaign. This signature line served to remind the consumer that Java Coffee Bags contained real fresh-ground coffee and that it could be brewed conveniently by the cup.

The second phase of the print campaign followed naturally from the first. Exhibits 6 and 7 present ads designed for use after the initial introduction of the product. In this series of ads the major benefit stressed was the convenience of not having to deal with the complications of using regular ground coffee (whether in an automatic coffee maker, drip pot, or percolator). The headline questions were immediately answered with the logo. The product was the hero of these advertisements as it hung from the "J" of the logo. In the background were visuals that reinforced the headline (visuals are indications of photographs).

Layouts for Java outdoor boards were also presented to the client. These boards were simple. They consisted of a single phrase and employed the device of a coffee bag hanging from one of the letters on the board. The bag

EXHIBIT 6
Layout for Print Advertisement

EXHIBIT 7
Layout for Print Advertisement

extended off of the board. This embellishment created a visual surprise for the viewer. The headline on each board played off the bag concept, thus reemphasizing the packaging convenience of the product.

In addition to the print and outdoor ads, the agency suggested a number of specific radio and television commercials. All of these spots employed music and stressed many of the same copy points used in the print ads.

A FOCUS GROUP EVALUATION OF THE COFFEE BAG AND THE PROPOSED CREATIVE STRATEGY

After presenting an analysis of the situation facing the Morning Treat Coffee Company, as well as their recommendations for advertising and promotion, the agency suggested conducting a small research project to "get a reading on consumer reactions to all this." The agency proposed that a focus group interview be conducted prior to their moving toward even regional introduction of the coffee bag through a mass media campaign. Mr. Gallo agreed that such a project would be useful.

In order to assess consumer reactions to the coffee bag and the proposed creative strategies, the agency conducted a focus group interview using female coffee drinkers. Following discussions with Mr. Gallo and as a first step in conducting the research, the agency developed the set of six objectives for the focus group interview. These objectives were as follows:

1. To assess acceptability of the coffee bag concept.

[handwritten: uses ~~before~~ for focus groups – can adv in their own language]

2. To discover apprehensions, negative feelings, or uncertainties toward the coffee bag.

3. To examine perceptions of taste compared with that of regular and instant coffee.

4. To assess likeliness of use.

5. To evaluate potential product names.

6. To have the group evaluate and critique proposed creative campaign strategies.

A random sample of adult females was selected from the Baton Rouge telephone directory and contacted regarding possible participation in the group interview. Women who were not coffee drinkers were eliminated. Those who agreed to participate were sent a sample of the product along with a letter thanking them for their cooperation. Eleven women agreed to participate in the group interview. Of these, six actually attended the session. The entire session, which lasted about an hour and a half, was recorded on audio tapes.

The session was held in the evening at the agency's office. The agency's conference room was set up with living room type chairs, a low coffee table, and other tables for refreshments. The session was moderated by a male principal of the agency who had considerable experience in moderating focus groups.

At the conclusion of the session a short demographic questionnaire was administered to the six participants. See respondent profile.

The day after the focus group session was held, the agency reported to Mr. Gallo that the results of the session were encouraging. Mr. Gallo immediately indicated that he did not want to discuss prematurely the project prior to receiving a formal written report and analysis of the session. In addition, he requested a transcript of the session which he wanted to read prior to evaluating the agency's formal report on the outcome of the research project. Mr. Gallo emphasized that all discussion of the results of the session should be postponed until he had ample time to study the transcript and the agency's formal report.

RESPONDENT PROFILE

Occupations: retired teacher, high school counselor, program director, office manager, product planner for IBM, and personnel employment manager

Marital status: married—4, single—1, widowed—1

Number of children under 18: zero—5; two—1

Education: Bachelors degree—1, Masters degree—5

Average number of cups consumed each day: average = 4 cups (1 cup—1, 2 cups—1, 3 cups—2, 7 cups—1, 8 cups—1)

Approximate household income:

$15,000–24,999—1
$25,000–39,999—4
$40,000+   —1

Ages: 30, 31, 31, 34, 56, 66

The agency submitted a complete transcript of the session and its formal report to Mr. Gallo for his consideration. Mr. Gallo was particularly concerned with the group's reactions to the proposed product name Java and their evaluations of the proposed creative strategies. The Appendix presents the segments of the focus group session most relevant to these issues. A meeting was arranged at the Morning Treat Company office a week later to discuss the conclusions that could be drawn from the focus group project.

QUESTIONS FOR DISCUSSION

1. Why are focus groups so popular among advertising researchers?

2. What are the major advantages and disadvantages of the focus group data collection methodology?

3. What major criteria should be used in evaluating the procedures followed in conducting a focus group?

4. What specific conclusions can be reached

from reviewing the transcript of the session? What changes in the agency's recommendations do the findings suggest?

5. What changes in the procedures followed in conducting the focus group interview session described in the case would you recommend?

f.g. can make predictions for mkting prod.

is f.g. representative of TM

leader should be same as members

ie: sex, race, social class

location

Evaluation of focus Groups.

Criteria: what were MTC ed info needs? Did they get their answers?

general goal was to get general info + succeeded.

APPENDIX
TRANSCRIPT OF FOCUS GROUP SESSION

Moderator: I thank you for coming tonight and your help is greatly appreciated. What we intend to do is to explore a new concept in the coffee industry—coffee bags—and this will take place as a group discussion. And we will consider several questions about the product. The tape recorder here will be used only to transcribe what we say. No names or anything like that—everybody's anonymous. And I urge everybody to express your opinions. Anything you want to say, positive or negative. I'm not selling these bags. I don't get any commission off of them, and so I don't have any interest in them. And feel free to serve yourself refreshments. You can get up, move around, and the rest rooms are down the other end of the hall down there. So, we probably should start out with everybody introducing themselves and give a short history of what you do. You can start, Carol.

Carol: I'm Carol _____, and I work as an office manager with a large association, and I'm in charge of setting up and coordinating the association.

Linda: I'm Linda _____, and I'm manager of a personnel office. I've been there about 13 years. I spend a lot of time at my job.

Dianne: I'm Dianne _____, and I work for Product Planning—I work in Product Planning for IBM.

Jean: My name is Jean _____, and I work part-time as a freelance graphic designer or advertising person but the biggest part of my day is spent working as a program director for a psychological testing company.

Katherine: I'm Katherine _____, and I'm a retired school teacher. I'm having a good time now. I don't miss the paper grading at all.

Vivian: I'm Vivian _____, and I'm a high school counselor.

Moderator: Okay. Well, I'm Mike, and I'm your discussion leader. The first question I want to deal with tonight is what do you think of the coffee bag concept. I guess all of you have tried it by now, and just what are your comments?

Katherine: I think it would be a handy thing to have, myself. I can think of times that I would have loved to have had a coffee bag with me.

Linda: It would be a lot easier to carry around than a jar of instant coffee, that's for sure. It's nice that it's premeasured too.

Vivian: I would find an instant coffee that was packaged that way of more use, because this really has to be—you have to have boiling water to really dissolve it, and it takes two or three minutes, where instant coffee is ready as soon as you put the water on it. And I didn't think this was as good as most of the instant coffees.

Jean: I think as a concept it's really good—I mean, certainly it's parallel to tea—you know, put a tea bag in and pour the water over it. But personally it's not something I would really use. But I think the concept is good for many cases.

Moderator: Okay. If you had to pick one aspect—just one—what do you like most about the coffee bag?

All: Convenience.

Moderator: Okay. What do you like least about the coffee bag?

All: Taste.

(AT THIS POINT THE GROUP CONTINUED TO DISCUSS THE PRODUCT ITSELF, APPREHENSIONS AND UNCERTAINTIES TOWARD THE COFFEE BAG CONCEPT, PERCEPTIONS COMPARED WITH REGULAR AND INSTANT COFFEE, AND THE LIKELIHOOD OF USE. THIS LENGTHY DISCUSSION IS OMITTED FROM THIS TRANSCRIPT.)

Moderator: Okay, let's change directions

just a little bit now. Let's talk more about—other than taste and all—let's talk about maybe a name for the coffee. If you were to name this product—let's say you haven't seen the package, you don't know what's on the package—if you just knew about this product, what names would you come up with to sell it?

Carol: I'd keep it simple, like tea bag coffee bag. Because somebody at work—I said I have to go to this silly thing to test coffee or something—no offense, but you know—and I was showing—I said, here, I need to test this. She said, what is it? I said it's a coffee bag like a tea bag. I said you have to keep it simple when you're comparing them.

Dianne: The first thing that came to my mind when you asked that question was something with which I could identify—the bag. Which is a tea bag. Like flow-through coffee bags.

Moderator: Well, the company itself is called Morning Treat. Do you think that just calling it coffee bags is too generic a name?

Linda: It might well be if other manufacturers come out with the same product. Then you have *The* Coffee Bag or something like that. But I think Morning Treat in some ways gives the wrong impression, because it's for convenience.

Moderator: Anybody else think of any names?

Dianne: You know, you think of other products that came on the market as firsts that I think of, like Kleenex. I mean, how many of us say, May I have a tissue please. They always say, Do you have a Kleenex.

Moderator: But that's a brand name that's become a generic name. Coffee bags is a generic name to begin with.

Dianne: That's right. I mean, I think of those things as firsts on the market and it would be a name that would be a catchall for it.

Moderator: Do you think that they would be disadvantaged if let's say some other competition came out and if they were coffee bags—just coffee bags—I don't know as far as copy-

right how it would be considered. Like Proctor and Gamble can come out with it and call it Sanka Coffee Bags. Do you think that would pose any problems as far as if you called your product just coffee bags?

Jean: I think it would.

Linda: You think about radio advertising. You don't have a product or an image to identify with. So you're advertising coffee bags. That's not going to—you know, how do you differentiate between this coffee bag and another manufacturer's coffee bag?

Moderator: So you're saying you might need a brand name to associate it with.

Linda: Right. To identify it.

Moderator: Any names that come to mind?

Jean: Are you saying that you need a name instead of coffee bags, or some catchy thing to go with it?

Linda: I think it needs something more than just coffee bags.

Moderator: Vivian, were you going to say something?

Vivian: Well, a lot of those brand names that have come out and become generic names like Kleenex and so forth, the sound of that name doesn't have that much to do with the product.

Dianne: That's right, all it is is a catchy name.

Vivian: So I don't think you need to necessarily have something that says coffee bags. You need some catchy name and once that's established—

Dianne: Like Sanka. Sanka has nothing to it that suggests coffee, lack of caffeine or anything.

Linda: But something like Easy Time would convey the simpleness of using it. Maybe it's too simple.

Moderator: Any other names?

Dianne: Bean Bags.

Carol: Something like One at a Time.

Moderator: One Bag at a Time? I couldn't resist.

Dianne: If it were a one word—just like we

were saying, like Sanka, Kleenex, Xerox. Where did the word Sanka come from though?

Jean: Turn it around. Bag of Coffee or something. Initials usually don't work.

Moderator: P.D.M., Coffee Company.

Katherine: We aren't very creative, are we?

Moderator: Okay. The next question. Somebody did—I think it was Jean—mentioned something about this. What do you think about the current name of the product—Morning Treat Coffee Bags?

Jean: Well, I just thought it made people think just of in the morning, when in fact coffee can be had at night or any time.

Linda: Maybe Coffee Treat.

Jean: I don't think Morning Treat is good. It seems to limit it in your mind.

Vivian: Quick Coffee.

Katherine: Presto.

Linda: Isn't there something?

Moderator: It's a cooker. Okay. I'll tell you a name someone has come up with. If you hate it, that's fine. I mean, don't—my feelings are nothing, because I don't care. What do you think about the name Java?

Jean: Isn't that the name of a kind of coffee?

Moderator: Okay, it is the name of a kind of coffee.

Jean: I'm not talking about Kava, I'm talking about—

Moderator: You're right, a roast. It is a particular roast, you're right. But what do you think about making it the brand name and calling it Java Coffee Bags.

Linda: It gives you a coffee association and gives you sort of an exotic—that gives me an exotic feeling.

Katherine: Well, I think it's repetitious to have Java and Coffee Bags.

Vivian: Yeah, because Java is sort of a slang term that means coffee.

Linda: I think it might raise your expectations, particularly on this brand. To me, that gives it a real rich mellow connotation, and I think on this particular line the expectations—

Katherine: It indicates real roast coffee.

Linda: It's got a nice—sounds good—nice and short. You know, sort of sticks with you.

Katherine: But I'd call it just Java Bags.

Moderator: Just Java or Java Bags or Java in a Bag, maybe.

Dianne: What's the Spanish term for coffee, *cafe?*

Vivian: *Cafe.*

Moderator: French is *café.* I don't know about the Spanish.

Jean: But still, if you were to do your specialty coffees, would that form sort of a conflict.

Moderator: You would have to advertise it with some sort of label on the box that says the different roasts that they have, which they do have.

Moderator: I will now show you some preliminary layouts for an introductory creative campaign for coffee bags using the name Java. Please comment on whether or not you like the approaches taken and why. Be honest. Also, remember that these are only roughs and not finished layouts. The drawings represent indications of photographs.

I would first like to get your impressions of some package designs. Here is the package design currently used by the Morning Treat Coffee Company and on the back is a proposed design using the name Java. The same basic design is used on package boxes of eight, sixteen, and forty-eight individual bags. [See Exhibits 1 and 3.]

Carol: I really like the colors used in the Java package. The browns remind me of coffee—a rich tasting coffee.

Linda: These are coffee beans, but what is the background?

Moderator: A butcher's block.

Linda: Oh. I agree with Carol. I like the brown tones very much. I think it's appealing but I wonder if the bright orange of the original package might stand out better on the grocery shelf.

Katherine: I don't know. Personally the orange package with the yellow and white lettering scares me off. It's not very esthetically pleasing.

Dianne: It really doesn't make any difference to me. I don't think the design of a package affects my purchases.

Jean: Oh sure it does.

Dianne: Well not consciously, at least.

Katherine: "Java" coffee bags bothers me. Isn't that redundant?

Linda: Grammatically maybe, but I think it's got a nice flow to it. I wouldn't think that it would bother the average consumer.

Vivian: I like the simpleness of the Java package. It's not cluttered like the Morning Treat package. To me that's very important in getting a consumer to notice the package on the shelf—simple design.

Moderator: Now I would like for you to look at a couple of layouts that are representative of a series of layouts for an introductory print campaign for Java Coffee Bags. [See Exhibits 4 and 5.] Look at the ads briefly and then comment on them.

Vivian: As I said about the package design, I like the simple, uncluttered appearance of these ads. They are very appealing. A lot better than those old Folger's ads. I get so tired of Mrs. Olson or Cora or whatever her name is.

Jean: For me, the one that says "The world's quickest coffee maker" is the most appealing. For me "quick" is an important benefit. I hate to take time to make coffee. I've got more important things to do.

Vivian: Do you really think it's quicker than some of those automatic coffee makers—they're pretty fast.

Linda: If you count the time that it takes to measure the coffee and all that it would be. All you have to do with the coffee bag is drop it in the water.

Katherine: I like the headline that emphasizes small. For me that's convenient. You can drop it in your purse and take it anywhere with you. Saying "The world's smallest coffee maker" and having the coffee bag over the cup of coffee is eye-catching. It sort of makes you say, "That's a clever little product."

Moderator: Carol, you were going to say something.

Carol: Oh well, I was just going to say that I agree with Vivian about the appearance of the layouts. I think it was a good idea to use coffee mugs. They always make me think of rich coffee more than a coffee cup.

Moderator: Any other comments?

Linda: Oh the "Fresh ground coffee by the cup." Is that going to be on all the ads?

Moderator: Yes. It's called a tag line.

Linda: Well it's a good idea. It sums up what the coffee bag is.

Katherine: I think you should put it on the package too. If not on the front then on the back or side somewhere.

Moderator: Now I want to look at a second series of ads that would be a continuation of the introductory ads that you have just seen. [See Exhibits 6 and 7.]

Linda: Oh that first one was written for me. I always make a mess when I make coffee. I don't know what it is, but I inevitably spill a little. I'm really not that messy all the time. This ad really hits home.

Jean: The second one was written for me. I hate making coffee. This ad describes it perfectly. Any coffee that will take the bother out of brewing coffee I'll buy.

Vivian: Well again, I like the appearance of the ads. It's good that the coffee bag is displayed prominently. I think they go well with the first advertisements that you showed us. I can relate with the bother of making coffee too. It's a good idea.

Dianne: What are these things right here?

Moderator: It's an indication of coffee grounds in a filter.

Dianne: Things you have to dump out and throw away.

Moderator: Right.

Dianne: I can relate to that. It's so much easier just to throw away the coffee bag when you're finished.

Linda: Those grounds are messy. Especially when you spill some on the floor. Yuk.

Katherine: Is there any copy that goes with these ads?

Moderator: Yes. These lines here indicate where the copy will go. However, I have not included the actual copy because I just want your immediate opinions on the ad concepts. If you're lucky, 6 percent of your readers will read the body copy. It's really secondary. Any other comments? If not, that will bring the session to a close. I do thank you all for coming tonight; you have been extremely helpful. I'll be glad to answer any questions that you may have. Feel free to help yourself to more coffee and cookies.

There is probably no greater health fear among Americans today than the threat of cancer. One doesn't need the most recent government statistics on the annual number of deaths caused by this disease to feel its impact.

During the past fifteen years several national, regional, and local organizations have emerged to help cancer patients deal with the myriad of emotional and physical adjustments that are part of a cancer operation and its aftereffects. One of these organizations is the United Ostomy Association (UOA), which concerns itself with the problems of patients (both cancer and noncancer) who have lost part or all of their intestines or urinary tract and must often wear an apparatus which enables their bodies to function properly. While the UOA and other organizations have been of immense help to cancer patients, their efforts to help both patients and the public at large are often hampered by a number of communication obstacles.

BACKGROUND OF THE UNITED OSTOMY ASSOCIATION

In 1949 a small band of gastrointestinal ostomy* patients came together at the Valley Forge General Hospital in Phoenixville, Pennsylvania, and formed the first ostomy group. In 1956 the first effort at forming a national organization was held in New York City. In these early years individual groups thrived in their own communities and exchanged information through small circulation newsletters, correspondence among members, and periodic meetings.

---

*Ostomy literally means to form an opening, and such an operation creates another body opening, allowing the passage of air, food, elimination, and so on.

This case was prepared by Charles H. Patti.

With the publication of *Ileostomy Quarterly* and the listing of all known groups, an exchange of ideas among members was facilitated. Nationalizing was given further impetus through the publishing of *Ileostomy Manual,* the first practical guide for good ileostomy care. Also, an educational filmstrip on ileostomy care and management was developed by the Ileostomy Association of Boston and Los Angeles.

After several preliminary organizing meetings, the first national convention was held in September 1962 in Cleveland, Ohio. Twenty-eight groups including 115 members became charter members at this first meeting. A name (United Ostomy Association) was selected, officers were elected, a constitution constructed, and most importantly, the goals and direction of the organization were specified. The United Ostomy Association was to be a national group of individuals united in one main purpose: to provide help and encouragement to the new ostomate.

To accomplish their goal, the UOA would have to serve and communicate effectively with many publics—members, nonmembers, the medical and nursing professions, and the community. One measure of the Association's success is the number of ostomates who become members of the Association. Today, there are over 300 local chapters of UOA representing a paid membership of over 20,000.

ACCOMPLISHMENTS OF THE UNITED OSTOMY ASSOCIATION

The progress and development of the UOA have been quite impressive. Among the Association's major accomplishments are:

1. Financial solvency. The Association was penniless in 1962 but has been self-sustaining to

the point of producing an annual budget of well over $100,000.

2. The *Ostomy Quarterly* was started in 1963 and continues to be successful.

3. *Colostomies—A Guide* and the *Ostomy Review* were published in 1968 and are but two of a long list of publications now available through UOA.

4. In 1965 a cooperative program for foreign groups was started and in 1970 the World Work Committee was formed.

5. The enterstomal therapist emerged as the professional in stomal care.

6. Ostomy prostheses have undergone vast improvements because of the concern of ostomates, therapists, and manufacturers.

To help ostomates, the UOA has broadened its concept of assistance. In a current UOA brochure the aim of the Association is defined as:

> The United Ostomy Association, Inc. is dedicated to helping every ostomy patient return to normal living through mutual aid and moral support; education in proper ostomy care and management; exchange of ideas; assistance in improving ostomy equipment and supplies; advancement of knowledge of gastrointestinal diseases; cooperation with other organizations having common purposes; exhibits at medical and public meetings; and public education about ostomy.

Despite the progress and successs of the UOA, Don Binder, UOA's Executive Director, points out some of the major problems facing the organization:

> Although we are very proud of the accomplishments of the UOA, we are aware that much more needs to be done. We estimate that there are approximately 1,000,000 ostomates in the U.S. and Canada. Each year there are about 100,000 new ostomy surgeries performed. This means that there are nearly 980,000 ostomates who do not belong to the UOA.

> Furthermore, we feel the general public knows almost nothing about this type of cancer. We would like to overcome this lack of awareness and knowledge for several reasons.

> First of all, awareness and knowledge will enhance early diagnosis. This type of cancer can be cured by early diagnosis, and the more people know about the disease, the greater the chances are for cure.

> Secondly, there are a number of physical and emotional adjustments associated with an ostomy operation. Partial or complete removal of the small or large intestines frequently involves the patient to wear an "appliance." Proper utilization of an appliance requires education and training. Although some basic training is provided by the medical profession, there is a need for continuing education and training. One of the main goals of the UOA is to provide such education.

> Also, many ostomates experience some lack of self-confidence as a result of having the operation and wearing an appliance. Doubts about returning to a "normal" life are common. The facts are that the vast majority of ostomates, even those required to wear an appliance, can live a completely normal life, including active participation in athletics, work, and bearing and raising children.

CURRENT SITUATION

During the past year Don Binder and the Executive Committee of UOA have observed with great interest the national advertising campaigns for many public health related organizations. The American Cancer Society's "Anti-Smoking Campaign," Alcoholics Anonymous, March of Dimes, "Take Care of Your Body Before Pregnancy," Muscular Sclerosis, HEW's Venereal Disease Information Campaign, and the Heart Association are just a few of the

EXHIBIT 1
Campaign Ideas of Agency A

I. CREATIVE STRATEGY

Cancer of the intestines or urinary tract is one of the severest forms of the disease and frequently results in an ostomy operation. Although the vast majority of such operations are successful, the patient experiences a wide range of physical and emotional problems. The UOA can help . . . but you need to learn more about this disease.

II. CREATIVE TACTICS: "SHOCK"

In both print and television, pictures will be used of people who have had the operation and are experiencing physical limitations and social rejection. For example, inability to return to prior employment, limited participation in sports, and difficulty in meeting others.

III. RATIONALE

People will take care of themselves only if they are dramatically shown the unpleasant consequences. Our advertisements will "shock" people into the desired action—joining the UOA or seeking information about ostomies.

growing number of public health organizations that have used mass media successfully.

At a recent UOA Executive Committee meeting, the following external communications goals were established:

1. To help convince the estimated 980,000 non-member ostomates in the United States and Canada to join the UOA.
2. To inform the general public about this particular type of cancer and the advantages of early diagnosis.
3. To foster increased acceptance of ostomates.
4. To overcome the general public's misunderstanding of the disease and the operation.
5. To persuade health care professionals and workers that the UOA does provide valuable assistance to ostomates in returning to a normal, active life.

To accomplish these goals, the UOA became interested in considering a mass media advertising campaign. Such a campaign would have to be designed so that it could be used on a national basis as well as by the 300 local chapters whenever public service announcement time or space became available.

A number of advertising agencies expressed interest in developing the campaign for the UOA and after talking with several of them, Mr. Binder and the Executive Committee decided to ask the three most promising agencies to summarize and submit their respective approaches. Each agency was given two weeks to decide on a campaign idea and submit it to the UOA.

At the next Executive Committee meeting the three campaign ideas (see Exhibits 1, 2, and 3) were discussed and there was considerable disagreement as to what campaign idea to use.

Each campaign seemed to have some advantages and disadvantages, and after several hours of deliberation the Executive Committee still could not come to an agreement. Finally, Don Binder invited the Account Executives from the three agencies into his conference room and said,

EXHIBIT 2
Campaign Ideas of Agency B

I. CREATIVE STRATEGY

Cancer of the intestines or urinary tract is a serious form of the disease and deserves the attention of everyone. There is a great deal of misunderstanding about ostomy and you owe it to yourself and others to learn more about it. The UOA can provide all the necessary information.

II. CREATIVE TACTICS: "FACTS"

All advertisements will stress facts—what the disease is; how many ostomy operations there are annually; the operation success rate; etc. Rather than showing people, cold, hard, statistics will dramatically point out the significance of the disease. Prominently shown in the ads will be the name, location, and the toll free number of the UOA and a local chapter.

III. RATIONALE

The most direct and powerful way to generate increased awareness and get people interested in the UOA is simply to present the facts. When receivers of this message see the figures that indicate the impact of the disease, they will react by taking the kind of action we desire—calling or writing the UOA or a local chapter.

"I want to thank each of you for presenting us with your ideas. We are very excited about the possibilities of accomplishing our communications objectives through advertising and we believe the ideas you have presented are very useful.

"Our problem is that we see potential in all three campaign ideas and obviously only one can be used. Therefore, we have a proposal to make to you. We would like each of you to submit your campaign idea to copytesting. You have our list of communications goals and if you will prepare your campaign ideas in a form suitable for testing, we will help support the research to the total of $5,000 per agency.*"

---

*It was agreed that the suitable form would be a 30-second television commercial in a prefinished format of 35 mm slides with voiceover.

Copytesting Procedures

Each agency was given $5,000 and six weeks to complete the copytesting of their campaign ideas. They were also given freedom to select the copytesting method of their choice. Described below are the procedures used by each agency and the results of their tests.

Agency A: "Shock." This agency exposed 75 housewives from a local church group to the "Shock" commercial. The commercial was among the other two prefinished commercials which were prepared by Agencies B and C. The respondents were brought into a viewing room and were told that they were going to see segments of game shows and some new commercials and then would be asked a few questions about the game shows and the commercials. The stimuli consisted of approximately twenty minutes of videotape in the following order:

EXHIBIT 3
Campaign Ideas of Agency C

I. CREATIVE STRATEGY

Although cancer of the intestines and urinary tract is a serious health problem, the vast majority of patients do return to a healthy, normal, active life. The UOA understands the physical and emotional problems associated with the disease and helps people overcome such problems.

II. CREATIVE TACTICS: "FUN"

All advertisements will show ostomates of all ages, engaging in normal, active activities—working, playing tennis, swimming, socializing, etc. Copy will stress the fact that it is impossible to tell if you have had an ostomy operation and that the vast majority of ostomates return quickly to all their previous activities. Furthermore, the UOA and their local affiliated chapters help all this happen. Therefore, call or write the UOA or a local chapter to find out more about this form of cancer.

III. RATIONALE

By associating pleasant activities with the disease and the operation, people will be encouraged about their own lives and the lives of others. People like to see pleasant things and they will see the possibilities for improving the quality of life through our advertisements. With this hope, they will be more likely to contact the UOA or a local chapter.

Part I
　　Prefinished commercial for "Facts," Agency B's commercial (30 seconds)
　　Prefinished "Shock" commercial (30 seconds)
　　Prefinished commercial for "Fun," Agency C's commercial (30 seconds)

Part II
　　Five-minute segment of Game Show 1
　　Five-minute segment of Game Show 2
　　Five-minute segment of Game Show 3

Part III
　　Reexposure to the three prefinished commercials (one minute, 30 seconds)

Next, the respondents were given a questionnaire and thirty minutes to complete it. In addition to various questions about the game

shows, the respondents were required to give their reaction to the tested commercials. These reactions were measured by the responses to Question 4 on the questionnaire (see Exhibit 1-A).

Agency A had been using this methodology for testing commercials for some time; therefore, they had a good feeling for what a "good" score was. The data in Exhibit 1-B reveal how the three tested commercials scored.

Agency B: "Facts."　Agency B contracted with a local research firm to have a booth set up in the mall of a large shopping center. Shoppers were invited to enter the booth to participate in the testing of "a few new commercials." Once a shopper agreed to participate, he or she was shown one of the three test commercials and

EXHIBIT 1-A
Question #4 in Agency A's Copytest

	Extremely	Moderately	Slightly	Slightly	Moderately	Extremely	
Unattractive	____	____	____	____	____	____	Attractive
Relevant	____	____	____	____	____	____	Not relevant
Unbelievable	____	____	____	____	____	____	Believable
Inoffensive	____	____	____	____	____	____	Offensive
Unrelated	____	____	____	____	____	____	Connected
Not persuasive	____	____	____	____	____	____	Persuasive
Inaccurate	____	____	____	____	____	____	Accurate
Objectionable	____	____	____	____	____	____	Not objectionable
Deceptive	____	____	____	____	____	____	Truthful
Appropriate	____	____	____	____	____	____	Inappropriate
Dishonest	____	____	____	____	____	____	Honest
Different	____	____	____	____	____	____	Same
Unclear	____	____	____	____	____	____	Clear
Obscure	____	____	____	____	____	____	Precise
Not applicable	____	____	____	____	____	____	Applicable
Unified	____	____	____	____	____	____	Not unified
Influencing	____	____	____	____	____	____	Not influencing
Sincere	____	____	____	____	____	____	Insincere
Uninteresting	____	____	____	____	____	____	Interesting
Factual	____	____	____	____	____	____	Misleading
Incomplete	____	____	____	____	____	____	Complete
Genuine	____	____	____	____	____	____	Artificial
Vague	____	____	____	____	____	____	To the point
Understandable	____	____	____	____	____	____	Not understandable
Distasteful	____	____	____	____	____	____	Tasteful
Appealing	____	____	____	____	____	____	Unappealing
Uniformative	____	____	____	____	____	____	Informative
Unique	____	____	____	____	____	____	Ordinary
Unimpressive	____	____	____	____	____	____	Impressive
Annoying	____	____	____	____	____	____	Amusing
Natural	____	____	____	____	____	____	Unnatural
Not Instructive	____	____	____	____	____	____	Instructive
Unusual	____	____	____	____	____	____	Common
Realistic	____	____	____	____	____	____	Unrealistic
Confusing	____	____	____	____	____	____	Not confusing

Question 4: I feel the commercial for _____ is:

EXHIBIT 1-B
Results of Agency A Copytest

Commercial	Relevancy	Credibility	Attraction	Aesthetics	Overall Score
"Shock," Agency A	4.2[a]	4.8	1.6	1.3	2.98
"Facts," Agency B	4.4	3.9	1.6	1.2	2.78
"Fun," Agency C	3.2	3.0	3.8	3.2	3.30
Norm 1	4.4	3.8	5.1	4.8	4.53
Norm 2	4.6	4.1	3.6	3.1	3.85
Norm 3	1.8	1.2	2.4	3.1	2.13

Norm 1: Average scores for impulse, grocery items.
Norm 2: Average scores for major appliances, furniture, etc.
Norm 3: Average scores for corporate image advertising.
[a]A 6 is the best possible score and a 1 is the lowest possible score.

then given a "product knowledge" test (see Exhibit 2-A). Agency B had used this methodology many times in the past and was convinced that the best commercial for any product or service was the one from which the viewer gained the most information. To make certain that the product knowledge tests were reasonable, the agency had commissioned two Ph.D.'s—one in education and one in communications—to prepare the test items.

The results of the testing are shown in Exhibit 2-B.

Agency C: "Fun."   Over the years Agency C had developed what it believed was the most valid procedure to test the effectiveness of a television commercial. The technique is an in-theater viewing by local groups recruited from churches, service clubs, and other organizations. The respondents view a 30-minute videotape of forty, 30-second, prefinished commercials. Among these commercials are the three test commercials. Therefore, in this particular test, the respondents saw thirty-seven commercials for a wide variety of goods and services and the three United Ostomy commercials.

The specific placement of the test commercials within the reel was determined on a random basis. The respondents were given a questionnaire (see Exhibit 3-A) and requested to evaluate each commercial immediately after exposure. There is a ten-second pause between each commercial.

The results of this testing are shown in Exhibit 3-B.

After the six-week testing period, each agency submitted its report and Don Binder and the Executive Committee of the UOA were left with the task of deciding which creative execution to use. Unfortunately, the data indicated conflicting results; therefore, the selection of the "best" commercial was difficult. In a group meeting the Committee discussed the copytesting results and finally decided that each member should vote for one commercial and briefly explain why the particular commercial was selected. The results of this vote are shown in Exhibit 4.

QUESTIONS FOR DISCUSSION

1. Which one of the three copytesting procedures do you feel is best? Why did you select that copytesting procedure?
2. On the basis of the results of the copytesting procedures, which creative strategy and tactics should the Association use? Why?

EXHIBIT 2-A
Product Knowledge Test Used by Agency B

1. What is the name of the organization that sponsored the commercial you just saw?

   _____

2. An ostomy is:
   a. An organization to help doctors become licensed
   b. An opening in the body
   c. A medical diagnosis
   d. The name of a magazine in the health field
3. Each year, there are approximately _____ ostomy operations:
   a. 5,000
   b. 25,000
   c. 100,000
   d. 1,000,000
4. The ostomy operation success rate is approximately:
   a. 10%
   b. 20%
   c. 40%
   d. 80%
5. The toll free number to call for the name and address of your local ostomy association is:
   a. (800) 321-400
   b. (800) 322-5500
   c. (800) 333-3000
   d. (800) 313-1000
6. Based on the information you just saw in the commercial, how likely is it that you would join the United Ostomy Association (assume you are an ostomy patient)?
   _____ Very likely to join
   _____ Somewhat likely to join
   _____ Don't know
   _____ Somewhat unlikely to join
   _____ Very unlikely to join
7. Would you like to receive additional information about the United Ostomy Association?
   _____ Yes
   _____ No

EXHIBIT 2-B
Results of Agency B Copytest

	Recall	Fact 1 (Question 2)	Fact 2 (Question 3)	Fact 3 (Question 4)	Fact 4 (Question 5)	Intention to Buy/Act	More Information
"Facts" (n = 48)	62%	64%	66%	57%	51%	28%	38%
"Fun" (n = 51)	58	60	28	26	42	64	51
"Shock" (n = 50)	43	51	46	39	36	27	18
Norm 1 (n = 4,882)	73	68	53	43	19	72	29
Norm 2 (n = 3,212)	69	71	62	41	22	56	36

Norm 1: Average scores for all goods tested during past 24 months.
Norm 2: Average scores for all services tested during past 24 months.

EXHIBIT 3-A
Questionnaire Used by Agency C

Instructions:	Please evaluate *each* of the commercials according to the scales shown below. As you make your evaluations, assume you are "in the market" for the product or service advertised.

Commercial #	*Appeal* (1 means not appealing at all and 5 means very appealing.)	*Conviction* (1 means that the commercial was not at all convincing in getting you to buy or use the product service; 5 means that the commercial was very convincing.)
1	1 2 3 4 5	1 2 3 4 5
2	1 2 3 4 5	1 2 3 4 5
3	1 2 3 4 5	1 2 3 4 5
4	1 2 3 4 5	1 2 3 4 5
5	1 2 3 4 5	1 2 3 4 5
.		
.		
.		
40	1 2 3 4 5	1 2 3 4 5

EXHIBIT 3-B

Results of Agency C Copytest

Product Category	Number of Commercials[a]	Sample Size[b]	Average "Appeal" Scores	Average "Conviction" Scores
Food and beverage	15	3,842	4.1	3.8
Furniture and major household appliances	12	2,760	3.1	1.8
Personal care items	20	4,641	2.6	2.7
Corporate/institutional	9	1,854	1.7	1.4
Not-for-profit organizations	9	2,102	2.1	2.2
UOA, "Shock"	1	180	1.9	2.1
UOA, "Facts"	1	180	3.1	2.6
UOA, "Fun"	1	180	3.6	2.9

[a]Represents the number of different commercials tested during past three years.
[b]Represents total number of respondents during past three years.

EXHIBIT 4

Results of Executive Committee Vote for "Best" Commercial

Name of Commercial	Number of Votes	Summary of Rationale
"Shock"	4	Admittedly not an attractive commercial, but it is strongly "believed" by respondents. Its 4.8 score in "credibility" in the copytest done by Agency A is significantly higher than that of "Facts" or "Fun." We need to establish credibility and "Shock" does it best.
"Facts"	6	This commercial is considered the most "relevant" and consistently outperformed "Shock" and "Fun" in terms of providing information. One of our primary objectives is to provide information about the UOA and "Facts" does it best.
"Fun"	5	Not only is this execution the overall winner in two of the three tests, it also had the highest "intention to act" and "more information" scores in Agency B's test. Clearly, this commercial will attract more viewers than either "Shock" or "Facts."

29

ATLANTA JOURNAL AND CONSTITUTION

Mr. Ferguson Rood, Research and Marketing Director of the *Atlanta Journal* and the *Atlanta Constitution,* was still perspiring from the three-block walk in the hot August sun back to his office from the meeting he had just been to at Rich's Department Store. At the meeting he had been told that Rich's, the newspaper's largest advertiser, wanted to test the effectiveness of TV and radio advertising versus newspaper advertising during their upcoming Harvest Sale. He had promised to make his suggestions for the research plan in 48 hours and felt he had much work to do in that short time. He wondered what recommendations he should make for the study and was concerned that the research design and questionnaire be developed so that the study would represent fairly the effectiveness of the *Atlanta Journal* and the *Atlanta Constitution.* As he began to review his notes from the meeting, he picked up the phone to call his wife and tell her he would be home very late that evening.

BACKGROUND

The *Atlanta Journal* and the *Atlanta Constitution* are a union of two of the largest-circulation newspapers in the South. The *Atlanta Constitution,* winner of four Pulitzer Prizes for its efforts in the area of social reform, was founded June 16, 1868. The *Atlanta Journal,* founded February 24, 1883, became the largest daily newspaper in Georgia by 1889. Also a winner of the Pulitzer Prize, the *Journal* is the Southeast's largest afternoon newspaper.

In 1950 the *Atlanta Journal* and the *Atlanta Constitution* were combined into Atlanta Newspapers, Inc., a privately held company. The two newspapers maintained independent editorial

This case was prepared by Kenneth L. Bernhardt, Georgia State University.

staffs, and there was very little overlap of readers.

To provide the advertisers and potential advertisers with information necessary to help them make their advertising media decisions, the newspaper did a considerable amount of research each year. Most of the research was designed to be used in selling advertising to a wide range of advertisers, and it included data on retail trading areas, shopping patterns, product usage, and newspaper coverage patterns. In addition to Mr. Rood, the research department had two other trained market researchers and one secretary.

Although there are other daily newspapers in the Atlanta trading area, all but the *Journal* and the *Constitution* have very small circulations. The newspapers' principal competition for large advertisers come from radio and TV stations.

Rich's Department Store was the largest advertiser for the *Journal* and the *Constitution,* accounting for a very significant percentage of their advertising revenue. Founded in 1867, Rich's had grown to a company with stores distributed throughout the Atlanta area. The company was classified as a general merchandise retailer and carried a very wide line of products including clothing, furniture, appliances, housewares, and items for the home. Rich's dominated the Atlanta market, with a large percentage of department store sales and of all the sales of general merchandise.

The merchandising highlight of the year was the annual Harvest Sale, first held in October 1925. The sale typically ran for two weeks and had become a yearly tradition at Rich's.

MEDIA EFFECTIVENESS STUDY

Before preparing his proposal to Rich's for the media effectiveness study, Mr. Rood reflected upon the events of the past 24 hours. The day before, he had received a phone call from the vice-president and sales promotion director of Rich's, inviting him to the meeting at Rich's the next day. Having been told that Rich's research director and the research director of WSB-TV and Radio would also be there, Mr. Rood had been a little apprehensive before going. At the start of the meeting he was asked if the Atlanta newspapers would be interested in participating in a cooperative research study aimed at measuring the effectiveness of various advertising media during Rich's September Harvest Sale, its largest annual sales event. It became immediately apparent that the research director from WSB, Mr. Jim Land, had met with the Rich's people the week before and was undoubtedly the source of the idea to conduct the study. A document was then passed out that had been prepared by WSB and was entitled "Suggestions for Rich's Media Research." This document, which is in the Appendix, outlined the objectives of the study, a suggested methodology, together with a questionnaire.

The suggested objectives for the project were: (1) to measure the ability of TV, radio, and newspapers to help sell specific items of merchandise in Rich's Atlanta stores; (2) to determine how each advertising medium complements the others in terms of additional units sold to various segments of the customer population (age, sex, charge account ownership, and other factors); (3) to determine what each advertising medium contributed in regard to additional store traffic. Mr. Rood's broadcasting counterpart stated at the meeting that "If Rich's is interested in conducting research to measure the effectiveness of various advertising media, WSB-TV and WSB Radio will be happy to assist." Rood had no choice, so he volunteered the support of the newspapers in conducting the study.

The Rich's research manager then asked if the media would participate financially in the study. Mr. Rood suggested that each of the three

media participate equally, and he committed the newpapers to $500 for a study that he figured should cost between $2,500 and $3,000 for interviewing. Mr. Land indicated that Cox Broadcasting would be willing to put in $500 each for TV and radio.

They then discussed how the research could be conducted. The WSB proposal suggested in-store surveys, with a separate survey conducted for each item of merchandise tested. The survey would be conducted by Rich's employees working overtime in appropriate store locations during the peak shopping hours. The tabulation of the results could be handled by the broadcast station's computer. Care was to be taken to ensure that the TV, radio, or newspaper advertising for the individual items would not be "stacked" in favor of one particular medium. The proposed questionnaire (see the appendix) included questions on how the respondents happened to buy the merchandise at Rich's, if they recalled seeing TV, newspaper, or radio advertising, and if they bought anything else. Questions were also asked concerning age and ownership of a Rich's charge account.

Mr. Land stated that WSB was not trying to take business away from the newspapers and that Mr. Rood had nothing to fear. His recommendation was that Rich's not take anything away from the newspaper advertising budget. He suggested that the amount of space purchased in the newspapers be the same as the previous year, with additional monies being committed to the broadcast media. The Rich's sales promotion director then discussed some of his thoughts concerning the study. He indicated that Rich's had been sending 400,000 direct-mail pieces to announce the Harvest Sale; this year they would send 200,000, diverting the other money to broadcast. This would make $7,600 available for broadcast, and another $12,000 to $15,000 would be made available to purchase broadcast time.

The Harvest Sale was to open with courtesy days on Monday and Tuesday, September 21–22,

EXHIBIT 1
Rich's Harvest Sale Ad

with the sale beginning the evening of the 22nd and running for thirteen days. While decisions concerning which sale items were to be included in the study and the media schedules to be used were not yet available, some progress had been made. Approximately ten items were to be researched, and the newspaper ads on Sunday, September 20, would include all or most of the ten items. Newspaper ads for the items would be repeated Monday and Tuesday with emphasis on the *Journal*. The interviews were to be conducted Monday through Wednesday.

On Sunday and Monday, with a possible spillover to Tuesday because of availablity, Rich's would run 120 thirty-second TV commercials on most commercial stations. During the same time they would run 120 thirty-second radio commercials on a list of stations which had not yet been determined. With both TV and radio, WSB was to get the lion's share if availability could be arranged. Mr. Rood felt certain, in view of the client and the research, that WSB would manage to come up with several prime-time commercial openings even if it meant bumping some high-paying national advertisers.

Ten items were mentioned as possible subjects for the research. The ten final items selected would come mostly from this list, although one or two other items might be chosen. The items mentioned were (1) a color TV console, (2) custom-made draperies, (3) carpeting, (4) Gant shirts, (5) Van Heusen shirts and Arrow shirts at 2 for 1, (6) women's handbags, (7) Johannsen's shoes, (8) pant suits, (9) a Hoover upright vacuum cleaner, and (10) a GE refrigerator.

Mr. Rood, who had not said very much at the meeting, then asked for 48 hours to review the proposal. Everyone agreed to this, and Mr. Rood promised to present a counterproposal in two days.

Even though it had been rather obvious who initiated the idea for the study and at first Mr.

Rood felt that the newspapers were being "set up" by WSB, it had been basically a friendly and relaxed meeting among friends. Mr. Land and Mr. Rood had worked together in the Atlanta Chapter of the American Marketing Association and had a great deal of mutual respect for each other. Mr. Rood thought Mr. Land was a tough competitor, and he understood that Land had been successful using awareness type studies in Cox Broadcastings' other markets to gain additional advertising for broadcast.

When he returned to his office, Mr. Rood pulled out some of his files on Rich's. He noticed that the amount of advertising had been fairly constant, approximately 40 pages over the two-week period, during the past three Harvest Sales, and that basically the same products had been promoted. A typical Harvest Sale ad is presented in Exhibit 1.

Mr. Rood reasoned that he should assume confidence in the effectiveness of the newspapers. He felt if the study were conducted properly the newspapers would get their share of media exposure and influence. The other decision he quickly made was that in preparing his comments on the proposed research, he would take Rich's point of view rather than that of the *Atlanta Journal* and *Constitution*. He then began to review the events of the day and the WSB proposal in light of what he felt Rich's needed to know. He also knew that whatever he proposed would have to be acceptable to Mr. Land. Noting the lateness in the day, he began work on the counterproposal.

QUESTIONS FOR DISCUSSION

1. What general research methodology should Mr. Rood recommend in formulating his counterproposal?
2. How should Mr. Rood's proposal differ from the WSB proposal? What aspects should remain the same?

Appendix
WSB Suggestions for Rich's Media Research

Objectives

If Rich's is interested in conducting research to measure the effectiveness of various advertising media, WSB-TV and WSB Radio will be happy to assist. As a basis for discussion, here are suggested objectives for this project.

1. Measure the ability of TV, radio, and newspapers to sell specific items of merchandise in Rich's Atlanta metro stores.
2. Determine how each advertising medium complements the others in terms of additional units sold to various segments of the customer population (age, sex, charge account ownership, etc.).
3. Determine what each advertising medium contributed in regard to additional store traffic.

How The Research Could Be Conducted

The project could consist of a series of in-store surveys. A separate survey would be conducted for each item of merchandise tested. The more items tested, the more reliable the results of the overall research project. If possible, all of Rich's stores in the Atlanta metro area should participate in the research.

Each survey could be conducted by placing interviewers (Rich's personnel working overtime) in appropriate store locations during peak shopping hours with instructions to complete brief questionnaires with customers purchasing the item being tested. (Questionnaire is on next page.) The interview could cover how the customer got the idea to buy the item, other planned purchases in the store during the same visit, charge account ownership, and any other pertinent data. Each interview would last less than a minute and would not bother the customers.

The sample size would vary, depending upon the number of stores participating, the type of merchandise, and the sales volume. Interviewers would strive to include all customers purchasing the items during peak hours. Tabulation of the results could be handled by the WSB computer.

Careful Attention to Items and Media Schedules

In order to make the research valid and meaningful, the items to be tested must be selected carefully. In addition, care should be taken to ensure that the TV, radio, or newspaper advertising for these items is not stacked in favor of one particular medium. Close attention to the items being tested and the media schedule for each is necessary.

Possible Questionaire for Rich's In-Store Survey

How did you happen to buy this merchandise at Rich's?

Saw on TV	( )
Heard on radio	( )
Saw in newspaper	( )
TV and radio	( )
TV and newspaper	( )
Newspaper and radio	( )
TV, Radio, and newspaper	( )
Saw on display	( )
Other_____	( )

Asked of Customers Not Mentioning a Medium: (questions 2, 3, 4)

2. Do you recall seeing this merchandise advertised on TV?

Yes	( )
No	( )

3. Do you recall seeing this merchandise advertised in the newspaper?

Yes	( )
No	( )

4. Do you recall hearing this merchandise advertised on the radio?

Yes	( )
No	( )

5. Are you buying anything else at Rich's today?

Yes	( )
No	( )
Maybe	( )
Don't know	( )

6. Do you have a charge account at Rich's?

Yes	( )
No	( )

7. In which group does your age fall?

Under 25	( )
25–34	( )
35–49	( )
50+	( )

STORE_____

TIME OF INTERVIEW_____

30

HI-POWER BEVERAGE COMPANY

Hi-Power Beverage Company produces and markets several carbonated and noncarbonated lines of canned fruit- and cola-flavored soft drinks. Charles Iverson was the product manager for Upper C, a vitamin-enriched fruit drink line sold in the canned juice sections of grocery stores. The key promotional tool for the line was network television advertising supplemented with spot TV in seasonally appropriate markets.

Iverson's usual procedure in the development of campaign strategy was to simply turn the problem, with relevant market data, over to the agency. The agency's account person, Katherine Cordaro—of Cordaro, Oritt, and Harmon, Inc.—would review the data, consult with Iverson in deciding upon a selling proposition, and then become somewhat reclusive until she returned with a "winning" campaign idea.

Ultimately, this single idea (along with an obviously poorer idea) would be developed into a storyboard and then presented to Iverson and the group product manager, Paul Waters. The presentation was usually supported by impressive multimedia techniques. In this way, even a relatively mediocre concept could be made to look good. After a few minor changes, Iverson and Waters would ordinarily decide upon the better of the two ideas. The agency would then move quickly to production and scheduling, where the media commission structure would begin generating revenue.

Now Iverson was beginning to question the procedure. He felt that there must be a better approach toward developing advertising campaigns for his company.

DEVELOPING ADVERTISING TACTICS

Over lunch one day Iverson stumbled into a conversation between two members of Hi-

This case was prepared by William R. Swinyard, Brigham Young University.

Power's marketing research department. They were discussing some intriguing ideas from a study done by a researcher named Irwin Gross. As Iverson left the lunch, his head was swimming with the possibilities suggested to him. In approaching ad strategy, the advertising agency could either (1) moved quickly through the creative execution stages and on to scheduling, thus maximizing the company's media expenditures, or (2) spend far more time and money in the development and production of three or four solid *alternative* creative executions, copytest them, pick the highest-scoring execution, then move to media placement.

"Maybe if we spent more money in developing and testing alternative ideas," Iverson reasoned, "we could come up with a better campaign."

Iverson discussed his views with Waters, who agreed that this method promised much. They were certain, however, that the agency would resist. The men were not disappointed, for Cordaro marshalled all of the agency's political clout to squash the proposal. Finally, virtually under duress, Cordaro agreed to try the idea on a one-time basis.

The instructions given to the agency by Iverson and Waters included the following: develop at least three alternative executions for a new campaign for Upper C. "We don't just want three ideas or storyboards," the agency was told. "We want three finished commercials." Only by having the finished commercials to test did the two men believe that a copytesting organization could give them worthwhile feedback about which execution performed best.

Hi-Power's marketing research department provided recent survey data about the relative importance of product attributes for Upper C's product class. Iverson and Cordaro examined a summary table of these data (see Table 1) and

TABLE 1
Consumer Perceptions of Enriched Fruit Drinks

Attribute	Attribute Importance Weight[a]	Consumer Evaluations[b]			
		HiPower	Brand A	Brand B	Brand C
Taste	.40	8	9	7	4
Calorie content	.18	7	5	7	4
Price	.15	6	8	6	10
Color	.02	6	7	7	6
Nourishment	.25	9	6	8	5

[a]Refers to the relative salience of each attribute to consumers in discriminating between the purchase of one brand versus another.
[b]On a 10-point scale, where 10 is the preferred rating.

concluded that the product's nourishment offered the most potential for positioning the brand. They translated this attribute into the selling proposition of "vitamin enrichment."

CHOOSING AMONG ALTERNATIVES

Five months and $90,000 later the agency presented three finished commercials, all 30 seconds, and each having a completely different theme (see Exhibit 1). "These are all solid campaign concepts," Cordaro said. Iverson had to agree, but he did feel that "Pantomime Man" was an especially effective execution.

The next step was to submit the commercials to a copytesting organization. Although Hi-Power had used one such organization from time to time, Iverson wanted more information about what services were available. He went to the company's marketing research department for advice.

He thought that he would have to ask only, "Which advertising copytesting service is best?" but he found that the answer was not at all straightforward. As the senior researcher put it, "That all depends on what you mean by 'best' and on which hierarchical model of behavior

change you believe characterizes your product." Three popular services were described to him (see Exhibit 2 for details). It was also suggested that he study some papers by Krugman and by Ray, which Iverson dismissed as being too esoteric. The researchers shrugged and suggested that he might start with copytesting service A.

Two weeks later, when the Firm A test scores had come in, Iverson looked at them with some dismay (see Table 2, column a). They simply did not confirm his expectations of the performance of the commercials. Waters, too, was disturbed, for his personal favorite of "Show Girls" came in well below "Saturday Afternoon," which he felt was a relatively mundane commercial.

Neither of the two men was satisfied. They decided to have the three commercials tested by another copytesting agency. "We have spent over $90,000 on the production costs of these commercials," Iverson said, "so a few thousand extra for testing is hardly consequential." They set up a test with Firm B. When the results came in (Table 2, column b), Iverson and Waters were simultaneously delighted and puzzled. On the one hand, the test results confirmed their own expectations—both "Pantomime Man" and "Show Girls" were highly evaluated—but these

EXHIBIT 1
Summary of the Three Upper C Commercials

PANTOMINE MAN

A 30-second commercial in which the video depicts the silhouette of a gymnast jumping on a trampoline, doing rolls, flips, and other intricate maneuvers. The trampoline is not seen—the video is cropped well above it.

A voiceover speaks about Upper C's energy power, vitamins, and minerals, which combine to provide energy for, and a pick-me-up after, physical activity.

The camera closes on a slow zoom-in on a can and glass of Upper C.

SATURDAY AFTERNOON

A 30-second commercial in which the video and audio portray a plot line in which a grade-schooler comes into the kitchen, tosses his mit on the table, screen door slamming. His mother and he exchange delighted phrases about his baseball victory, while she makes a display of getting the Upper C from the refrigerator, opening the can, and pouring him a large glass. Label is in constant view.

Final scenes show boy drinking from glass, mother saying, "It makes me happy that you like things that are so good for you as Upper C."

Close on slow zoom in on a can and glass of Upper C.

SHOW GIRLS

A 30-second commercial in which video and early audio depict the parade walk of show girls, in Las Vegas costume.

Voiceover on low-level audience noises speaks of the wear and tear of a tough day—and how refreshing a pick-me-up would be . . . that even adults need a full supply of vitamins.

Final scene in dressing room of show girl, where she pours a glass of Upper C, samples it, looks at the camera, and says, "It sure helps out after a tough day."

---

results directly contradicted the scores from testing service A. In addition, the previously high-scoring "Saturday Afternoon" now scored quite low.

Their feelings of confusion became those of bewilderment when they tested the commercials a third time—this time with Firm C (see Table 2, column c). Waters turned to Iverson: " 'Saturday Afternoon' is getting scores like a yo-yo, and 'Show Girls' is back down near the bottom again. Surely our friends in the marketing research department will help us understand what's happening here." "I hope so," Iverson

replied. "Or we'll be forced right back into our old system of one idea, one commercial. We just have to reconcile this dilemma."

QUESTIONS FOR DISCUSSION

1. What are the strengths and weaknesses of each of the three testing procedures?
2. What additional information would be useful in evaluating the testing procedures?
3. What action should Hi-Power take based on the results of the three research tests of the three executions?

EXHIBIT 2

Description of Three Copytesting Techniques

COPYTESTING SERVICE A

The technique is an in-theater viewing, by local groups (from churches and other organizations). Respondents view a TV pilot, interspersed at expected intervals with commercials. Among the commercials is the test commercial.

Respondents, who believe that they are at the theater to evaluate the TV pilot (in fact, they sometimes are), complete a questionnaire about the pilot at the conclusion of the show.

Twenty-four hours later an interviewer from the firm telephones each of the respondents "to collect some additional information." At this point the interviewer questions the respondent about recall of commercials shown with the pilot, using open-ended questions such as, "I'm going to read you a list of products, some of which were advertised last night and some of which were not. Please think about each product and tell me whether you recall seeing that product advertised last night. Do you recall a commercial for . . ."

Respondents who claim recall are asked the brand advertised. The percentage of respondents recalling correctly form an awareness "score" for the test commercial, which can be evaluated against a "norm," or average for the product class.

COPYTESTING SERVICE B

Firm B uses pupilometric techniques, supplemented with attitudinal responses. One respondent at a time is exposed to several commercials, which the respondents view by peering in a light box. While they watch the ads, a motion picture camera continuously photographs their left eye, recording changes in pupil size throughout the "control" commercials and test commercial. Firm B has experimentally established that pupils respond to emotional activity.

Up to one hundred respondents participate in each test, and the pupil response, along with some paper and pencil attitude measurements for the brand, are combined for the entire sample of respondents. These are then transformed into an indexed score, which is compared with a norm for the product class.

COPYTESTING SERVICE C

Firm C's technique involves a behavioral response measure. The copytesting technique involves moving a well-equipped viewing-room (contained in a motor home) to the parking lot of a large supermarket.

Shoppers are invited to participate in the test as they leave their cars and approach the store. In the van they are shown a series of commercials. In some cases (test condition), the test commercial is included in those shown. In other cases (control condition), the respondents would see all commercials except the test commercial.

After viewing, all respondents are given a complimentary booklet of cents-off coupons—good for 10¢ to 25¢ off on specific grocery products. Among the coupons is one good for cents-off on the test product. The respondents then proceed with their shopping.

At the close of the day, Firm C people collect all redeemed coupons, which had been coded to reflect whether they had been given during the test condition or control condition. A comparison is then made on differential redemption rates of test versus control coupons.

The differences between test condition redemption and control condition redemption are transformed into a percentile score, in which the norm for the product class is 50 percent.

TABLE 2
Test Scores from Three Organizations

| Commercial | Firm A | | Firm B | | Firm C |
	Score	Norm[a]	Score	Norm	Percentile[b]
Pantomime Man	3	10	5.4	3.8	34
Saturday Afternoon	17	10	1.5	3.8	73
Show Girls	4	10	6.5	3.8	20

[a]Scores above or below the norm reflect above or below average performance respectively.
[b]50% is an "average" score.

4. Was the decision to use the "vitamin enrichment" proposition a wise one? Could this decision have exerted an influence on the outcome of any of the testing procedures? Would the nature of the executions have any possible effect on test results?

Mr. James Martinez, President of El Rancho Grande, was confident that he had an idea that would enable his company to become at least somewhat less than totally dependent on the national supermarket chain under whose private label his firm's output was marketed. Although he was satisfied with his firm's arrangement with the supermarket chain, the even modest success of a product under his own label was important to him from a psychological standpoint.

El Rancho Grande was a relatively small food-processing and canning company located in south Texas. The firm produced three basic types of canned products—tomatoes, peppers, and Mexican sauces. These products were packaged in a variety of can sizes ranging from seven ounces to six pounds.

The El Rancho Grande contract with the supermarket chain did not preclude the canning, labeling, and selling of products under the El Rancho Grande label. Realistically, however, Mr. Martinez was well aware of the formidable obstacles to his firm's achieving distribution in retail food stores, much less a respectable sales volume for one of his conventional products in such stores. In light of these obstacles, he proposed to distribute a food specialty item eventually through gift, gourmet, and other specialty stores. At the present time he felt the product could be sold on a mail-order basis. The whole proposal hinged to some extent on the Texas mystique.

THE TEXAS MYSTIQUE

Mr. Martinez felt that the time was right to capitalize on an apparently sustained wave of national interest in the cowboy mystique in

This case was prepared by John H. Murphy and Leonard Ruben, The University of Texas at Austin.

general and the state of Texas in particular. Fueled by considerable national media attention, Texas chic seemed to have captured an enduring place in the national consciousness. Within the state this same trend was reflected in a marked increase in state pride and a closer identification with people, places, and things uniquely Texan.

A number of consumer products had successfully utilized their Texas heritage in their marketing efforts. In addition to Texas beers, boots, cowboy hats, and Western wear, a large number of novelty items were available. These items included, Texas ties, a wide variety of T-shirts, belt buckles, jigsaw puzzles, cookbooks, kites, and beer mugs. Three of the more unusual of these products are briefly described below.

Artesia: A mineral water promoted as 100 percent pure and sparkling from the Texas Hill Country. The product was retailed in supermarkets in six packs of twelve-ounce bottles and quarts by a firm based in San Antonio. The water taken from the famous Edwards aquifer was advertised in full-page magazine advertisements as a healthful drink alone or as a mixer and was positioned against Perrier.

The Ice of Texas: Ice trays that produced cubes in the shape of the state of Texas. It was advertised as the state's "official" ice tray that made cubes with a distinctive flair. The product was sold through mail orders and a range of gourmet, kitchen ware, and specialty stores.

Texas Cutting Boards: A 1¼-inch thick maple butcher block board shaped like the state of Texas. These cutting boards were available in two sizes and promoted as being individually handcrafted in Texas. The boards were expensive and available through mail order plus gourmet, specialty, and department stores.

THE PRODUCT

Mr. Martinez's product idea to be marketed under the El Rancho Grande label was a sauce for use as an appetizer or snack with chips or in the preparation of Mexican food. The new product was a slight variation of a product produced for the supermarket chain. The chain's product was branded under the chain's private label and identified as "Home Style Mexican Sauce."

By substituting jalapeño peppers in place of serrano peppers and adding carrots to the recipe for the chain's sauce, Mr. Martinez created a product he named "Texas Style Jalapeño Sauce." The ingredients as listed on the can were: fresh tomatoes, onion, jalapeño peppers, carrot, iodized salt, and coriander. Variations in the proportion and variety of jalapeño peppers produced three versions of the sauce—mild, warm, and hot.

In order to get some feedback on likely acceptance of the new sauce, Mr. Martinez had some of his employees offer samples to adult shoppers as they exited supermarkets in a nearby community. Shoppers were offered a choice of tortilla, corn, or potato chips and three bowls of sauce marked mild, warm, and hot. After trying one or any combinations of the chips and sauces they wished, the shoppers were asked several questions to gauge their reaction to the sauce.

Although extremely informal, the results of this test were encouraging. Over 70 percent of the adults sampled reported they liked the product and would consider purchasing it, assuming it was competitively priced.

Encouraged by the shoppers' reaction, Mr. Martinez began to make plans to market the sauce. He decided that the sauce would be promoted as a specialty/gift item with a very high price relative to the cost of the ingredients and processing; the product would be canned only in seven-ounce cans and sold only in six packs.

PACKAGING AND ADVERTISING

Mr. Martinez employed the services of an advertising design studio to produce the product's label and packaging (see Exhibits 1 and 2). In addition, the design firm was asked to produce several different creative approaches for direct response advertising to be placed in print media.

A subjective evaluation of four alternative approaches reduced the number of what were felt to be reasonable treatments to two. Three different sized magazine ads (1/3, 1/6, and 1/12 page) using each of the two strategies are presented in Exhibits 3 and 4.

AN ADVERTISING TEST

Mr. Martinez was reluctant to commit to anything beyond very modest production or promotion of the new sauce without conducting some empirical research. He felt that before he proceeded, an advertising test should be de-

EXHIBIT 1
Individual Can of the Product

EXHIBIT 2
Six Pack of the Product

signed to gain insights into several basic questions regarding the product.

First, it was necessary to determine what level of demand the new sauce would generate through direct response advertising. Second, the test should be designed to evaluate the alternative creative treatments. Finally, there were the important issues of which individual magazine's audience would be most responsive and whether residents of Texas were better prospects than nonresidents.

Mr. Martinez suspected that some combination of state, regional, or city magazines would be best for the test. Although he was aware of the availability of regional and single-market editions of several national magazines, he wondered about how many of these magazines might have split-run capabilities for testing the two creative treatments and if this type of test would be appropriate.

The total media costs for the test could not be justified beyond $12,000; Mr. Martinez felt that any test should be as inexpensive as possible. Naturally he felt the larger ads would pull best but he was not sure he could afford to pay for these versions. He realized trade-offs would probably be necessary in conducting any research that sought to answer some or all of the basic research questions he wanted answered.

QUESTIONS FOR DISCUSSION

1. Are there any additional evaluations or reviews that Mr. Martinez should conduct prior to designing a formal test?
2. In light of financial constraints, should Mr. Martinez attempt to answer so many questions through a single test?
3. What general form should a test designed to provide data useful in answering Mr. Martinez' questions take?

EXHIBIT 3
Advertisements: Creative Strategy A

EXHIBIT 4
Advertisements: Creative Strategy B

SECTION 8
MANAGING THE ADVERTISING PROGRAM

All organizations—the large, multimillion dollar advertiser of detergent, the public library, the manufacturer of machine tools, and the local jewelry store—face a common advertising problem: how to organize for the development of the most effective advertising effort. Although every organization does not employ an Advertising Manager, someone must ultimately be responsible for coordinating the communications between the organization and its external publics. One of the most important functions of the Advertising or Promotion Manager is to plan, coordinate, and evaluate the advertising program.

One of the basic decisions is determining who will perform each of the various advertising functions. Today, most large advertisers retain advertising agencies to develop and execute their advertising campaigns. Agencies provide expertise in developing verbal and visual messages, familiarity with marketing and promotion problems, and objectivity in creating advertising for their clients.

A choice preferred by most retailers and industrial advertisers is to hire an in-house staff of advertising professionals who devote their full-time attention to the advertising of their employer's products or services.

A third alternative is to utilize the services of the large number of free-lance advertising professionals (copywriters, designers, media specialists, research firms, and the like) that are readily available in most markets.

Each of these alternatives varies in its potential effectiveness, convenience, and cost. Eventually, every marketer selects the alternative or hybrid that best fulfills the firm's needs and matches its style of management. Intelligent selection from among the three choices require management's ability to:

1. *Evaluate the potential ability of the alternative to develop effective advertising.* This includes knowing how to select advertising professionals and how to judge their past performance.
2. *Foster an environment that is conducive to producing the most effective advertising.* This includes creating the proper balance between guidance and creative freedom. This also requires careful attention to clear com-

munication between the parties involved and a sensitivity to the personalities involved.

3. *Develop standards against which a particular alternative's performance can be measured.*

Again, the cases that follow require you to make management decisions that fall into one or more of these areas. In analyzing the cases, also keep in mind that: (1) there is no "right" system for every organization, and (2) an organization's personality and management style are extremely important variables in creating a successful marriage between the firm's management and advertising professionals.

The Portage Grocery Company (PGC) is a dynamic grocery company situated in a midwestern state. The company, which experienced a growth rate in retail sales during the past year of approximately 18 percent, operates 80 stores throughout the state. Approximately one-half of them are corporate-owned stores and the balance are franchised stores which carry the corporate identity of Portage.

Many of the franchised stores are located in the smaller rural sectors of the state, with most of the corporate-owned stores located in metropolitan areas. The Portage stores had a combined sales of approximately $380 million last year, while the major competitor in the metropolitan areas had 60 stores and sales of approximately $580 million. The Portage Grocery Company is a relatively young and innovative company whose growth during the past decade has exceeded the growth of most regional chain grocery companies in the United States. All stores are supplied from one warehouse situated in the largest metropolitan area of the state. Although four new stores are on the drawing boards, it is anticipated that during the 1980s all future stores will continue to be supplied and operated from one central warehouse.

The stores are jointly advertised by an advertising program developed and implemented from the corporate headquarters. All stores including franchised stores are assessed .8 percent of retail sales for advertising. Added to this amount are all forms of co-op advertising. Next year it is anticipated that the advertising budget will be approximatly $3.4 million. It is also anticipated that the next year's advertising budget will be allocated similarly to the current budget—that is, one-third spent on newspapers

This case was prepared by Richard W. Skinner, Kent State University; and Terence A. Shimp, University of South Carolina.

in the smaller market areas (including rural), one-third spent on newspapers in the metropolitan markets within the state, and approximately 25 percent on TV and radio advertising. The balance is spent on outdoor and direct-mail advertising.

Several years ago the company began to use TV advertising. Approximately one-fourth of the budget for the past two or three years was allocated to TV and radio production and placement. Management was convinced that the dollars invested in TV were worthwhile, however, they did not expect to increase expenditures on this medium in the foreseeable future. No formal research program evaluating the TV advertising had been conducted; however, the company had won awards for its TV comercials.

Much of the credit for the success of their TV advertising must go to Tom Wilson, Director of Advertising. He had been with the company for eighteen years and in his present position over six years. Wilson is an extremely inventive and imaginative individual. His efforts to sell top management some of his ideas had been supported by one of the directors of the company who is a vice-president of a very large advertising agency. This director had been very helpful to Wilson and had instructed him in contacting the right people to produce TV commercials. The agency of which the director is vice-president has no interest in the PGC account since it concentrates exclusively on industrial accounts.

Richard Helms, the President of Portage Grocery Company, had for some time been concerned that there was a need for more formalized outside advertising assistance. He believed that Tom Wilson worked too long and hard and that he needed to learn some other aspects of the business; additionally, perhaps real savings could be effected by outside professional help. The President, however, had *not* been displeased with the quality of the past TV advertising.

A few days ago during an informal lunch, several of PGC's executives discussed the broadcast advertising being done by retail food chains. After some discussion there was a general consensus that larger grocery chains had increased their broadcast advertising. Some remarked that Food Fair, which had left TV, had returned in a big way. Somebody else commented that they had read that all of the top ten chains were using TV to some extent. The conversation prompted the President to give some additional thought to the future regarding the Portage Grocery Company's advertising. He also began to do more reading in advertising trade publications.

These trade publication articles prompted the President to request a meeting in one week with Tom Wilson, Director of Advertising, and Bill Green, Vice-President of Retail Operations. Both men were instructed by the President to be prepared to defend their position regarding the efficacy of employing an advertising agency that would be responsible for all broadcast (TV and radio) advertising. The President indicated that he had a definite opinion about the matter but certainly would be receptive to changing his opinion if logical arguments could be presented.

Green welcomed this opportunity, as he had for some time advocated retaining a full-service ad agency to handle the broadcast portion of the budget. Green, however, had not been able to sell Wilson on the idea and the President had seen no reason to persuade Wilson to change in view of the good work he was doing. Wilson disagreed with Green and maintained that no one understood the food retail business like those involved in it; he thus believed that the in-house agency that he had been operating should continue.

The President opened the meeting with the following statement:

"Tom and Bill, I just finished looking over some figures for the last three years. I want to commend both of you for the job you have done. I know that much of the success must be credited to the two of you. I take great pride in our team effort. Despite inflation and the financial crisis, the future for the Portage Grocery Company looks bright.

"Now, to the main issue of our meeting. Our discussion during lunch and some reading started me thinking about the advertising program. In what I am about to recommend, I am in no way implying or suggesting that I am anything but pleased with the results of our advertising program. However, I recommend that we obtain some outside help for Tom in developing and implementing our broadcast advertising program. Note that I only said broadcast advertising. It is my conviction that our own advertising staff can do the newspaper advertising more effectively and efficiently than any outsider.

"I have read about the increasing development of 'boutique shops.' These are creative specialists who probably could aid us significantly in creating and producing our broadcast messages. In addition, we could utilize media-buying services which would negotiate and place our broadcast advertising. These are options that are available today that were not a few years ago. The opponents to these types of specialists call this approach to advertising 'piece-mealism.' It is my understanding, however, that many advertisers are experimenting with piece-mealism.

"There are several reasons for my recommendation. Basically they consist of the following:

1. I would like Tom to have more time to plan and to keep abreast of the changes in the industry.
2. The creative specialists or boutique people should be able to add a fresh dimension to our broadcast advertising which our own staff could not achieve. They may be able to do this without the higher cost that would come with a full-service agency, as the full-service agency is likely to have more overhead.

3. The media-buying agency provides a specialized service which negotiates and places broadcast advertising. It is a matter of fact, according to the Association of National Advertisers, that independent media services have been a desirable development for advertisers since more efficient buying practices has resulted from their advent.

4. The fee structure for several media-buying services is 5 percent for spot TV buying, 5 percent for radio, and 1.85 percent for network TV buys. For a total media job, which includes newspapers and magazines, the fee is about 3.75 percent. This, of course, is significantly less than the 15 percent received by a full-service agency.

5. According to trade publications we can expect increased competition from our competitors via the broadcast media; thus, we must continue to do an outstanding advertising job. The creative specialists should enable us to do this job more effectively and efficiently as we employ them only when we need them, and creativity is their business.

6. A number of experts predict that advertisers in the future will tend to rely not so much on internal capabilities as on limited internal capabilities plus wide outside services.

"In summary, Tom needs more time for planning, and so on. The boutique people and media-buying specialists will permit us to continue an excellent broadcast advertising program at an efficient cost figure."

These was a pause, then the President looked at the Vice-President of Retail Operations. Bill Green seized this opportunity to speak:

"I agree with you in principle; however, I sincerely believe you are only taking half a step when we should go the full way, that is, a full-service agency.

"Tom and I have discussed this several times, but I have never had support from anyone else in management. Tom, I know, does not agree with me. However, I am pleased that the subject has emerged again. I think that Tom understands that my desire for a full-service agency in no way reflects on the job that he and his staff have done. My concern is lack of continuity that would exist if Tom should leave the company, get sick, or be promoted.

"There are a number of factors that I believe support my position. These factors are:

1. We will spend approximately $800,000 in broadcast advertising. This is a significant amount and requires skills in production and placement that are not comparable to newspaper advertising. I agree with the concept that an agency is probably not adequately staffed to handle a retail food chain's newspaper advertising. It also seems logical that a retail food chain could not be expected to be adequately staffed to produce and place broadcast advertising. The point is that while our TV commercials have been good, they perhaps could have been better.

2. A full-service agency generally has the following departments and people:
   a. *Copywriters.* Skilled writers who develop ideas and write advertisements exclusively for broadcast media.
   b. *Art directors and artists.* People who supply the visual framework for the advertising message.
   c. *Media department.* This department places the advertising messages developed by creative departments.
   d. *Production department.* Responsible for mechanical production of ads.
   e. *Account People.* Responsible for detailing problems, development and implementation of plans.
   f. *Research department.* Researchers who may be trained statisticians, psychologists, economists, and others to provide facts that will provide a basis for themes and image development. It just does not seem logical that we, specialists in food merchandising, could satisfactorily perform

...I just defined nor could we
... to seek out and retain on our
... people who could effectively
... the tasks.

...n athletic teams are usually champi-
... ...ause of their bench strength. A good
agency will have a depth of personnel that
our own advertising staff could not expect nor
afford to maintain.

4. We've seen a strong movement by agencies
toward compensation by fees such as cost-
plus with commissions rebated to the client.
Under this type of arrangement we have to
pay only for what we get. This results, I
think, in greater objectivity by the agency
and more complete service.

5. A very significant advantage of using an
agency over establishing an in-house capability is the greater flexibility that would be
possible with an outside agency. It would be
difficult if not impossible to temporarily
abandon TV or reduce it drastically for one
year with an in-house agency as the overhead
would be too great. We would have this
flexibility with an outside agency.

6. Also, a full-service agency with research
capabilities would provide us with considerable input for formulating effective merchandising strategy that would appeal to the
ever-changing consumer tastes and would
enable us to be one step ahead of our
competitors or in step with those competitors
who also have a full-service advertising
agency.

"I recognize that many of my arguments in
favor of a full-service agency are equally applicable to the use of creative specialists and media-
buying specialists to supplement our own advertising staff. I seriously question that we have the
expertise or know-how to seek out and, even
more important, the ability to effectively control
these specialists. It would be very difficult to
coordinate the use of these specialists with our
overall desired image. A full-service agency

would tell us via research not only what image
we should strive for but how to obtain that
image.

"I doubt that we could find a boutique shop
that really understands the retail food business.
Also, I seriously doubt that the size of our
broadcast budget would impress the media-buying people sufficiently for them to take a real
interest in our company on the basis of the
relatively small commission."

The Advertising Director for Portage Grocery
Company, Tom Wilson, was becoming increasingly impatient as the Vice-President spoke,
since he had heard many of the arguments from
Bill Green before. However, he would have to
agree that Green had spent some time preparing
for the meeting.

Tom liked Bill as they worked together for the
company for several years. They were golf
partners in the company's golf league and their
families frequently socialized. However, on the
point of retaining a full-service advertising
agency, they seemed to widen the gap in their
thinking each time it had been discussed, so
much that recently they had tended to avoid the
issue.

When the Vice-President paused, the Director
of Advertising quickly interjected:
"The last two points you just made are equally
applicable to a full-service agency. I seriously
doubt that we could find a full-service advertising agency with the expertise or knowledge of
food retailing, and, even if we could, I doubt
that a good agency with all the departments and
people that you made reference to would be
interested in our company with a total broadcast
budget of $800,000.

"I appreciate the concern of both of you as to
my work load; however, I don't think either of
you has heard me complain. I have heard you
[the President] say on more than one occasion
that the principal reason for the success of the
company is the combination of ability, experience, and youthful enthusiasm of our officers
and department heads. I like to consider myself

a part of that team. I sincerely believe that I can be most effective and contribute more to the growth and profit of this company by continuing with what might be called an in-house agency. I like my work. My only request is that I be permitted to add the necessary staff when needed and to use the people my staff believes will do the best job in production.

"According to industry sources, for many years following World War Two, the average number of employees per one million in billings for an agency has dropped drastically. Does this mean that with only a $800,000 budget we might expect an average of two people to work on our account? Perhaps a more appropriate question would be, why do we need an average of two employees devoted to our relatively small budget?

"Perhaps one of the most significant arguments I can advance in favor of an in-house agency is the obvious need to coordinate broadcast advertising with print advertising. It is difficult to comprehend how we would do this effectively with a full-service agency. Under our present arrangements, coordination is quite simple since the same people work on both forms of advertising.

"I also am quite concerned as to whether an outside advertising agency would devote sufficient time and money to learn the food retailing industry, assuming they do not now have a food retail account; more important, how long will it take them to become familiar with us, our stores, and our market area?

"Before we make a decision, I strongly encourage Bill to think about the flexibility that we now have which, most probably, would be lost with a full-service agency. There are a lot of things that we take for granted now that would necessitate additional communication with and approval from the agency.

"I agree with the President that food chains will use more broadcast advertising in the future; however, I think we have a jump on our competitors by two or three years, and I also believe we can maintain this leadership by

continuing as we have operated. My impression of the 'boutique' people is that they become overly concerned with the creative process so as to impress their peers and to aid in obtaining new accounts. In other words—they would tend to use us to advance their prestige. I do not think the media-buying services would be interested in us either. It is my impression that they tend to operate for nationwide accounts and we would be too small to justify their time and expense. Frankly, I sincerely believe we do as well as they could in our market. It is my understanding that the media-buying specialists have not delivered the miracles once promised. As you are aware, we devote considerable time to our placement and buying functions. We know the people, they know us, there is a mutual trust. We have and should continue to have buying and placement expertise within the company.

"With an in-house agency, when our people have ideas, they will fight for them; they will talk up and talk back. I guess what I'm really saying is that communications is a critical management tool. With an in-house agency we can provide this communications more efficiently, directly from the firm to the consumer, and at the same time be in a position to interpret the consumer's reaction. Thus, we can identify problems and make adjustments so much more quickly than we could if we relied on outside advertising assistance—whether full-service or boutique.

"Do you realize that if we were to use a full-service agency—let's assume an agency of some size that would have other accounts—what might happen if the agency lost one or two sizable accounts! The result might cause the agency almost to disintegrate or at least retrench drastically. In effect, we no sooner get one account executive trained to the retail grocery business than we have to start all over and retrain another one.

"In addition, agencies, buying services, and creative specialists are all accustomed to persuading consumers to buy products—anywhere they can. We in retail advertising urge the consumers to buy products from us, not else-where. The large department stores do not have outside agencies. Big department stores' in-house agencies turn out more advertisements than many full-service advertising agencies. Our problems are unique to food retailing—agencies do not understand them; thus we can do the job, I believe, more effectively and efficiently."

At this point in the meeting the President's secretary knocked at the door and indicated that the warehouse union steward wanted to see him. Thus the meeting was quickly adjourned.

QUESTIONS FOR DISCUSSION

1. What factors or considerations, in addition to the ones raised in the discussion, should have a bearing on Portage's decision whether to utilize outside specialists in developing and/or placing their broadcast advertising?
2. How important are the "human relations" aspects of the situation in reaching a decision?
3. Which of the three alternative courses of action would you recommend to Portage? Why?

CONTINENTAL FASTENER CORPORATION

John Tobin is the Advertising Manager for Continental Fastener Corporation (CFC), a company that manufactures metal and plastic fasteners that are used in a variety of applications, primarily the electrical and appliance industries. Continental Fasteners spends about $300,000 annually on advertising and during the past year, Ed White, VP-Marketing, has been encouraging John Tobin to "do something different with the advertising program."

Because he realizes that there is very little physical difference in CFC's product category, Mr. White encouraged Mr. Tobin to seek out a "consumer goods" advertising agency to get more "creative" ideas for the advertising program. Mr. Tobin tended to agree so he invited several agencies to talk with him about handling the account. After three weeks of meetings with six different agencies, he narrowed the choices down to two agencies—Paulsen & Partners (a medium-sized industrial agency and CFC's current agency) and a medium-sized consumer goods agency, B & P Advertising.

B & P Advertising has offices in six U.S. cities, and in five of these cities CFC has district sales offices. B & P's presentation was also very different from that of Paulsen & Partners. It provided a fresh look in print design and it also presented a very attractive package design. Although B & P had never handled an industrial account, it was quite confident it would be able

to put CFC in the number one market position very soon. At the time, CFC held nearly 20 percent of the market and the two industry leaders held 38 percent and 29 percent market shares, respectively.

Paulsen & Partners' presentation emphasized an updating of CFC catalogs and launching a new direct-mail campaign. They too suggested a print campaign, although their suggestions for copy and layout were not nearly as appealing as that of B & P.

In terms of compensation, B & P suggested a fee of $75,000 per year and it would rebate all media commissions. Production would be marked up 17.65 percent. There would be no additional charges for creative time.

Paulsen & Partners suggested that they stay on the same compensation system they had been using for the past eight years—15 percent commission, plus $40 per hour for creative time. Again, production would be marked up 17.65 percent.

John Tobin had until the next morning to give his recommendations to his boss.

QUESTIONS FOR DISCUSSION

1. Which agency—Paulsen & Partners or B & P—would you recommend? Why?
2. What are the key considerations affecting your recommendation?
3. What additional information would be useful in evaluating the two agencies? Why?

This case was prepared by Charles H. Patti.

Jane Gordon and Mary Wolfberg had formed their advertising agency, Gordon & Wolfberg (G & W), on the basis of a mutual respect for each other and their complementary talents. The two principals in the agency had been friends since their high school days in Evanston, Illinois, and both had studied advertising at the University of Illinois. After graduation the two friends had gone their separate ways. Ms. Gordon had taken a media buying job in the Dallas office of a large Chicago-based agency and after two years had moved to an account executive position working with a large package goods client. Ms. Wolfberg had initially taken a job as copywriter/artist with a struggling agency but after nine months the agency lost its principal account and folded. Next Ms. Wolfberg's artistic talents landed her a position as a creative artist with Hallmark Cards in Kansas City.

As a result of professional contacts established through the local ad club, Ms. Gordon had received a job offer to become the advertising manager of a large manufacturing firm whose offices were in Dallas. At that time the firm had media billings of roughly $1.2 million. Although the offer was attractive, she viewed the situation as an opportunity to establish her own agency. Ms. Gordon suggested that the firm's present Vice President of Marketing could handle the job in a "partnership" with her new agency.

After considerable discussions, the owner of the manufacturing firm, who was extremely unhappy with the results of the firm's advertising efforts, bought Ms. Gordon's idea and agreed to fire the present agency as soon as Ms. Gordon could assume responsibility for the firm's advertising. Ms. Wolfberg instantly accepted Ms. Gordon's proposal that they jointly form an agency to handle the manufacturer's account.

This case prepared by John H. Murphy.

Ownership of the agency was divided 60/40 between Ms. Gordon and Ms. Wolfberg. Both of the principals began their new enterprise with considerable enthusiasm and dreams of quickly adding significant new accounts. During the first two years of the agency's operation several small clients were picked up by G & W. However, both the principals were dissatisfied with their efforts to add at least one major account.

In an attempt to correct this perceived shortcoming, Mr. Jack Miller, a seasoned and highly successful account executive from a major Dallas agency, was hired to concentrate on pitching prospective new clients. Ms. Gordon and Ms. Wolfberg each gave Mr. Miller 10 percent ownership in the agency, which became Gordon, Wolfberg, Miller, & Friends (GWMF).

Since GWMF's formation, the agency had grown to about 25 accounts and handled media billings of about $7.5 million. The agency employed about 40 individuals and hired outside free-lance talent such as photographers or copywriters when the workload justified additional help.

As fate would have it, on a Monday morning developments with three different clients reached the point where a decision was sorely needed regarding what action to take. These developments required the immediate attention of Ms. Gordon, Ms. Wolfberg, and Mr. Miller. To handle these problems adequately, the three principals would have to agree upon a course of action to resolve each by the next morning.

SURE FINE DAIRIES

The first of the problem areas involved an important client, the Sure Fine Dairies. Sure Fine Dairies executives had approved GWMF's recommendation to place $125,000 in outdoor showings and a spot radio schedule for $57,000 to support the 12-week introduction to a new line of natural yogurt flavors. Further, it was understood that an additional 12-week campaign to reinforce the initial efforts would probably be approved.

At the same time Sure Fine wanted GWMF to develop six multimedia displays which would present the history of Sure Fine and show the procedures used to process dairy products. The displays were to be used for special events or programs (for example, the state fair) and three would be housed permanently at Sure Fine Dairies.

In order to produce the type and quality of displays Sure Fine wanted, GWMF would require special film work, sophisticated audiovisual equipment, plus the hiring of a photographer and talent for the voiceover to be used. An estimate on the expenses involved in producing the displays was as follows:

Audiovisual equipment (cost to agency)	$7,621
Materials (cost to agency)	567
Talent, sound, production (cost to agency)	1,000
A/E supervision time = 50 hours, @ $35/hr.	1,750
Total	$10,938

In figuring their estimates of costs to develop the six displays for Sure Fine, GWMF followed the accepted agency practice of marking up all work contracted outside by 17.65 percent. Thus, the estimate presented to Sure Fine for its approval was $12,559.

When the account executive from GWMF presented the estimated costs and requested Sure Fine's approval, the Sure Fine marketing manager balked at the additional charges for agency markup on "outside services" ($1,621). The marketing manager said that he did not mind paying commission to the agency on the media advertising but that he objected to a fee being charged on other services. Further, he suggested that perhaps GWMF did not appreciate Sure Fine's business and that he wanted a special deal if the markup was a standard practice. The account executive told the market-

ing manager that he would check with the principals of GWMF and come by on Tuesday to discuss the situation further.

WOODY'S

The second problem involved Woody's, a regional chain of fast food restaurants. The chain had multiple locations in Dallas, Fort Worth, Houston, San Antonio, Amarillo, Beaumont, Tyler, and Lubbock. Periodically, Woody's ran a burst of advertising promoting a "Buy-One-Get-One-Free" weekend sale. These weekend promotions had been extremely successful in the past. Woody's management had always been extremely pleased with consumer sales during these promotions and felt such sales contributed heavily to business in nonsales periods. Woody's executives gave most of the credit for the success of the promotion to GWMF's high-quality creative advertising strategy and executions.

Through an unexplainable error, most likely on the part of GWMF's new assistant traffic manager, fifteen 30-second and eighteen 10-second television spots promoting the "Buy-One-Get-One-Free" sale had not appeared as originally planned on the Friday evening prior to the sale. To make matters worse, sales during the promotion were about half of their usual level for an average weekend during such a sale.

Mr. Woody Burkehart, owner of Woody's, was extremely upset after watching the 10 P.M. news only to discover that his ads did not appear. Mr. Burkehart attributed the dismal sales performances to the scheduling error. "The promo never had a chance after we missed those front-end spots. This error robbed the spots and newspaper ads that did run of their impact. If there had been time, I'd have canned the whole promotion after the foul-up on the opening spots."

The account person who handled Woody's apologized for the scheduling problem and pointed out that two other factors contributed to the poor sales performance: (1) light snow and sleet made travel by car dangerous during much of the weekend in most of the markets served by Woody's, and (2) competitive advertising and price promotion by other fast food restaurants was unusually heavy over the weekend of Woody's "Buy-One-Get-One-Free" promotion.

Mr. Burkehart rejected these explanations. Further, he literally demanded that Ms. Gordon and Mr. Miller be in his office the next morning to discuss some sort of "make good" on the botched promotion, the likelihood of such a situation's occurring again, and the future of the relationship between GWMF and Woody's.

HOMEWOOD SAVINGS & LOAN

The third client that would require attention the next day was Homewood Savings & Loan. Homewood had been a solid client of GWMF for 3½ years but recently had become unhappy with the quality of the creative efforts of GWMF.

In the fifteen years since its founding, Homewood had grown from a single location in Dallas to eight branches plus a downtown headquarters and presently had deposits of over $300 million. However, in the last six months new accounts had lagged to a trickle despite the fact that the service areas of the branch locations had experienced strong growth.

When the Marketing Manager at Homewood, who was under pressure to correct the meager new accounts problem, complained to GWMF's account executive about the "stale" creative efforts, the A/E responded that the campaign represented the creative people's best efforts. Further, the A/E explained that the present efforts built logically on past Homewood promotions and advertising. Finally, the A/E suggested that Homewood's media budget of *only* $350,000 was a stumbling block to the develop-

ment of the sort of impact that was necessary in the highly competitive Dallas financial market. (As a result of fee work and preparation of collateral materials, GWMF considered Homewood an excellent client.)

Homewood's Advertising Manager questioned whether GWMF's creative group really devoted much time or energy to his account. The Advertising Manager went on to say: "Don't tell me you're not capable of a stronger creative execution of our ads. It sure seems strange that Mr. Miller is going around town touting your shop's expertise in creativity and showing award-winning commercials for almost all your clients except us!"

The A/E's conversation with ad manager ended on a very sour note. In so many words, the ad manager threatened to fire GWMF and look for some new creative blood. The Advertising Manager ended the discussion with the following request: "The executive board of Homewood is meeting for dinner and a working session to review our marketing efforts tomorrow evening at the Petroleum Club. Please ask Jack Miller to join us around seven o'clock. Better still, ask Jack to meet me here at the office about five so we can talk prior to meeting with the board."

QUESTIONS FOR DISCUSSION

1. How should GWMF respond to each of the situations involving their clients? What are the likely implications of GWMF's response?
2. Are the immediate problems related in any way? How?
3. What general principles of client/agency relationships are involved in the three situations?
4. How might each of these problems have been avoided?

The Williams advertising agency had devoted over six months of effort to the development of a new advertising campaign for their biggest client, Wensley Industries. The campaign was for a new product which was scheduled to be introduced in September. Bill James, the agency Management Supervisor, had informed Wensley's Advertising Manager, Alfie Thomas, of the progress on the campaign at various stages of development but had not revealed the creative strategy. He had explained: "Alfie, we think we have a great idea but we don't want to expose it to you until it has had some preliminary pretesting. It would't be fair to ask your approval at this stage."

Alfie was fully informed on details of media recommendations and budgets and had given Bill James authority to make certain television buys for the introduction of the new campaign in about four months. He was, however, impatient to see the creative recommendation and was irritated somewhat that he had not been involved in its development. Secretly he believed he was very creative and could make substantial contributions. Bruce Jenkins, the agency Creative Director, who headed up the team working on the campaign, had insisted that the creative work should not be revealed until the agency was ready to recommend it. He said, "Alfie is a good guy but he's not very creative. If he gets into it he'll foul it up."

In late April, Bill called Alfie and said the creative plan was ready. Further, Bill asked Alfie to come to the agency's New York headquarters for a Wednesday afternoon meeting to discuss it. He also asked Alfie to schedule a meeting the following week with Ted Alford, Wensley's General Manager, and other top executives. Bill said, "If you approve of the

This case was prepared by Robert E. Anderson, The University of Texas at Austin.

idea, Alfie, and okay the budget for further pretesting, we should try to get tentative approval from top management." Alfie realized that if further testing were required, the time schedule to prepare the campaign for fall release would be very tight but he reluctantly agreed to arrange the meeting with Ted Alford.

Alfie flew to New York for the Wednesday afternoon meeting. John Williams, Chairman of the agency, presented the campaign to Alfie and gave the rationale behind it. It was a very daring campaign, which was sure to attract public attention but might invite substantial criticism. Mr. Williams described the preliminary research that the agency conducted at its own expense and noted that several focus groups' reactions to the campaign were favorable. Now he wanted to have an animated storyboard prepared and pretested at an estimated cost of $13,500 to be paid by the client.

Alfie responded enthusiastically. He recognized the creative excellence of the campaign and knew that it would be unique in the industry. He telephoned Ted Alford and reconfirmed the meeting with top management for the following Wednesday morning. He caught an evening flight back to the client's midwestern headquarter city.

The next day Alfie called Bill James and the following discussion ensued:

Alfie: That was a great meeting, Bill, and an exciting creative approach. I think we have a winner. I'm sure Ted will go along so why don't you get the animated storyboard started right away.

Bill: Okay. It will cost about twenty-five hundred bucks to make it, but if we get with it maybe we'll have it ready to show Ted next Wednesday.

Alfie: The budget of $2,500 is okay. Try to have it ready. Now, do you have any plans for an alternative campaign? If Ted shoots this down we should be ready to show him something else. Otherwise we'll never make those fall schedules.

Bill: We weren't planning on getting this campaign turned down. We really don't have an alternate. Let's just give this our best shot and if Ted won't buy it, we'll just have to start over again.

Alfie: But Bill, we just don't have time. We have to get some kind of tentative approval Wednesday. I'm all for this campaign, but I don't want to be left hanging if Ted thinks it's too dangerous. I'd look foolish.

Bill: We'll all look foolish if we come in with a shoddy campaign thrown together over the weekend. And besides, Bruce wouldn't have his heart in it as long as he thinks his big idea has a chance.

Alfie: The heck with Bruce. If this idea bombs it's my hide not his. Get another creative director to develop the alternate.

Bill: That won't work. He wouldn't have the background for the campaign. Let me talk this over with John Williams and get back to you.

Alfie: Okay, but be sure you understand. I want an alternative campaign, and until you get one there's not going to be a meeting with Ted Alford.

QUESTIONS FOR DISCUSSION

1. Given the facts of the situation, what is your assessment of Alfie's position?
2. How should Bill James handle the situation?
3. Could an irate Alfie actually fire the agency in this situation? Knowing that Wensley is the agency's biggest account, how should John Williams react to the situation? What are his risks?

INDEX OF CASES